9780553088984

Secret studies in the Soviet Union have not been able to dismiss these events.

Now, a growing body of information offers strong evidence that the earth has played host to extra-terrestrial beings—on both sides of the Iron Curtain!

The details of this evidence, both written and graphic, have been kept hidden in the files away from the public gaze.

UFO'S FROM BEHIND THE IRON CURTAIN brings this unpublished material into sharp focus for the first time

NO MATTER WHAT YOU CHOOSE
  TO BELIEVE,
THIS BOOK WILL FASCINATE AND
  EXCITE YOU!

UFO'S From Behind the Iron Curtain

by Ion Hobana and Julien Weverbergh

RLI: $\dfrac{\text{VLM 9 \quad (VLR 8-11)}}{\text{IL 9-adult}}$

UFO'S FROM BEHIND THE IRON CURTAIN
*A Bantam Book / published by arrangement with
Souvenir Press Ltd.*

PRINTING HISTORY
*Souvenir Press Ltd. edition published 1974
Bantam edition/June 1975*

*All rights reserved.
Copyright © 1972 by Uitgeverij N. Kluwer N.V., Deventer
English translation Copyright © 1974 by A. D. Hills
This book may not be reproduced in whole or in part, by
mimeograph or any other means, without permission.
For information address: Souvenir Press Ltd.
95 Mortimer Street, London W1N8HP*

Published simultaneously in the United States and Canada

Bantam Books are published by Bantam Books, Inc. Its trademark, consisting of the words "Bantam Books" and the portrayal of a bantam, is registered in the United States Patent Office and in other countries. Marca Registrada. Bantam Books, Inc., 666 Fifth Avenue, New York, New York 10019.

PRINTED IN THE UNITED STATES OF AMERICA

The assistance given by the Bruges UFO circle GESAG is much appreciated.

J.W.

Julien Weverbergh, who wrote the original foreword and book in Dutch, is entirely responsible for chapters 1, 2, 3, 5 & 7 and that part of chapter 4 referring to Czechoslovakian UFOlogy; likewise for the Russian section.

Contents

Foreword   1

PART ONE

The Evidence Assessed

1. The "Tungus Miracle" (Russia) 1908: food for UFOlogists   10

   Ten million trees destroyed in one explosion—Leonid Kulik goes in search of a comet which cannot be found—A mini-bomb is exploded from a cable above a small wood—Professor Fessenkov's doubts—Professor Zigel demolishes the comet-theory—The genetic structure of tree-cells strikingly altered—Spaceships with motors supplied with energy deriving from anti-matter

2. Russian UFOlogists fight against the same odds as their Western colleagues   31

   Professor Zigel pleads for the establishment of an international organization for UFO research—Jacques Vallée delivers a lecture in Moscow—The Stoljarov Committee unleashes a storm in the Russian Academy for Science—The Russian scholar who waits to see which way the American UFO cat is going to jump—Frequent sightings of UFO's in Russia—Russian astronauts report seeing flying cylinders—"Voices from space" command a woman to murder a scholar—Not a single theory can claim to explain the UFO phenomenon—Konstantin Tsiolkovsky, father of space-travel and ETI speculation—Space-travel and telepathy will one day be joined together indissolubly

3. Two famous Russian examples: Robozero (1663) & Karelia (1961)   53

   Russian UFOlogists cautiously approach the thorny problem—His Highness the Archimandrite receives a UFO report—"From the clearest of all skies a great fire descended upon Robozero"—Meteorite, comet, ball-lighting or space probe? Forester Vasili Bradski's telegram—Green ice-floes—The medal of gold for a case of proven cold-bloodedness—Craters, indefinite tracks and inexplicable substances are constant factors in UFO literature the world over

viii CONTENTS

4. UFOlogy in Poland, Czechoslovakia and Hungary 66

A Polish weekly takes the initiative in a thorough study of the saucer question—The UFO photographed over Muszyn—The Ministry of Information issues a brochure—Janusz Thor plagiarizes Menzel—Dr. Hynek undertakes a lecturing tour in his native Czechoslovakia—The UFO Information Centre in Prague—Two Czechoslovakian books on UFO's—Bànky Robert is not allowed to demonstrate the non-existence of aeroplanes on Hungarian T.V. channels

5. The Akademski Astronomsko-Astronautiki Klub at Sarajevo (Jugoslavia) give an exemplary lesson to UFOmaniacs 79

UFO's over Golgotha? AAAK's name is taken in vain—A conical object seen in Jugoslavian skies—Fixing the weight of a UFO—A stratosphere balloon "examines" Jugoslavia with a scientific purpose, or perhaps some other—Did the 1954 UFO wave reach the Balkans?—Orthothenic lines on Jugoslavian maps

6. Emil Barnea from Cluj (Rumania) offers some important clues 93

25% of UFO photos are authentic—UFO photos by the American Rex Heflin—Dr. Hartmann hangs a "UFO" on an invisible thread—Police interrogation methods of sceptical and spiteful scientists who cherish prejudices—A picnic in Baciu Wood—The Rumanian Emil Barnea's photos are remarkably like Heflin's—Florin Gheorghița investigates the facts—The conclusions of the Belgian Delcorps

7. The UFO phenomenon and Rumanian mass media 108

Swedes and Frenchmen show that they know all about UFO's in Rumanian papers—Some newspaper correspondence gets into trouble—A Rumanian professor hopes for an international UFO observation point—150 amateurs and professional astronomers are requested to keep a look-out for UFO's—In Bucharest a scientific circle is established—Comparative drawings once again underline the universal character of the Rumanian sightings

CONTENTS ix

8. Silver discs, satellites, balloons and other disputed flying objects 126

   UFO reports collected like stamps—A strange manifestation over the Carpathians—Movements untypical of balloons—During accelerations orange changes to red—Dr. Ion Xantus hangs a satellite on a thread—Producer Nacu sees a silver disc—Broadcasting Station YO–5–TZ is disturbed—A student of physics sees a UFO for two minutes

9. The Rumanian sightings underline the universal character of UFO phenomena 150

   The many-sidedness of UFO manifestations—Did the angel's glad tidings take place by means of the Montgolfier Balloon?—UFO-formations, flight manoeuvres, landings—"A square face with odd eyes"—Domes, cylinders, triangles, cones, deltas, satellites—The cowboy hat over the chicken shed—A UFO in the monastery garden—Six photos of a UFO over Colibița—UFO's are sighted by people from all walks of life

PART TWO

Documentation relating to Flying Saucers behind the Iron Curtain

Bulgaria	192
Hungary	198
Jugoslavia	202
Poland	210
Czechoslovakia	214
Rumania	221
Russia	280

Appendices:
A. Bibliography 292
B. Letter to 150 Rumanian amateur astronomers 303
C. List of Illustrations 305
D. A table reconstructing the Banat sightings 306

FOREWORD

On 21st February 1959 dock-workers in the Polish port of Gdynia see a radiant object fall into the harbour basin, and their account of the matter is so accurate that the spot where it fell could be ascertained exactly. The port authorities send three divers to the scene who, after going down into the ice-cold water and reporting that their investigations are hindered by a thick layer of mud, nonetheless come back to the surface with a piece of metal. The newspapers then report that the metal bears not the slightest trace of rust—which might well suggest that it may indeed be a fragment of the object concerned. After being examined by the Polish navy it is sent to Gdynia's Polytechnic University. The final results of these two examinations are not known, and neither do we know as yet what the object is and what happened to it. It did however come to light that certain "misfortunes" occurred during the investigations, as a result of which some of the material was lost. This story bears some striking likenesses to the one about a piece of magnesium which people said derived from a UFO picked up in the Brazilian Ubatuba (see Bibliography 4 and 7).

This does not mean that there was necessarily anything "mysterious" in itself about this odd affair: if we suppose that the object sighted was, for instance, a rocket of any kind or origin then we can understand both the concern of the authorities involved and their reticence about the results of the examinations. But what is really "mysterious," in fact very much so, is the outcome of the story as it was told in Gdynia: several days after the "object" had plunged into the harbour men guarding the beaches met a strange figure which was clearly male dragging himself exhausted along the sand. This creature spoke no known language and was dressed in a "sort of uniform"; a part of his face and hair appeared to be burnt. The man was taken to the university hospital, isolated and examined. But it was at once apparent that it was impossible to unclothe the creature as the "uniform" had no means of opening. It was not of ordinary material such as wool or leather but of a metal which could only be cut open by means of special tools and after a great deal of effort. The doctors noted that their "patient's" organs were quite different from ours: the blood system was new to them and the number of fingers and toes was not the normal one. The creature remained alive until a kind of armband was taken off and the "mortal remains" were sent for further examination to the Soviet Union. Polish UFOlogists readily link up the metal object and the living being with unidentified flying objects and everything associated with the latter.

Any critical and sceptical reader who is familiar with our usual approach to reports such as these will read this account of a story that appeared in Polish newspapers of the time (inter alia *Wiezoor Wybrzeza*) with a certain amazement. He will feel that we are using the story as an example of UFO hysteria and expect us to refuse categorically to have anything to do with this sort of tale— Eastern European UFOlogy is riddled with such stuff. The reader will hope we shall do this not only because the accounts tend to be incredible but also because they threaten study of the real problems arising from the observations of "genuine UFO's." Surely our previous UFO research published in the press and other mass media was a clear attempt to free the UFO phenomenon from the labyrinth of prejudice, bathos and mysticism with a view to helping the establishment of proofs that they "exist."

Thus we disappoint any critical and sceptical reader. A case like the one just given—and there will be several other similarly mysterious cases carefully selected by us— we do indeed include in our list of UFO reports recorded in Poland and it does have a part to play when it comes to any judgment upon Polish UFO's and the whole Eastern European UFO situation. The reasons for this are that whenever anywhere in the world genuine UFO activity is reported it seems to be associated with phenomena which for the sake of convenience we describe as "rumours." These rumours may come from any part of the world and are identical in pattern. They involve the following main features:

1. The digging-up of "old," "historical" examples: that is, aspects of local archaeological and historical UFOlogy.

2. Reports of "UFO fragments" which after being sent to "official" laboratories are never heard of again.

3. The sudden appearance of strange-looking craters and imprints in remote places; reports of odd holes in ice or curiously melted patches of snow; mysterious marks on road-surfaces etc. Such reports are considered by UFOlogists as being worthy of their attention and local or national authorities often investigate the matter.

4. Meeting unusual people, regardless of any facts about "vessels" having landed in their vicinity.

5. The numerous reports of aerial or sky phenomena by conscientious people who lack scientific training and thus dismiss them without further analysis as misinterpretations of aircraft, balloons or some of nature's less familiar manifestations.

6. Newspapers' growing tendency to give prominence to UFO matters in general.

Before making some comments about this list we should point out that in this section of our work concerning UFO phenomena in East European countries we cannot simply ignore the whole issue and neither do we wish to do so. We say this mainly because throughout the second part of our book there is the constantly recurring theme that the UFO phenomenon in these countries is *exactly the same as anywhere else in the world, as is also the case with the "rumours" about such phenomena*. When we began this book on East European UFOlogy it was not obvious to us in advance that we should arrive at this conclusion, but we were forced to it as we acquired ever more material. It was in fact a surprise to us that what we described as rumour could also occur in those countries. We have included a considerable number of these "rumours" in this volume, together with authentic UFO material. We ourselves regard a few of the accounts as obvious nonsense, and there are some that are clearly observations of balloons, though made in a striking manner. There are also certain "mysteries" like the 1908 Tungus case, for instance, as well as a list of historical UFO phenomena which we have made as complete as possible. We make this point particularly because the areas we mapped out are from a UFOlogical point of view ones which hitherto were fallow. A further reason for choosing some of the "rumours" is connected with the lack of any tenable hypothesis about the origin of the UFO phenomenon. The studies in this field consider two possibilities: either that the UFO is entirely physical in nature, or that it is psychical. "Rumours" about observations of flying saucers or fragments of them become extremely important if they are indeed physical, regardless of whether or not they are of extraterrestrial origin. Such details could be of prime importance in any attempt to approach the subject scientifically and methodically. As for the possibility that they may be psychical, it should be pointed out that mass hysteria and misinterpretation can hardly be responsible, and this has been shown in authoritative literature on the subject quite clearly (including our own previous work).

Paranormal phenomena are sometimes brought in to account for the UFO, and people who hold this view do not believe in excluding radar echoes, imprints, photos and films of them.

Although we ourselves are weaned from this mystical way of thinking, we were of the opinion that, in case the UFO should prove to be psychical in origin, then our own contribution to the whole problem should not be deprived of the "rumours" emanating from the Eastern European countries, especially if these "paranormal" hypotheses should prove to have a basis in reality. Here one might point out also that Sheila Ostrander and Lynn Schroeder record in their excellent and authoritative book *Psychic Discoveries behind the Iron Curtain* that the UFO question is being studied in the Soviet Union from this angle. In a recent book on the question of UFO crews, the Belgian author of the present book demonstrated also, through statistics, that the UFO phenomenon is primarily a *luminous* phenomenon, but a luminous phenomenon of *manipulated* and/or *corporeal* light. We must get used to thinking in terms of UFO = light rather than UFO = metal. This particular luminous phenomenon and its effects are undoubtedly analogous or, rather, parallel to certain paranormal phenomena in the literature in this field. But we are dealing—still according to J. Weverbergh—with a relatively recent phenomenon which, being simultaneously subjective and objective, escapes the known scientific disciplines. We exclude the possibility that the UFO is a product of the imagination only, but even supposing that this does prove to be the case then our own material on the subject can and will be used as a basis for social and scientific investigations—which would take place because of the millions of people who would be vitally concerned. If we were to exclude all the "rumours" then it would imply that we would know in advance what a UFO is; or suggest that we were fully informed on the matter and could tell grain from chaff; and that we should know exactly where the borderline lay between rumour and authentic UFO phenomena. But such is not the case and moreover we would not be acting in our full capacity of imparters of information if we were to suggest we possess *a priori* knowledge in this field.

Concerning this function of ours as providers of information we would also like to add that it seemed from readers' reactions to previous UFO books that some of them imagined all we had in mind was to provide innumerable contributions to the fascinating subject of ETI (extraterrestrial intelligence) and to the attempts to prove the latter's existence. But this is definitely a false idea of our intentions, since all we had in mind was to provide the reader with as complete a picture as possible.

Neither have we had the aim of even *trying* to explain the UFO phenomenon, since as long as we do not know what it is, that is to say as long as the UFO is not physically measurable—which of course is a necessary basis for any scientific investigation—then any speculation about its origin is just that: speculation. Informed people in various scientific disciplines have studied the material about the UFO made available through the media, though not with the idea that there was "something peculiar" about them—only as a basis of possible hypotheses for further elaboration: a method of approach which may be termed quite false. The most important thing we might ask the scientific professionals to do is to study all the reports, including the "rumours," in order to develop a *method* of measuring the UFO, rather than collecting only materials and details which might lead to some explanation of the phenomenon. Certainly the publication of as many reports as possible is important at this juncture. Though it may seem that many details in these reports are quite superfluous, later on it may turn out that it is precisely these details which can prove useful for the formation of a methodology. Catalogues as such are especially valuable for building the first principles, like those developed by Dr. Jacques Vallée, Professor Saunders, the U.S.A.F. and the Frenchman Claude Poher, whose statistical treatments of the data have yielded positive results in connection with UFO observations from all parts of the world, especially as regards the duration of the phenomena and period in which they occurred (see also p. 119).

It seems a simple enough matter to suppose that the UFO must one day be made physically tangible, yet the very supposition is the cause of confusion on the part of the scientific establishment, because scientific people and intelligent laymen alike too quickly assume that everything which can be known about the UFO is in fact already known. If one wants to progress then all the careful calculations of azimuth, speed and velocity of the vehicle, use of polarised glass, photos, films etc. are of little avail *since they have been developed to deal with phenomena already known to us;* whereas UFO's are UFO's precisely because they are of *un*known nature . . .

The authors are relatively pessimistic since they suppose that the next step—that of investing capital in this field—cannot easily be undertaken, despite the fact that a steadily increasing number of scientifically minded people are convinced of the reality of the UFO: the Condon report alone is enough to persuade the complete sceptic to change his mind. It can seem amazing to the man in the street that a large part of the scientific establishment will have nothing to do with inexplicable phenomena: even the genuine UFO observation is considered unimportant, so unimportant in fact that investing money in this field of endeavour is considered a waste even by those convinced that these "phenomena" defy all known principles of physics. This attitude is regrettable but it is a hard fact—like the UFO itself. However, let us return to the "rumours."

From the way we have compiled these "rumours" one might think that the link between them and the actual manifestations is such that the latter are actually rumours too. But if there were no demonstrable distinction to be made between rumour and manifestation then the authors would not have interested themselves in the slightest in UFOlogy and we therefore reject this idea completely. We hope the reader will trust our intellectual integrity when we say that our Rumanian data in 1968 (a peak year UFOlogically) came from sources all over that country and from people entirely without any connections with each other and without our having told the witnesses of the phenomena about the vast amount of UFO details already in our files. We do not deny that there was a certain feedback from articles and publications on UFO phenomena but we do claim (as other serious research workers like Hynek, Bloecher, Michel and Vallée have done) that this feed-back is not as great as the sceptics would have one believe. After the 1971 publication of our study on UFO's in Rumania (of which there were 32,000 copies, all sold out within a few days) there was an increase in the otherwise very moderate rate of reports about UFO's: 55% of them in 1968 indicated sightings. Right up to 1972 there have been reports coming in (sporadically) with details about the UFO wave in 1968, in which year the Rumanian press carried articles about the objects then seen. Ion Hobana also notes that this press attention was the result of an increasing number of sightings since 1967 (see Table on p. 120). We can therefore assert with the utmost confidence (and we have the support of the above-mentioned foreign investigators) that press reaction is a consequence of UFO activity and rumour and not the reverse.

Furthermore we believe that the "rumours" arise because UFO's are real phenomena, though any normal, logical approach to the problem fails completely. We cannot prove that reports of UFO "fragments" and UFOnauts etc. come from a general concern and belief in their existence because we ourselves doubt that people have enough interest in the matter. The "rumours" come from people who apparently have no general UFOmania of any kind and often do not even know the term "flying saucer." It is especially important to us in our present endeavours that up till the end of 1968 the mass media hardly influenced (if at all) the people who produced the accounts of what they had seen, so that these reports are free from any other conscious or unconscious experiences.

In Rumania for instance, until the summer of 1968, the public was hardly if at all aware of the UFO problem through the mass media. Books about it were unknown, detailed sightings were totally alien to the few people involved, so that reporters, investigators and observers, in reproducing what they thought they saw, had no need to sort out in their reports the real experiences from descriptions based on what had been read, consciously or otherwise.

From 1967 on we received all sorts of reports the facts of which tallied with the details which usually are known solely in UFO circles where *complete* accounts are handled by the editors. (See also p. 38 in connection with our conclusions in Russian UFOlogy.)

The most enigmatic "rumours" appear to us to be the fifth type: reports of phenomena misinterpreted as aircraft, balloons, meteorites. These involve numerous versions of wrongly interpreted but familiar data—and at a time when there was authentic UFO activity going on. In the chapter where we analyse more closely the Rumanian wave of activity in 1968 we shall deal with this matter again. But for the present we shall just note that during times of increased UFO activity the number of reports also grows very considerably larger: the phenomena reported on are often wrongly interpreted and may thus appear to be of an unknown nature though they are in fact known. Why should people be in the habit of sending in accounts of their sightings of globe lightning, Venus, aircraft, balloons, radar inversions etc. during a wave of UFO activity and not do it at all when there is no such wave? And we must stress the fact that the details of these reports have been kept secretly hidden in files away from the public gaze. Are the accounts of genuine UFO observations, therefore, a matter of misinterpreting familiar aerial phenomena? No, because the manifestations are too convincing and well-documented; and in years when there is no UFO activity we do not find thousands of people spending their time writing about hundreds of objects difficult to identify which finally turn out to be "known" ones.

This is one of the many problems we deal with in this book. Like our readers we look forward to the solution to this and many other puzzles with the keenest interest.

PART I
THE EVIDENCE ASSESSED

1. THE "TUNGUS MIRACLE" (RUSSIA) 1908: FOOD FOR UFOLOGISTS

Ten million trees destroyed in one explosion—Leonid Kulik goes in search of a comet which cannot be found—A minibomb is exploded from a cable above a small wood—Professor Fessenkov's doubts—Professor Zigel demolishes the comet-theory—The genetic structure of tree-cells strikingly altered—Spaceships with motors supplied with energy deriving from anti-matter.

On the 30th June 1908 at about seven o'clock in the morning the sky above the Tungus *taiga* (forests) in Siberia was rent by what sounded like tremendous gunfire. Hundreds of farmers, hunters and fishermen saw an object in the sky travelling at great speed and emitting a light more dazzling than that of the sun; whilst later on the inhabitants of the village of Vanovara saw a brilliant ball of fire on the horizon which seemed volcanic and turned into a mushroom-shaped cloud. A deafening noise could be heard as far away as Kansk, 800 km from the village. (A train-driver in Kansk stopped his train, in fact, because he thought that one of his goods-wagons had exploded.) A hurricane arose above the *taiga* which tore roofs from houses and shattered windows. Shock waves encircled the world twice and were recorded in London on barographs. Huge waves flooded the banks of the Angara river and wood floating on other streams was thrown high into the air. Seismographs in Jena, Irkutsk and other cities recorded earth tremors and for three nights in succession people were able, in London and Paris, to read their papers without the aid of any artificial light. Around Moscow it was even possible to take photos at night, while in Siberia itself the clouds during wet weather were greenish-yellow according to the diary of Academician A. Polkanov, who was in the region during the days in question. The "yellowish-green" sometimes changed to a rose-pink tinge. Altogether the enormous ball of fire destroyed 20 million sq km of soil and tens of millions of trees.

For many years eye-witnesses and narrators talked about the "Tungus Miracle" so that in time truth and legend became virtually inextricably entangled together. As for science, there was a satisfactory explanation of the explosion in regarding it as the landing and bursting of a huge meteorite.

In 1921 people began the search for this meteorite in the Siberian forests but without success. In 1938 and 1939 aerial photography was carried out over the area of the explosion and during 1959–60 further expeditions went to Tungus; and today hardly a year goes by without further investigations of the region being carried out, laboratories in both Moscow and Siberia dealing with the relevant material and analysing it. "Tungus" has become in effect a special study or science in its own right. During the period 1908–69 77 different authors and groups have published 77 different "explanations" of what happened, but it was not until 1969 that the first well-arranged and exhaustive survey of the matter with various scientific conclusions was published. Since then it has been accepted first that the explosion above the Tungus *taiga* was caused by a cosmic body; second that the explosion must have taken place about 10 km above the earth's surface; and third that the upheaval was a nuclear or thermonuclear event having the power of a 10-megaton hydrogen bomb. A further conclusion was that during the object's journey through the earth's atmosphere both course and velocity were altered. The actual nature of the nuclear reaction still remains to be determined and likewise the type of object. . . .

12   THE EVIDENCE ASSESSED

As the Tungus event could prove in future years to be the first incontestable evidence that our planet was visited in a particular spot at a particular time by extraterrestrial beings, and since Tungus, as we shall see, stimulated discussion about ETI, it might be useful at this point to discuss in further detail the various stages of the Siberian investigations.

In 1921 Leonid Kulik of the Russian Meteorological Institute published a short statement about the 1908 Tungus meteorite. Self-taught as he was and without being able to boast of any systematic scientific training he was nevertheless inspired enough to grasp the fact that the Tungus affair was scientifically very important. As a result of his statement the Russian government supplied funds for an investigation, this being the first expedition to take place after the Russian Revolution five years earlier. Kulik set out without appreciating the appalling difficulties of his task awaiting him: the mere finding of the site was accompanied by considerable troubles.

The Siberian forests do not appeal as much to our imaginations as do the South American or African jungles, since in popular and semi-scientific literature they are hardly ever mentioned. Yet they are every bit as impenetrable, as desolate, hostile and inaccessible as the tropical wildernesses are. Up till the 1917 Revolution fewer Europeans had ventured to enter them than had gone into the southern jungles. So the idea of an expedition exploring what people thought was a fallen meteorite was hardly likely to occur at the beginning of this century to any scientist, adventurer or Tsarist regime. The population of the region was very thinly scattered and extremely primitive, so their accounts reaching Moscow about the terrifying acts of nature there were very far from the reality. This was a population which, afraid as it was of the place "where the God Ogdi had come down from heaven to earth and destroyed by fire all those who ventured there," would also make any investigation very difficult to carry out. Kulik and his men had to go through almost lifeless territory, carrying equipment to penetrate the frozen ground. The area was immeasurable and there was no question of any roads or even cart-tracks. When Kulik's European companions, ill and exhausted, left the Vanovara base he himself stayed on alone in the Siberian jungle, and after having traversed the last few terrible kilometres with the aid of only one guide in the frightful cold of the 1927 winter, Kulik at last reached the edge of his destination. He looked down from the Shahorma Mountains and beheld the remains of forests destroyed by indescribable forces—it seemed as though the whole area had been mown down with a gigantic scythe, since huge pine-trees, larches and other kinds of Siberian trees had been torn up by the roots. All the trees lay in a north-westerly direction, as if waiting for an explanation of the unusual "something" which had struck them down. The guide was filled with superstitious dread and refused to lead the way any farther, so the only thing Kulik could do was return (as he was unable to reach the centre of the damage) and hope to try again after the winter with braver and more numerous companions.

Kulik: "Now has the trade-union been on a jaunt this way or has a meteorite fallen?"

In the spring of 1928 Kulik, after having hacked his way through fallen forest, reached an open spot ringed with trees lying on the ground, all with their roots pointing in the same direction. Kulik's conclusion was

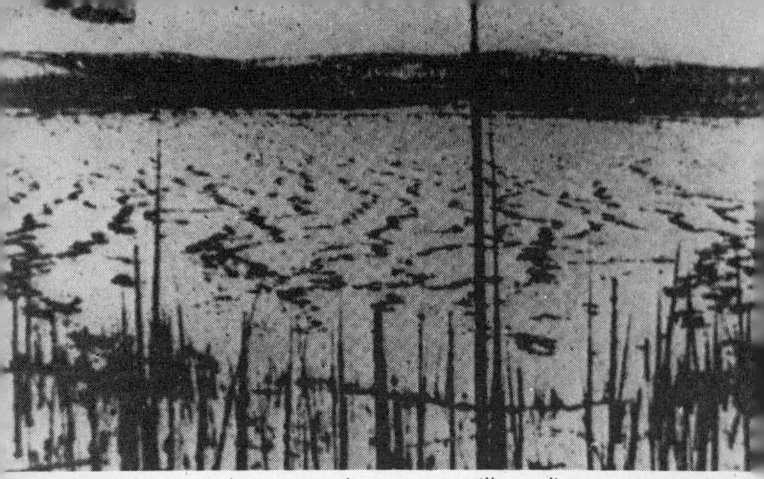

A swamp and some trees still standing
but bereft of bark and branches

left: Several kilometres from the explosion's epicentre.
Note the way the trees have fallen. Photo from the 1930s.

right: Tungus 1908: Broken-off trees in the epicentre
and around them some new ones which have grown
too fast. Pankov's Flora Expedition. (1961)

that he was now at the epicentre of the explosion and therefore face-to-face with his life's work; and so, together with his few colleagues, he began to draw up a balance-sheet of the awe-inspiring destruction. His first reports increased scholarly interest in the Tungus event over the whole world and Kulik was still certain that the catastrophe was caused by a huge meteorite. This was an acceptable and "normal" theory for those days and any other hypothesis was unacceptable. Nevertheless he did not come across any fragments of a meteorite and neither did he succeed in finding the crater which must have been made. What he did find at the epicentre near marshy land was vast quantities of fallen trees stripped of branches and leaves. They were all dead and their roots stuck up in the air. It was nothing but a landscape of dead poles where the explosion must have taken place. The first doubts about the meteorite theory now began to appear. Vasili Sytin, one of Kulik's colleagues, formulated the most absurd of the 77 theories: that the disaster was brought about by a very violent wind. But Kulik, who had boundless energy for solving the problem, obstinately clung to his belief that it must have been a meteorite. Finally it was assumed that fragments of the supposed meteorite would be found underneath 25 metres of frozen ground in the Siberian *taiga*'s permice. Marsh water, he thought, must have filled the crater. But half a century later it was to be clearly shown that the swamp in the epicentre was a normal *taiga* formation—the so-called thermokarsten.

In 1938–9 topographical measurements were made by aircraft and a series of photos taken, but the work was interrupted by the Second World War. Kulik, an enlisted volunteer, was killed near Kaluga in April 1942.

The 1945 Hiroshima and Nagasaki explosions with their intense light and mushroom-shaped cloud formation remind one of Tungus. The Russian magazine *Vokrug Sveta* published a short story in January 1946 by the science-fiction writer A. Kasantsev who suggested that the Tungus "thing" could well have been from another planet sending out a space-ship supplied with nuclear energy. The craft exploded when it tried to land in the Siberian forests. As this was in any case a nuclear explosion nothing would have remained of the space-ship, especially as it burst above ground. Thus there would have been no crater as no contact with the actual ground was made and this would explain why, right in the epicentre, some trees remained upright but dead whilst elsewhere large areas of trees were cut down. The trees at right angles to the shock waves only lost their tops, branches and leaves, but the trees at more acute angles to the direction of the shock had been cut down for miles around....

Kasantsev's theory was rejected by part of the scientific circles as being quite fantastic. "The object which landed in Tungus, and this is *beyond all doubt,* was a meteorite, not a space-ship," wrote Academician V. Fessenkov, while E. Krinov, the scientific secretary of the Committee for meteorite studies, also put in a word or two: "The explosion did not take place at an altitude of several hundred metres as Kasantsev claims but at the moment the object struck the ground. The resulting crater immediately filled with water. There is absolutely nothing mysterious about the Tungus meteorite or about its origin either." So much for that; but is it not a fact that the non-scientific conclusions reached by the science-fiction writer fit in better with the facts actually observed than the serious statements made by scholars do? We shall see.

From 1958 on, a number of new expeditions went to Tungus, consisting chiefly of young amateurs from Siberia, the Urals, Moscow and Leningrad. They looked on it as a holiday and initially supported themselves financially. Two groups of investigators were formed and these are still in being today. The first team was led by the geophysicist A. V. Zolotov, who still thinks it was possibly a nuclear explosion of cosmic origin. After some years various other Soviet scientists joined the group, such as E. K. Fedorov, M. A. Leontovici and B. P. Konstantinov. Zolotov is now held to be one of the leading Tungus specialists. The second group is led by G. Plekhanov and N. Koschelov, who maintain that a nuclear explosion certainly took place over the Tungus *taiga* in 1908 but that it must have had a natural cause: the "thing" which devastated Tungus was radioactive cosmic dust.

This second group has expanded and is now the official "Institute for Laboratory Research into Cosmic Objects coming down in Siberia and Eastern Russia."

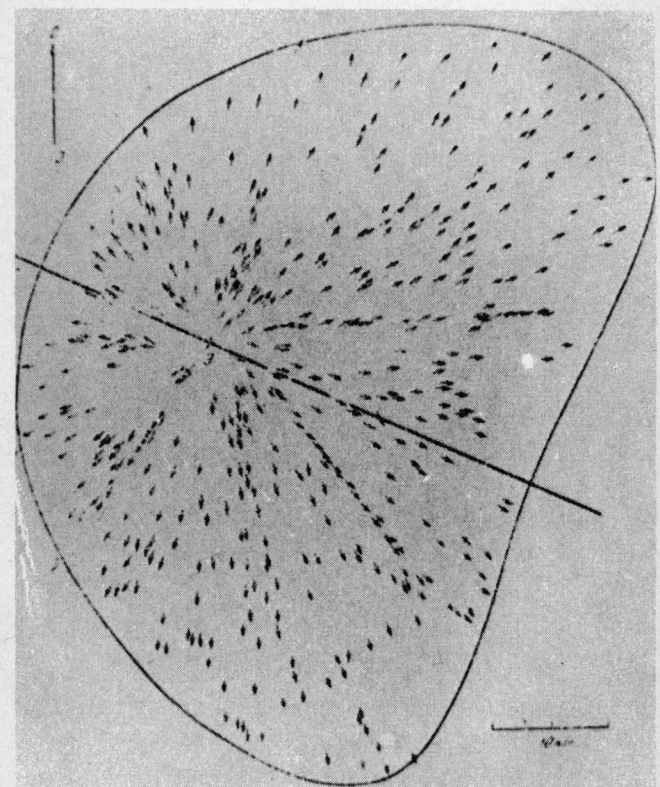

Tungus 1908: laboratory explosion, showing direction of fall of the trees as actually happened. (Zotkin and Tsikulin, 1965). Compare with the directions shown on the diagram of the disaster area, p. 19

In 1958 a team of genuine specialists from the Committee for meteorite studies led by Kiril Florenski went to Tungus in the footsteps of the early pioneer Kulik, and after years of research came to the definite conclusion that *"the meteorite* had exploded in the air." They had decided that this was what happened not simply by calculating the directions of the shock waves and the results but also by using barograms dating from 1908 which had been unearthed from the archives of the Geophysical Institute in Potsdam. From these they deduced that the displacement of air above the earth was at its maximum at a height of 5 km: at roughly this height the "thing" had exploded over Tungus, a conclusion which one year later was confirmed by other laboratory tests. I. T. Zotkin and M. A. Tsikulin simulated the disaster on a small scale by planting small wooden pegs in a 2 × 3 m plateau to reconstruct the disaster zone on a 1/10,000 scale; and to study the explosion and shock waves a miniature "bomb" was suspended above this mini-forest from a slanting cable. This "bomb" was run along the cable and set off at different speeds and various altitudes. By this method it was established that whenever the explosion took place below an angle of 27 degrees a "disaster zone" was brought about similar to the one which actually happened. Calculations now showed that the 5 km altitude was somewhat on the generous side and a maximum height of 10 km could be assumed.

The eminent authority Professor Fessenkov, now accepted as the "official" Tungus expert, who years before had indignantly rejected Kasantsev's theories, accepted the current conclusion. And the same Fessenkov was to admit and consider *beyond doubt* that the Tungus catastrophe was not caused by a meteorite, since not only was there no trace of one revealed by faultless magnetic methods of detection, but also the ice-layer (25 m thick) which gives the *taiga* its peculiar features, had been broken neither in the epicentre nor in the immediate vicinity. This ice—a remnant of the Ice Age—could not possibly, after any fracture or temporary melting brought about by an enormous object of the size needed to cause such damage burying itself, have joined itself together again without leaving a mark. It was further shown that the events were accompanied by a marked change in the earth's magnetic field which was apparent not only at Irkutsk but also at Greenwich; and a disturbance of such severity could not have been brought about by meteorites. Furthermore the light phenomena lasting three successive nights in 1908 could not be due to any cloud of particles of a terrestrial origin. No meteorite, regardless of size, could produce a dust-cloud so high in the atmosphere on the assumption that it plunged into our planet and exploded. Certainly any such cloud could not traverse in a few hours the distances separating Vanovara, London and Paris.

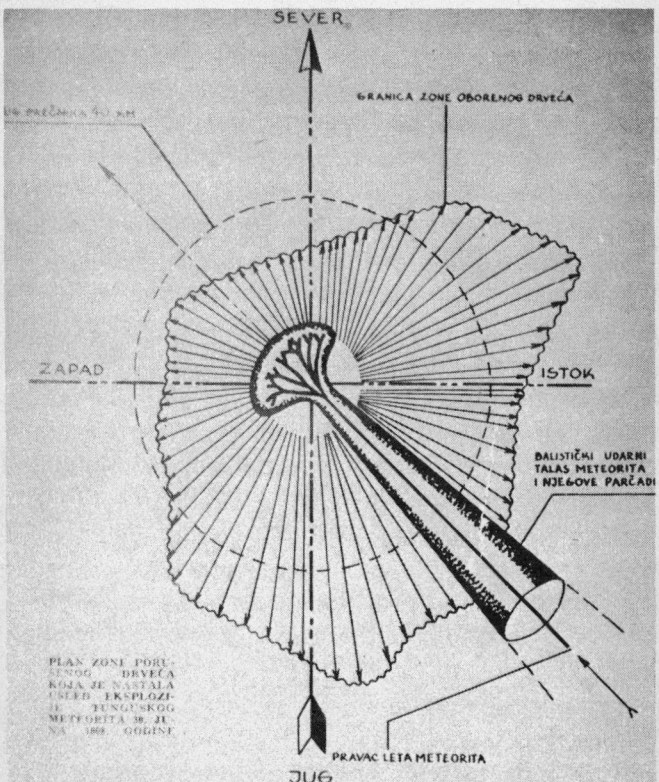

Rough outline of the disaster area: general direction of the trees and the path taken by the object.

Therefore not a meteorite, said Professor Fessenkov. But what *was* it then? Some other heavenly body was perhaps responsible for Tungus, Fessenkov said, and published the following sentence: "It is beyond all doubt that in 1908 a comet blew up above the *taiga* in Tungus." And note that he says "beyond all doubt"! Of all the heavenly bodies known to us only comets (apart from meteorites and asteroids) can ever come into contact with us; this was the reason for altering the idea of cause from meteorite to comet, after the former theory had been rejected round about 1960 by even the most conservative scholars. Not that this was a brand-new idea, since an American astronomer, Wipple, had favoured this notion in 1930 and he was soon supported by the Soviet astronomer I. S. Astapovitch. It was the particularly bright skies during the nights of 30th June and 1st and 2nd July both in Siberia and Central Europe which were the chief reasons for adopting the comet hypothesis: this light could have been caused by the comet's tail within the earth's atmosphere. Professor Felix Zigel was the one to bring in most arguments against the comet theory.

However acceptable this hypothesis may seem it does not withstand thorough criticism. What, after all, would have happened if a comet really had hit our planet? The centre of a comet is solid ice hundreds of metres (and in some cases kilometres) in diameter. Such a gigantic block of ice contains many fragments of substances like those of meteorites. On the surface a comet is covered with a relatively thin layer of cosmic dust and the centre consists of gases like methane and ammonia in the ice as well as H_2O. When therefore a comet approaches the sun and its centre becomes warmer the gases liquefy and form a tail stretching out for a distance of millions of kilometres. These gases escaping under pressure drag the cosmic dust into the tail. Now the hypothetical Tungus comet cannot have been small in view of the fact that the energy released has been estimated today, after studying the havoc caused, at 10^{23} ergs at least. If in 1908 a comet of that size had contacted the earth a crater several kilometres across and hundreds of metres deep would have been made, whereas it was already known that the epicentre showed no trace of such a thing; and neither did the now famous swamp show any evidence of violent damage. Furthermore the complete absence of any fragment at all of whatever it was that exploded renders the comet theory as doubtful as previously it had that of the meteorite. No relic of either comet or meteorite was ever discovered and as for the nocturnal light which made it possible for people in London and Paris to read their papers this cannot possibly have been due to the comet's tail. Our planet has on several occasions had experience of such things (as in 1861, 1882, 1910) without there having been side effects akin to the light phenomena and magnetic disturbances so typical of the 1908 case. The tails of all the comets approaching the earth had seemed very bright and huge even when the comet itself was tens of millions of kilometres distant. If a comet had really collided with us in 1908 the enormous object would certainly, in view of the amount of energy released, have been noticed in the skies long before. It is certain that the constantly enlarging tail could not have escaped the notice of a single person. For the sake of completeness we might add that people on the 1961 expedition did indeed find grains of silicate and magnetite in the vicinity of the explosion; but similar amounts of the same metals from meteorites are found all over the world; and furthermore it has been proved that these had nothing to do with the 1908 explosion.

There is yet another reason for supposing that it was not a comet which caused the disaster, and this has to do with ballistics. The felled trees—carefully mapped by the meteorite service—show without doubt that there were two shock-waves: one before the explosion, caused by violent air displacement as the object raced through the atmosphere, and the other after it had burst. By means of electronic calculating machines and by reconstructing the flight as seen by eye-witnesses, the aircraft designer A. Monotskov proved that the "thing" slowed down its velocity, which at the moment of impact was 0.7–1 km per second in place of the usual 10–60 km per second for normal comets and meteorites. This velocity is close to that of modern jet aircraft and if it had plunged down at this speed (an insignificant one for planetary bodies) then according to the laws of aerodynamics it would have needed a mass of one thousand million tons to bring about the destruction which has now been assessed and mapped. Certainly such a huge weight is nothing unusual for objects flying through space; but assume—and this does not agree with the facts—a diameter of only one kilometre for the thing: where are the remains of such a monster? So both meteorite and comet theories, which *are above all doubt*, must be thrown away.

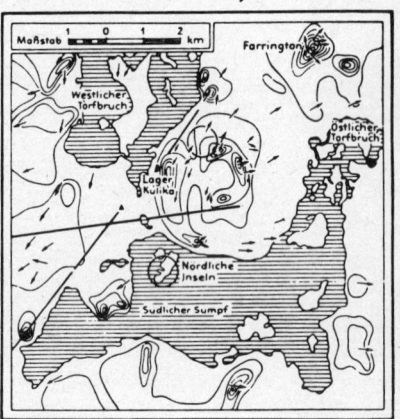

Exact map (Tungus 1908) of the centre of the disaster area (circa 2400 sq km). The arrows show the way the trees fell. According to V. G. Fessenkov the "comet" exploded in the ringed areas. He postulates three explosion sites to account for the change of direction shown by the "comet" during its flight over the *taiga*.

But let us consider another hypothesis which today finds increasing favour—the one which says that the explosion was nuclear or thermonuclear. The American scientist Libby, a Nobel Prizewinner, is one of the important defenders of this faith and the point at issue here is: Was the nuclear explosion over Tungus in 1908 of natural or artificial origin? Before going into the matter let us look at the arguments leading to this theory.

What are the Tungus facts? About 17–18 km from the epicentre Zolotov found trees stripped bare and set on fire by light radiation during the explosion. A living tree will only catch alight when any square centimetre of its surface is exposed to a light radiation of 60–100 calories. From this it has been deduced that the energy generated by the explosion must have amounted to around 1.5×10^{23} ergs. These figures represent several tens of percentages of the total energy, other figures deriving from different and quite independent data having given values of 10^{23} to 1.4×10^{23} ergs. The proportions of such parameters are typical exclusively of nuclear explosions—not chemical ones.

If one knows the most important parameters of the explosion then one can calculate the temperature involved: Tungus generated a heat of several tens of millions of degrees—so intense that living trees were set on fire for distances of 15–18 km. One of Kulik's closest collaborators, E. L. Krinov, noticed that on some trees there were small branches only partly charred because they had been protected by larger ones, and more recent investigations have led to the conclusion that the fire was in fact a result of the sudden development of heat—not a consequence of a forest fire which would have consumed the small branches entirely. Another curious fact was the discovery that the degree of burning was not the same everywhere over any one particular tree—from which it was deduced that the conflagration cannot have arisen from *underneath* the trees. The burn-scars cannot have been caused by the hot gases that escaped because if they had been the explosion would have had to have been scores of times stronger, with the result that trees still further from the epicentre would have been uprooted. All this points to the fact that the fire induced by the radiation was the consequence of a nuclear explosion. Sufficient evidence lies in the fact that in various observatories people discovered microbarograms dating from 30th June 1908 which registered infrasonic shock-waves with a frequency varying from 0.001 to 0.1 Hz. Frequencies of this order are typical of very large nuclear explosions in the atmosphere.

As far as the magnetic disturbances are concerned, and the three successive nights of light in western European cities, a group of physicists at Tomsk, led by Plekhanov, published in 1960 their findings after comparing the American Bikini atomic explosion in 1958 with the Siberian one half a century earlier. Bikini brought about changes in the gravitational fields of the planet very similar to the ones at the time of Tungus. The 1958 explosion also caused a greater nocturnal light intensity, though rather less pronounced than the 1908 one must have been. The lighting-up of the clouds in colours ranging from yellow to pink is the result of contact with radioactive dust thrown into the atmosphere.

So it seems that at the end of June in 1908 a nuclear explosion took place above the Tungus *taiga*. There is still the question of whether the explosion was thermonuclear or of a more ordinary nature; and whether natural or artificial. In this connection the surprising results of the "flora expedition" led by G. P. Plekhanov and Koschelov were published in 1969 after a special investigation of the area, when it turned out that larches and birches aged between 40 and 50 years (which had therefore germinated after the explosion) which should normally have been 7–8 m high were in fact 17–22 m in height; that is, they had reached a size which "normal" trees of this type would attain only after two or three hundred years. Thus their genetic structure had been radically altered in 1908, a phenomenon which could have been caused by radioactivity. After careful measurements had been made of countless sections of tree-trunks it appeared that the annual rings in the wood made before 1908 were 0.4–2 mm thick, whereas those made after that date were 5–10 mm in thickness. Many trees alive today which had experienced the catastrophe had over a period of 50 years increased their girth four times!

Unusual developments of this sort are typical of vegetation exposed to radioactivity. In the laboratories of the Valga Geographical Institute detailed examina-

Cross-sections of larches from the disaster-area:
1. A 40-year-old tree with 5 mm rings of growth.
2. A 95-year-old tree with annual rings of 1.0 mm till 1908 *and* 3.2 mm *after* this date.
3. A larch ravaged by fire in 1908. Annual rings till that date 1.2 mm and 5 mm afterwards.

tions were made of more than 100 sections of trees from the disaster area. Seven to fifteen samples were taken from each so that over a thousand were studied altogether, and it was shown that the great majority whether alive or dead had undergone radioactivity either after the explosion or when it occurred. The outer 10 to 15 rings showed increased radioactive content as a result of the most recent tests. The most important fact about all this is that the *increased radioactivity of the annual rings laid down in and just after 1908 presupposes the presence of artificial radioactive isotopes.* During the examination of charred pieces of wood use was made of a very sensitive spectrometer and the presence of the radioactive isotope cesium 137 was confirmed.

As the nuclear hypothesis won more followers, various theories grew (like those of the astronomer Urey) about natural atom and hydrogen bombs, radioactive meteorites, comets and other bodies plunging through our atmosphere and exploding so that trees were attacked radioactively. These theories have not stood the test of time, however, nor has the hypothesis that a comet exploded and produced nuclear or thermonuclear fall-out naturally. The comet was assumed, because of the released gases, to have been 50–70 m in section, which was again impossible in view of the slow speed with which the "thing" described its ballistic arc.

The English science magazine *Nature* published an article in 1965 by the American Nobel Prizewinner Libby reporting the presence of radioactive carbon 14 in North American trees. He demonstrated that tree deposits from 1909 showed increased radioactivity, and this was confirmed by the Soviet Academician A. P. Vinogradov. Libby is an ardent champion of the theory that there was a nuclear explosion above Tungus in 1908, but he tends rather to speak of it as an "anti-meteorite." It is very probable that he is right in thinking that it was cosmic anti-matter that plunged into the atmosphere at that time and brought about a destruction of both matter and anti-matter; this is a theory put forward by the American meteorite specialist La Paz as early as 1948. It is of course pure theory as it is based entirely upon hypothetical possibilities, and Soviet scholars like Plekhanov, Zolotov and Fessenkov are quite right to protest that their American colleagues are not taking enough notice of the Tungus data so carefully established. Whatever exploded over Tungus had a force equal to 10 megatons, and to develop energy of that order one needs an "anti-meteorite" of 300–400 grammes. If we assume that such an "anti-meteorite" did actually penetrate our atmosphere, then it could not have caused the ballistic waves which now make it possible to calculate the trajectory which the "thing" must have gone through. The power of the ballistic waves was by nature thousands of times smaller than that of the original explosion yet big enough, if need be, to make us assume an object several metres across; and an "anti-meteorite" is not "a body several metres in diameter." Besides, nobody has as yet ever seen an "anti-material" object: the existence of such a thing rests entirely upon the formulae of a scientific working hypothesis. Also an object of this nature would inevitably explode as soon as it was in contact with matter. That is to say, penetrating the solar system would mean an explosion, but this would be millions of kilometres from our own planet. An explosion of anti-matter is nevertheless a possibility if one accepts the theory that a space-ship blew up over Tungus—a space-ship driven by anti-matter. This idea was put forward by the Soviet scholar V. N. Mehedore after he had studied the conclusions of the various teams investigating the affair. The explosion of a motor powered by energy from anti-matter would show all the traits known to us of a nuclear detonation.

A strong argument in support of this idea of an artificial cause could be deduced from a reconstruction of the trajectory the object traversed, though this line of investigation has up till now not led to any definitive conclusions. The following is the essence of the case:

According to the material published in 1964, the object was assumed to have taken a route from south to north (south variant). Zolotov and his colleagues came to a different conclusion after they had studied the trees struck down in the disaster area. The object's trajectory agrees with the longitudinal axis of these trees knocked down by the ballistic shock; a trajectory which shows a striking reversal of direction as it runs first from west to east—roughly—and then back (east variant—see map). The most cogent arguments for the south variant were brought forward by Professor Astapovitch who based his findings on numerous complicated calculations connected with the earthquakes

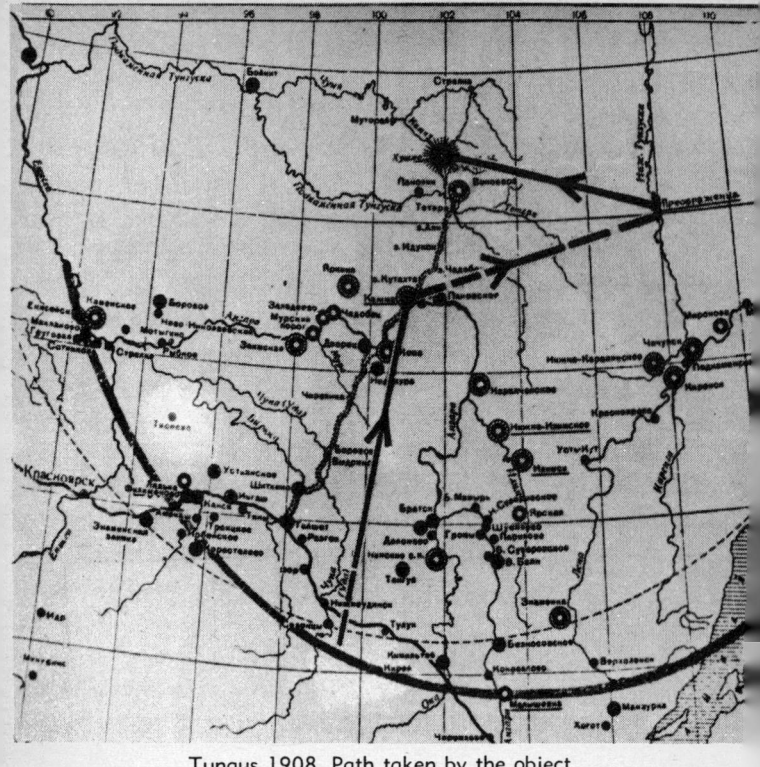

Tungus 1908. Path taken by the object.
Note the odd turn.

and electrical changes registered during the object's flight, as well as on the evidence of witnesses living in the area (though often miles from each other) who either actually saw the flight or heard one of the two sound waves. The calculations and conclusions of both investigators, working independently of each other, proved to be accurate on checking regarding the explosion's epicentre. Zotkin and Tsikulin's laboratory tests already mentioned, in which the explosion was simulated in miniature, showed that the opinions concerning the south and east variant were not necessarily in contradiction to each other or mutually exclusive; that is, the Tungus object altered course in its flight so that it was rightly supposed that it was manoeuvred by "someone."

After it had penetrated the atmosphere the object took a southerly course as far as Keshma, but thereafter, in the vicinity of Preobrajenka, turned suddenly eastwards. An astronomer attached to the Polish (now Czechoslovakian) Tatranska observatory noticed a "fireball" on 30th June 1908 which suddenly changed course over Poland, thus defying all the laws of mechanics. If this was the same object—which can hardly be doubted in view of the fact that the astronomers' times agree—the Tungus "meteorite" or "comet" carried on a peculiar form of ballet before exploding. There are finally several facts, connected not only with direction and speed but also with height, which persuade us that the object was guided (and guiding a "something" of natural origin is quite impossible to us.) Concerning agreement about this change of course there can hardly be any more doubt about the character of the object which blew up over the *taiga* in 1908; it shows the features of an extraterrestrial object guided or teleguided by intelligent beings. But to deduce from that, as does the writer Kasantsev in 1946, that it blew up as the result of an accident, seems to us to be far-fetched, though within the framework of the human imagination absolutely all hypotheses could be valid alike—the Tungus outburst might have been of an experimental nature done on purpose by ETI to study the effects on our planet or simply to draw attention to its existence. Absurd? At the beginning of September 1971, an international scientific congress was held in the far south of Soviet Armenia, in remote Byurakan, which will perhaps prove to be of lasting importance historically: research workers from Russia, America, England and other East European countries including Czechoslovakia and Hungary came together to discuss the possible existence of inhabited worlds elsewhere, and the availability of methods for contacting civilizations in space. In general Russian astronomers are more inclined to speculation in this field than are their western colleagues, as is Dr. Victor Ambartsumian, chairman of the conference and director of the observatory at Byurakan, which is equipped with a large radio-telescope. During discussion of the means of making our existence known to others in space a number of scholars proposed detonating hydrogen bombs in the areas of (relatively!) near galaxies where there was reason to believe that intelligent life had developed....

A possible connection between the "Tungus miracle" and UFO phenomena is something which anyone can make, and if intelligent beings are responsible for the presence of "flying saucers" in our atmosphere, it is very likely that they also brought about the Tungus explosion; the UFO's are probably still searching for the wreckage or have at least drawn conclusions from the blast which make it feasible for them quite easily, we think, to appear in our atmosphere. Who will settle the matter? Homo sapiens?

2. RUSSIAN UFOlogists FIGHT AGAINST THE SAME ODDS AS THEIR WESTERN COLLEAGUES

Professor Zigel pleads for the establishment of an international organization for UFO research—Jacques Vallée delivers a lecture in Moscow—The Stoljarov Committee unleashes a storm in the Russian Academy for Science—The Russian scholar who waits to see which way the American UFO cat is going to jump—Frequent sightings of UFO's in Russia—Russian astronauts report seeing flying cylinders—"Voices from space" command a woman to murder a scholar—Not a single theory can claim to explain the UFO phenomenon—Konstantin Tsiolkovsky, father of space-travel and ETI speculation—Space-travel and telepathy will one day be joined together indissolubly.

In our previous works we paid a great deal of attention to research into UFO sources and their reliability, and we concluded that only a fairly limited number of publications concerning flying saucers deserve to be regarded as reliable; but that on the other hand those few—with the exception of the publication by Captain Edward J. Ruppelt—are by scientific investigators who are known nationally or even internationally. Since Professor Allen Hynek, Jacques Vallée, Professor James E. McDonald and the commissions for compiling the Hearing and Condon Reports have all taken a public stance in this matter of flying saucers, anyone wishing to write on the subject can no longer afford to ignore the scientific works of these scholars. It is also thanks to these scientific publications that western UFOlogy is now slowly but surely disentangling itself from a welter of prejudice, ridicule and mysticism. Like their western counterparts the Russians also have their authorities, or rather, authority, and that in the person of Dr. Felix Zigel, Professor of Higher Mathematics and Astronomy at the Moscow Aeronautical Institute. He is trying to establish a world organization of UFO research and we know there are many other people in Russia with scientific training who are in tacit agreement with him. Although UFOlogy is not entirely taboo in that country, people have to proceed very carefully if they wish to pursue it. The influence of important "anti-UFO" scholars is considerably greater than it is in the U.S.A. today, and the attacks made there by the scientific establishment on those who study UFO's are fiercer and more spiteful.

So an important characteristic of Russian publications about UFO's can be seen in the way the authors often employ historical (see the Robozero case from the seventeenth century, p. 54) or present-day American UFO sightings for the purpose of interpreting their own flying-saucer observations. Whatever the tendencies of the publications about UFO's might be the number of them is very small. Official Russian documents about UFO's, comparable with those in the archives of the U.S. Air Force, are not at our disposal since the Russian air arm did not keep any sort of Bluebook project such as that kept in the U.S. since 1947. One might look in vain for special organizations in Russia dealing with UFO's solely, like the American NICAP. The absence of such institutions means there are no magazines about UFO's. The editors of Russian daily papers do not make a practice of reporting UFO observations, although *Pravda* does sometimes sporadically give a brief account "from official sources" about the results of the Condon investigation; and in 1967–8 *Izvestia*, *Komsomolskaia Pravda* and several local papers like *Sovetskaia Latvia* reported UFO sightings. During the same years articles about the problem by Russian and American authors did appear in several weekly and monthly magazines in the home market, such as *Smena*, *Ogoniok*, *Tekhnika Molodieji*, and *Vokrug Sveta*, while it became apparent through a now famous article by Zigel in the December 1967 edition of *Sputnik* (well-known abroad) and in an interview with him in the *New York Times* that flying saucers are in fact reported even in Russia and that importance is attached to them "officially." The Moscow science publishers—Nauka—brought out an important book in 1967 in which a number of authors speculated about the possibilities of ETI and extraterrestrial life, and it was for this book that Zigel wrote the chapter on the UFO's. The book was called *The Inhabited Cosmos* and was under the general editorial guidance of P. Konstantinov, Vice-President of the Academy of Sciences.

The fact that Russia kept quiet about UFO's until the 1960s has its reasons. First of all the Russian authorities just after the Second World War (the Cold War period) felt that UFO reports whether from abroad or originating at home had to be linked with psychological warfare tactics since these "mysterious" and excited accounts were looked upon as likely to have the sole purpose of creating unrest and fear amongst the people. The second cause—an extension of the first—is that the Russian authorities, just like their colleagues in the West, did not know what to do apart from debunking all such accounts or hushing them up. For this reason Dr. Donald H. Menzel's book written in the U.S. in 1953 was published in large numbers in a Russian translation only in 1962—the original title being *Flying Saucers*. Menzel's book has been fiercely attacked, yet in Russia it enjoys more "respect" than was ever bestowed on him in his homeland.

Fortunately the end of the Cold War during the 1950s brought *inter alia* an exchange of information between scholars of East and West, when the Soviet authorities found that the UFO was as big a problem over here as it was to them. To their considerable surprise they discovered that a small but respectable number of scientists in the West not only took the matter seriously but actually studied it! Two important international congresses were held in Moscow: the first in 1965 concerned telecommunications, during which the three unknown satellites encircling the earth were discussed; and the second took place the following year—a world congress of mathematicians. In the course of this meeting the Franco-American

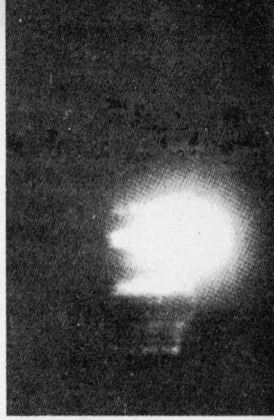
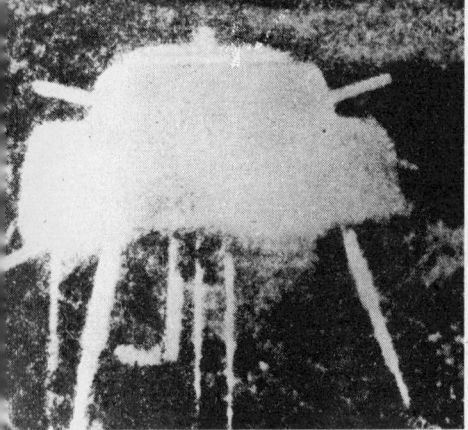

top left: One of the photos released by NASA of the object which McDivitt photographed and stated by NASA to be "Unidentified."

bottom left: Photo of a UFO which landed at Genova (Italy) and published by *Domenica del Corriere* on 8th September 1963. Striking likeness to the sketch of the Caucasus UFO (see p. 36).

bottom right: Leningrad, 1966. Photo taken by a Russian journalist (a friend of the Belgian author). It is very probably a falsification.

top right: A UFO photographed at night at Sherman, Texas on 2nd August 1965 by the television reporter Bob Campbell. Dr. Allen Hynek considered it to be genuine. Here too there is a remarkable similarity to the UFO photographed on 24th December 1967 by Damir Gradisj (see p. 206).

computer expert Jacques Vallée held a lecture on UFO's which encouraged Zigel (and others) to declare an attitude to the problem publicly. Though "publicly" must be treated with caution in this context, there was now more freedom to talk about UFOlogy in Russia and one could really imagine that an extremely skilled and respected team of workers under the leadership of the equally skilled and respected Prof. Edward U. Condon (of world repute) was busy studying the flying saucer problem in depth in California and Colorado. UFO activity in 1966 also increased strongly over Poland, China, Czechoslovakia and the Soviet Union; thus the Czech army magazine *Periscope* and the Soviet News Agency Tass announced to the whole world on 12th April 1965 that radio astronomer Sholomitsky had detected in the Pegasus constellation an "intelligent" source of radio waves. These circumstances made the 18th October 1967 the most important date in Russian UFO history so far, since on that day an official meeting organized by the Cosmonaut Committee was held in Moscow and over 400 people were present. The following authorities headed the committee-meeting: Major-General Porfiri A. Stoljarov, president; Dr. Felix Zigel, vice-president; Alexander Kasantzev, author, vice-president; and Arkadi Tykhonov, engineer, secretary. On 10th November of the same year the president and first vice-president of the committee were introduced to the public on Russian T.V. Professor Zigel showed sketches of the UFO sighted in the Caucasus in 1967 (see diagram) and photos of unknown flying objects. General Stoljarov stressed that his colleagues—called for the sake of convenience the Stoljarov Committee —had the particular task of exposing pseudo-scientific interpretations of genuinely odd and inexplicable phenomena. He requested all interested persons to come forward and support the cause of scientific and systematic research into the UFO problem.

As might have been expected, this appeal found an enormous response over the whole world, all the important newspapers reporting the founding of an "official" Soviet organization for the solution of the UFO problem. A lengthy article by Henry Kamm was devoted to this subject in the *New York Times* on 10th December 1967 and no less a person than Walter Sullivan pointed out in the same paper the affinities between the Stoljarov Committee and the Condon team which at that time was still functioning. That Walter

Sullivan drew the wrong conclusions about this is due solely to the fact that he was unaware, completely, of what the Russian UFO position was. But the Russian Academy for Sciences took fright at this sensational new development: the Stoljarov Committee, it said, was wrongly viewed by the Western press as an organization "officially" supported by the government like that of Condon; it was simply a free association of Russian scientists who wished to spend their spare time pursuing the problem. Like all Russian associations this one also needed the blessing of the government which it did indeed acquire, since people at the highest levels of the political executive were convinced of the serious nature of the problem: this was of course the same in the U.S.A. The Bureau of General Physics and Astrophysics section of the Academy for Sciences held a meeting during which Dr. L. A. Artsimovitch, Russia's Menzel, sharply attacked all UFO protagonists, invoking the honour of Russian scientists who were making themselves look ridiculous in the eyes of their Western colleagues (having said this, the story has it that he then furiously waved a copy of Walter Sullivan's *New York Times* article).

Sketch of the Caucasus UFO, 1967. Presumably shown on Russian television on 10th November 1967.

Even before the Academy had officially pronounced upon the matter Vladimir Lechkoutsov, secretary of the National Committee of Soviet Physicists, had granted an interview to a Canadian newspaper in which he denied the existence of any Russian organization for the solving of the UFO problem. This blow took effect and the Stoljarov Committee was forced to suspend its activities. On 27th February 1968 *Pravda* published in detail the official attitude which was signed by E. Mustel, chairman of the Astronomical Council of the Academy for Science, D. Martynov, president of the Astronomical and Geodetical Society —and Lechkoutsov. One of the statements was that not a single object had been sighted above Russian soil which could not be explained. People who reported seeing such things were deceitful—or simply lacking in scientific training. In brief, all the prejudices were once again aired which had already been answered in the famous October 1966 edition of *Science* in the article signed by Doctor J. Allen Hynek. The Russian bosses referred to Menzel's book of course, and they requested him to re-state his opinion in Russian newspapers, which he promptly did: in January 1968 he published his already familiar views in *Vokrug Sveta*, that the universe contains other intelligent life besides our own but that the UFO's are unconnected with any such civilization. Russian UFOlogy was finished. It only remains for us to quote in this connection from the French UFO magazine *Phénomènes Spatiaux* (No. 15, January 1968), a publication the Russian UFOlogists followed fairly closely. Tykhonov, the secretary of the Stoljarov Committee, wrote to the editor saying that the information the magazine had published about the establishment of a UFO committee in the Soviet Union was wrong. "As far as I am concerned," Tykhonov concluded, "being old and ill, I ask that you should take this letter into account."

Headlines in the *New York Times* (10th December 1967) arouse the wrath of Professor Artsimovitch.

Finally, at the end of 1968, the scientific authorities put a stop to all UFO research for good, when reports about the Condon Committee became gloomier, and more and more nonsense was being spoken and published about the subject by UFOmaniacs with or without scientific training—to such a degree that the whole affair was becoming ridiculous. Since then all is very quiet on the Russian UFO front and one might perhaps suspect the authorities of co-operating in a world-wide "conspiracy" aiming to conceal from "the people" the existence of UFO's for some sinister reason or other. But there is in our opinion no question of the existence of any such plot, and the Russian government has nothing at all to hide—seeing that scholars in that country have declared that UFO's do not exist. . . . Any government is likely to adopt the same attitude towards such a complex and "mysterious" problem as this one, where the verdict of specialists—in this case physicists and astronomers—is indispensable. The leading scholars in Russia have the same point of view in this matter as their equals in America: they do not study the facts because these are absurd; and absurd facts do not need to be studied. Even if they were convinced of the existence of UFO's they would still not consider them a worthwhile subject for their attention. UFO's make them shy and unsure of themselves because the subject has already had so much attention, in an atmosphere of secretiveness and mysticism, paid to it by lay people that it seems "unscientific" to them. Russian scholars would rather wait and see what happens in America first.

Despite the above-mentioned limitations we have enough material at our disposal to conclude that:
1. the Russian UFO period begins in 1946—the "modern" one;
2. Russian UFO's have the same features as anywhere else on earth;
3. although UFO sightings are not announced through the mass media the feed-back to the public and the observers appears to be the same as it is in the West;
4. Russian science circles approach the UFO problem with the same revulsion (or avoid it just as eagerly) as elsewhere;

5. the UFO phenomenon is likewise assumed to be of extraterrestrial origin.

In connection with this last point we should note that in Russian discussions the possibility of ETI, even in scientific circles, finds more favour than it does in the West; in this field Russia does indeed have a great and rich tradition to which we shall return later in this chapter.

In May 1946 the first accounts were heard of strange, saucer-shaped flying objects appearing at night, the reports coming both from "experienced" observers like pilots who saw these saucers in the form of "fire-balls" during their flights, and also from "inexperienced" people such as farmers and townsfolk who saw them from the ground. Both types of observer mentioned the enormous velocities and accelerations of these objects, which were quite unlike anything human beings could simulate in their aircraft built on traditional lines. It is remarkable that Dr. Zigel thus begins the modern UFO period a year or more earlier than the customarily accepted date of 4th June 1947 when the American Kenneth Arnold first noted them. We think this is correct since in both East and West "modern" UFO's had been seen already in 1945 and 1946. But what is scarcely known at all is the *number* of observations in Russia; we think it virtually certain that the list of fifty or so we note in the Documentation section covers the *published* ones. But this relatively unimportant number is not at all representative of the Russian total. In Russia (and according to a Gallup Poll 90% of observations are not recorded in the U.S.A.) the number is enormous, as anyone must agree who has touched on the subject with ordinary Russian citizens. The latter do not think twice about contacting newspapers to report them and the Soviet Air Force compiles dossiers on the phenomena when reported by pilots—but not otherwise. (There is a well-known file on UFO's seen over the Baltic regions of Murmansk, Harkov and Gorki by Senior Pilot Akkusatov, who has specialised in polar flights and repeatedly observed them.)

In spite of the fairly small number of published cases we think that UFO's are as often seen in Russia as in the West—and we base this opinion on what we have learnt in the course of our investigations into the matter in Rumania especially, and to a lesser extent in Russia itself. To begin with there seems to have been almost a UFO wave in the second half of the 1950s, as in July 1949.

One of the best-documented cases dating from that time is at our disposal thanks to the American Lloyd Malland, an authority on space-travel and a well-known author of scientific articles who mentions, in *The Official Guide to UFO's*, Special Issue of *Science and Mechanics*, 1968, the observation of a UFO in Kazakstan on 30th May 1958. We give a shortened version of this account:

"Between 21:20 and 21:30 Moscow time [G.M.T. is three hours later] some people on a small airfield in the Urals saw a strange object flying from the north. It shone like a star of magnitude 2 but there was no twinkle. It was visible in the Cassiopeia Constellation but was clearly no higher than 350 metres and had a velocity of 150 knots. The object veered to the west and accelerated to 400 knots (the speed of a turbo-reactor), flying over the airfield without any sound at all. Then suddenly it stayed motionless in the air for about 10 seconds. The light now emanating from it was quite spherical and *beams* of light could not be seen. The colour was that of a red rose. After thus pausing briefly the 'light' started again and went off at an angle of 45 degrees in a north-westerly direction for several seconds at 100–120 knots and suddenly stopped 45 degrees above the horizon. After this it moved until it was close to the control tower and the light began to pulsate. Did it then make a spiral ascent? Probably it did, though that is not the impression I have. At 80 degrees above the horizon it seemed to turn like a satellite around an (invisible) axis. When the object had become distant it appeared to be approached by a second light coloured like red stars. Both points of light circled around each other for a long time and finally disappeared from view. During this wave Russian Pacific coastal batteries shot at high-speed at brightly-lit UFO's on 25th July 1957 but without any result" (Reuter and Tass).

At the end of the 1950s the reports and rumours of UFO landings in Kazakstan and Uzbekistan in particular became increasingly difficult to brush aside, and at the same time there were stories current about "little green men" and "marsh inhabitants." In these remote areas, where rumour had it that UFO's skimmed low over the roofs of houses, this was enough to cause the holding of new religious services—see for instance the magazine *Science et Vie* in its July 1961 edition. It was L. A. Artsimovitch, the same man who was to stifle the activities of the Stoljarov Committee, who was given the task of exposing the mystique and silencing the rumours. Artsimovitch adopted the tactics he was to use again seven years later: he wrote articles in local newspapers accusing the American press of causing it all for the sake of propaganda and sheer sensation.

There was definitely a second UFO wave in Russia in 1966, the year in which America also experienced a UFO scare. The year after that appears likewise to have been a busy one for UFO's in the Soviet Union, and at the beginning of 1968 *Soviet Weekly* published an article that in the previous year in South Russia alone there had been more than 200 reliable reports of UFO observations. In the March 1968 edition of *Aurora,* the Russian information bulletin in Rumania, there was an account by Vasili Kuprevici, president of the Byelo-Russian Academy for Sciences, in which he stated that in his native province the number of UFO reports were steadily increasing; not only of objects seen with the naked eye but also of those detected with the aid of radar, photos, films and telescopes. (In our summary of UFO's in Russia various cases support this statement.)

Meanwhile Zigel had revealed in the April 1967 number of *Smena* that those UFO observations made by Russian pilots were identical with those familiar to him from the West; he also announced that Gorilek, who acted on behalf of the central Soviet aerological laboratory, had perceived UFO's by means of radarscopes. It is odd that Zigel makes no mention of the strange cylindrical objects which Russian astronauts had reported out in space two years before. During the 1965 Telecommunications Congress clear reference was made to the fact (we have our information about this from, amongst other things, the December 1967 edition of the UFO magazine *Clypeus*) that the crew of both Voskhod 1 and 2 had seen strange "cylinders" in space which were perfectly formed and had no apertures. Voskhod 1 started its flight on 12th October 1964 at 09:30 Moscow time, completed sixteen revolutions round the earth and landed the next day at 09:47 Moscow time. This was the first space-ship in which three astronauts—Komarov, Feoktistov and Egorov—were sent into an orbit around our planet together. A Western journalist who on 21st October 1964 attended a press conference about this event in the Grand Hall of Moscow University told us quite recently (1972) that Komarov, the most skilled cosmonaut Russia ever had (who four years later was to meet with a fatal accident in Soyuz 1), was very brief in his delivery although he was chief spokesman and answered more evasively than usual. During a question put by our informant about the possibility of meeting unexpected objects in space flights Komarov walked out without further commentary. Voskhod 2 began its journey on 18th March 1965 (09:00 Moscow time) and had two cosmonauts on board: Pavel Beljajev (who died in 1970 from a stomach complaint) and Alexei Leonov, who in the course of this flight was the first human being to step out into space. When the space-ship was given instructions to land as it was completing its seventeenth revolution, the automatic navigational system failed to function correctly. It then made an unexpected eighteenth orbit and descended under manual control on to an equally unexpected spot in the Urals. The cause of the defect was never discovered and the subject was not mentioned during the press conference which followed on 26th March. Furthermore there was no mention of the cylindrical objects seen by Pavel Beljajev during the flight...

The American James McDivitt likewise saw floating around his Gemini cabin a number of cylindrical objects on 4th July 1965. Is it possible that what was observed on 12th October 1964 and 18th March 1965 by Russians was the same thing seen by the American on 4th July 1965?

Photo of a UFO by James McDivitt, taken on 4th July 1965. This type of UFO is often reported by observers: see inter alia Rumanian catalogue no. 17 and 32.

In an interview with a journalist on the Barcelona newspaper *El correo Catalan* (published 18th November 1967) Zigel explains that in Russia, too, fragments of UFO's are preserved and studied (for this topic see the material reproduced concerning the Karelia crater, p. 61). Zigel mentions "certain metal fragments of an unknown composition."

With a few exceptions we have at our disposal hardly any Russian details about electromagnetic effects—e.g. the sudden cutting-out of automatic motors, the failure of electric current etc. But we can take one detail at secondhand from the magazine *Veac Nou*, in which an anonymous author sharply "denies" the "contention" that electromagnetic effects had been detected in Russia. Our comment here might be that the "denial" of the "contention" in this context—and in sharp terms too—only proves that reports about this phenomenon exist; moreover the number of them on this subject is greater, presumably, than the number we have been able to cover for the purpose of this book.

The same *Veac Nou* adjures its readers to consider it as nonsense that people could ever have been hypnotised by secret "rays." Yet the number of cases published in Western UFO magazines of people who as a result of "rays" sustained burns or were paralysed is legion: read, for instance Jacques Vallée's *Passport to Magonia*.

Similarly we do not know a great deal about Russian UFO observations where UFOnauts made contact with human beings or vice versa, if we leave more or less out of account the reported UFO landings in Kazakstan and Uzbekistan. As in America, the number of reported cases of contact between people and UFO crews is increasing in recent years in Russia, or seems to be; we ourselves were personally told of a case in which the UFOnaut was "only half visible and seemed to hover." In this connection we would like to cite witnesses from *Passport to Magonia* (1969):

In the Soviet Union not very long ago an eminent scientist in the field of plasma-research died in suspicious circumstances—he was killed by being pushed under an underground train in Moscow by a mentally deranged woman. The accused claimed that a "voice" from space had instructed her to kill this particular man and she felt unable to resist the order. I understand from trustworthy sources that Russian criminologists are worried about the increase in cases of this sort in recent years. Quite often mentally unstable people are known to run wildly across a street protesting that they are being pursued by Martians. But the present wave of mental troubles is an aspect of the UFO problem deserving special attention because it may be connected with the growth of the myth about human contact with higher spheres.

What is remarkable about the nature of this Russian "myth" is that it has developed in a way identical with its counterpart in the West and from the same types of observations. And this cannot be due to the press seeking sensational publicity (since in Russia this exists hardly at all) or to the workings of international groups.

As already stated, the UFO phenomenon in Russia is closely associated with the hypothesis that it is of extraterrestrial origin and there are three important Soviet publications in this respect which we shall now look at in detail.

First is Zigel in the 7th April 1967 edition of *Smena* (actually an early publication of his argument in *The Inhabited Cosmos*); second an interpretation and explanation of the UFO problem by Donald Menzel and James McDonald in the Spring 1968 edition of *Vokrug Sveta*, with an introduction by Professor Dobronravov; and third a series of articles by Jacques Vallée, Kasantsev, Makarov and Campbell in the August 1967 number of *Tekhnika Molodieji*.

Many of these ideas and conclusions are known to Western readers—certainly those of Jacques Vallée, James McDonald and D. H. Menzel—and we shall not refer to them again here. That Felix Zigel is such an outright champion of the theory that UFO's are of extraterrestrial origin, as many UFO magazines would have it, is apparently not the case to judge from the *Smena* article we have at our disposal.

In this account Zigel systematically investigates and rejects a number of theories (also known in the West) about the UFO problem. He first shows quite convincingly how shortsighted and inaccurate popular ideas in this connection are, since UFO observations are often based on reports by unbalanced or inexperienced people with no qualifications; and also that sightings of UFO's cannot be reduced to symptoms of any kind of hallucination. Second, he rejects Menzel's theory which derives from the "explanation" of UFO sightings as optical illusions, which is naturally an explanation that cannot possibly be valid for *all* such sightings. Third, he suggests that they cannot be secret machines constructed by human beings anywhere in the world. So are they natural phenomena of a practically unknown sort? Fourth, Zigel has his own ideas about these matters, for example that some of the UFO's could be plasmas formed in the stratosphere by ionized particles deriving from the earth's crust. An earthy bone to pick for the physicists, Zigel rightly says, adding at once the view that this theory is not suitable for *all* UFO's. These types of plasma are not in the habit of forming in the atmosphere after all and can hardly be considered as responsible for typical UFO manifestations like electromagnetic disturbances, fierce conflagrations of light etc. Fifth, Zigel describes as mere fantasy and speculation the hypothesis that "UFO's are space-craft of spatial origin and workmanship sent to our planet for contact and reconnoitring." Finally Zigel says: "Not one of the existing hypotheses can boast of authoritatively clearing up the UFO problem." But Zigel does not doubt the reality of the UFO itself and urges people to establish a scrupulously scientific, multilateral and international investigation.

V. V. Dobronravov, university physicist and mathematician, supports Zigel unreservedly in his introduction to Menzel's and McDonald's articles on the existence of UFO's but adds further speculation about ETI. Dobronravov reasons logically that communal groups must exist in the universe which are more developed than our own and he thinks that Man is as yet only at the beginning of an evolution which will enable him in the long run to achieve things comparable with the UFO phenomenon today. But he questions McDonald's proofs of the UFO's extraterrestrial origin, saying that McDonald's arguments "are inadequate and unconvincing." A strange way of thinking and reasoning; just as strange as, for instance, the arguments put forward by Carl Sagan and Joseph Skhlovsky (discussed later on in this chapter) that our planet was formerly visited by "beings of a different order of intelligence" but that we need not expect them to come here again for the next ten thousand years; which implies that UFO's have nothing to do with ETI. Whoever can see the logic of this argument is perhaps himself a "being of a different order of intelligence." In any case Menzel's and Dobronravov's "explanations" are just as unsatisfactory.

From the series of articles in *Tekhnika Molodieji* we would mention only the views of the physicist I. Makarov, which amount to an acceptance of the universality of intelligence and UFO reality. Unfortunately however Makarov also brings in the "explanation" that most of the UFO phenomena noted are the results of ball-lightning and their effects. A clincher par excellence, is this, since hallucinations, weather balloons etc. (the reader can fill in the rest) are no longer adequate as the "solution" of the riddle.

Interest in space-travel and ETI is considerable in Russia, both in scientific circles and amongst the ordinary people. Westerners are inclined to be amazed that nearly everybody there reacts enthusiastically to Russian space achievements and takes a lively interest in every next step towards the stars—while Western television organizations are snowed under with complaints about time-wasting commentaries on rocket-launchings, space-travel and journeys to the moon that leave no room for the football matches, detective and cowboy films, the homely quiz for the whole family. . . . Westerners are thus not generally at one with the enthusiasm and interest the Russians bring to the subject with their sense of national pride. Russia is at the centre of scientific space-travel and the father of this science is not, as is so often asserted, Wernher von Braun or Hermann Oberth, but the Russian Konstantin Tsiolkovsky.

Tsiolkovsky was the son of a woodcutter at Jevsk and was born on 17th September 1857. He spent his student days at Moscow University trying to launch rockets and devoured whole libraries of books about physics and astronomy. At Kaluga he was a lecturer in mathematics from 1882 and when not lecturing there spent his entire free time on "space-travel." He was known as an odd character but he worked out the rocket principle both practically and theoretically, so that his work is the basis of modern rocketry. He demonstrated that the only machine which could undertake space-travel was the rocket since, unlike the jet engine, it did not need air for its take-off into space. Although he built very interesting types of rockets and was the first man to construct wind-tunnels for his models, his importance lies in the field of theory.

One of his hypotheses was that the only method of gaining sufficient acceleration, at least with present energy-sources, to force machines away from the earth's gravitational field and thus enable them to fly into space, was to use the multi-stage rocket. Later (and better-known) pioneers have admitted Tsiolkovsky's great inspiration has enormously influenced their own work. We mention only Hermann Oberth, Ari Sternfeld (the chief theoretician relating to space-travel Russia possesses), Sergo Kheirolev (well-known Russian rocket-expert) and the American Robert H. Goddard, who can claim to be the first man (around 1920) to work on the building and manning of moon-rockets. Tsiolkovsky died in 1935. He was not concerned about building rockets simply to reach the greatest possible height but to reach the moon and investigate the nature of the universe. According to the opening lines of *Voilia Vselenoii*, the best-known of the roughly sixty books he wrote, he was "convinced that civilized beings exist elsewhere in the universe able to travel from planet to planet and help less developed worlds than their own if requested, and communicate with them."

Russians believe much more strongly than Westerners do in the existence of ETI and have in general more of an urge to contact it: this to them is the "sense" or "usefulness" or "importance" attaching to all space travel as a science and practical undertaking. Faith, desire and motivation have always been there since the days of Tsiolkovsky to the present. Kasantsev, the science-fiction writer who in 1946 maintained that the Tungus "miracle" was the result of a space-vehicle accident, declared in his opening lines that he had drawn his inspiration from Tsiolkovsky. Despite being laughed at by such scholars as Fessenkov and Krinov, Kasentsev was able two years after the story was published to defend his hypothesis in a meeting of the Astronomical Society of the Soviet Union. He found some appreciative listeners amongst such eminent astronomers as Mikhailov, Director of the Pulkovo Observatory, Parenago, Chairman of the Moscow section of the Astronomical Society, Vorontsov-Veliaminov, Academy for educational sciences, Baiev and Nabokov—see No. 9 of *Tekhnika Molodieji,* 1948. As may be deduced from our chapter about the Tungus event Kasantsev's theory is gaining ground and continues to do so; it is a theory grafted upon that of Tsiolkovsky (once considered as a crank) who is the creator of the long Russian tradition of ETI speculation. The foreign delegates to the above-named conference at Byurakan noticed to their astonishment that Russia carries on permanent research in the field of extraterrestrial intelligence. A 17-m radio-telescope is systematically studying the 50 stars which are (comparatively) nearby; in addition there are four other radio observatories attempting to find evidence of extraterrestrial civilizations in the intensive electromagnetic impulses emitted by other bodies.

It is not generally known to the Western reader that the hypothesis popularized by Erich von Däniken— that the "gods" were "cosmonauts"—actually stems from Russian scientific sources. A better and more convincingly documented case than von Däniken's is that of Dr. Viatcheslaw Zaitsev, for instance, who made a study of all the religions in the world with a view to discovering texts mentioning supernatural and wonderful "visions," "vanishings" and so on which might possibly be interpreted as manifestations of an extraterrestrial "something." Another source is the one mentioned earlier in this connection—that of Dr. Iosif Skhlovsky, who together with the American Carl Sagan wrote the most authoritative book to date on ETI, in which it is postulated that perhaps 20,000 years ago the earth was visited by a space-craft. It is the same leading Russian astronomer Shklovsky, of the Sternberg Astronomical Institute at Moscow, who listed as CTA 102 the above-mentioned "intelligent" source of radio-waves, which was found in the Pegasus Constellation by his colleague Gennady Sholomitsky, and afterwards published "officially." His student Nicolas Kardashev was to defend the idea, in the bulletin issued by the Soviet Academy for Sciences, that the signals involved might come from a super-race. An odd point is that Betty Hill, who together with her husband (also American) was said to have been examined by a UFOnaut crew—a fact that came to light under hypnosis—, drew a section of an astronomical chart (again under hypnosis) which she had seen on board a grounded UFO. She then pointed to a star which was the UFO's home port—and the star indicated on the map lay in the Pegasus Constellation. She drew this map two years prior to the Russian discovery; but that Dr. Sholomitsky was influenced by this American social worker was something only Dr. Menzel dared claim—the story of this medical examination of the Hill couple as described by Fuller in *The Interrupted Journey* is recommended.

A matter we mentioned in our foreword as one we wanted to deal with later for the sake of completion is that of the UFO and paranormal phenomena. After all, it is not totally inconceivable that space travel is connected with telepathy and telekinesis—Tsiolkovsky maintained they were closely connected. The Russian navy's newspaper said in 1967 that cosmonauts in orbit discovered an increased level of telepathic communication, so Tsiolkovsky's prophecy may one day well be verified. The most important aspect of telepathy is that thought may momentarily be transferred and the usual limitations imposed by the velocity of light abolished. If we assume that an extraterrestrial civilization has perfected these gifts then the UFO's are telekinetic phenomena, and it would be immaterial whether or not they have been "sent out" by such a culture living perhaps 1 to 10 milliard light-years away. Apparently research in this field has been much more advanced in the East than in the West, according to the book *Psychic Discoveries behind the Iron Curtain* by Sheila Ostrander and Lynn Schroeder.

Meanwhile there has appeared one of the most convincing publications known to us concerning the spatial origin of the UFO—even if this is evident in only an indirect way in the book, where one has to search for it tucked away in the last paragraphs—and this work is by the Russian Iuri A. Fomin, a doctor of telemechanics and automatism; two of the most important branches of the Russian space-travel programme. The publication was in the March 1970 edition of the French UFO magazine *Phénomènes Spatiaux,* supplied by the press agency Novosti—a very official Soviet organization responsible for sending to foreign newspapers articles by Russian authors. In the first part of his work Fomin deals with the problems which might arise if sophisticated and less-sophisticated civilizations come into contact; and he goes on to argue that we might, in order to traverse interstellar space, have to grapple with physical laws which are different from those we know at present and which so far have only a theoretical basis. Fomin adds that the principles of these laws have already been established in mathematical formulae. Many things occur today which puzzle us, and could be the result of contact with various forms of current cosmic phenomena, though the material so far familiar to us has not yet yielded up all its secrets. The hypothesis concerning the various levels on which the material might have existence, and the theory about the interpenetration of the worlds and their parallel being, both find a champion in Fomin; furthermore he is convinced that the multi-dimensionality of space is something which must be treated seriously. If, as he asserts, space has a fourth dimension, then any two points in it could lie together although in our own three-dimensional world they may be far apart. So Fomin thinks it probable that space's multi-dimensionality can be closely linked with the various levels of the material's existence. Our concept of time is an Einsteinian one of linear progression from cause to effect; but an inversion of this is not self-contradictory. If we bear this in mind, and we are almost used by now to the idea of interstellar contact, we may safely conclude, Fomin thinks, that extraterrestrial beings are aware of us because we have arrived at a decisive turning-point in our evolution. This of course presupposes that the increasing amount of UFO information and activity is closely linked with these questions.

All this reminds us of Dr. Charles Townes, Nobel prize-winner for the part he played in the discovery of the maser and laser principles, and Dr. Ronald Bracewell of Stanford University, a world-famous pioneer in the radio-astronomy field. Both took part in the September 1971 conference held at Byurakan (Russia) which debated the possible existence of inhabited worlds other than our own, and methods of contact. They suggested cautiously that the UFO problem should be dealt with on a world basis since UFO signals might well come from space although their significance escapes us as yet. "If there really is a form of ETI trying to contact us then it is quite possible that their messages reach us in signals or other phenomena as enigmatic to us as television pictures would be to the ancient Greeks. . . ."

3. TWO FAMOUS RUSSIAN EXAMPLES: ROBOZERO (1663) & KARELIA (1961)

Russian UFOlogists cautiously approach the thorny problem—
His Highness the Archimandrite receives a UFO report—"From
the clearest of all skies a great fire descended upon Robozero"
—Meteorite, comet, ball-lightning or space probe?—Forester
Vasili Bradski's telegram—Green ice-floes—The medal of gold
for a case of proven cold-bloodedness—Craters, indefinite tracks
and inexplicable substances are constant factors in UFO
literature the world over.

There is a very large number of published cases of strange light phenomena occurring in times long past. Often they have to do with comets or meteorites (see Menzel, who is not *always* wrong after all), which were interpreted by Europeans of past ages as evidence of God's Providence. One might well be sceptical about most of these "wonders," although there are UFOmaniacs who consider all such cases found in old books and manuscripts as authentic cases of UFO's; moreover, such people count upon the reader sharing their enthusiastic suppositions uncritically.

In the Russian magazine *Znaniya-Sila* (Science is Power) which was published on 8th August 1970 the 1663 "Robozero Case" was recalled. We quote from this below in full. Why? Because the whole matter is not only an excellent example of the way in which manifestations from earlier centuries could be approached but also stresses our own point of view that the Russians have made a strong commitment to the hypothesis that UFO's are spatial in origin: certainly this is not an official Russian view but in almost all the publications where these matters can be discussed somebody betrays the attitude typical of both scholars and publicists. We cannot escape the impression that such a one is the well-known scientific writer attached to that paper, Iuri Rostsius, who took up this old and "hoary" (and thus less dangerous) apparition as an alibi and in doing so subtly undermined the arguments about UFO's as normally applied to the modern phenomena. If we substitute, say, 1963 for 1663 and "glowing ship" for "great fire," "Waddensee" for "Robozero" —then we have a typical example of the frivolous manner in which Western UFOlogists pontificate about their explanations of the inexplicable. As we said, UFOlogy is not entirely taboo in Russia but circumspection is called for, and it is an attitude common in all walks of life in the Soviet Union. It is a kind of approach to the problem which still seems to trouble Western readers.

THE ROBOZERO CASE, 1663

If we suppose that what Robozero witnessed in 1663 was to happen today then the newspaper headlines would probably read: "Mysterious light over Robozero; Gigantic ball of fire creates panic; Fishermen sustain burns when fire-mystery approaches; Ball-lightning or space-probe over Robozero?" And so on. But Russian people in 1663 had no newspapers at all; it was only 40 years later under Paul I that they were to appear. I will not repeat the evidence given in those days but would rather quote several excerpts from the original document containing the account of what happened:

"To His Highness the Archimandrite Nikita, to His Highness the Starets Matvei, to His Highness the Starets Pavel, to their Highnesses the Starets of the Synod of the Monastery of St. Cyril; Most Venerable Lords, humble greetings from your servant Ivachko Rjevskoi. The peasant Levka Fedorov, domiciled in the village of Mys, submitted to me the following first-hand account:

On this, the fifteenth day of August in the year 1663, a Saturday, the faithful from the district of Belozero had gone to church in large numbers in the village of Robozero and whilst they were there a great crash sounded from out the heavens and many people left the church of God to assemble outside on the square. Now Levka Pedorov, the farmer already mentioned, was amongst them and saw what happened; to him it was a sign from God. Around the stroke of midday there descended upon Robozero a great ball of fire from the clearest of skies, not from a cloud; moreover it came from the direction from which we get winter and moved across from the church to the lake. The fire was about 45 metres on each side and for the same distance in front of the fire there were two fiery beams. Suddenly it was no longer there but about one hour of the clock later it appeared again, above the lake from which it had disappeared before. It went from the south to the west and was about 500 metres away when it vanished. But once again it returned, filling all who saw it with a great dread, travelling westwards and staying over Robozero one hour and a half. Now there were fishermen in their boat on the lake about a mile away and they were sorely burnt by the fire. The lake water was lit up to its greatest depths of nine metres and the fish fled to the banks. The water seemed to be covered with rust under the glow. . . ."

This document was first published in *Historical files compiled and issued by the archaeological commission,* part IV (St. Petersburg, 1842) under the title "30 November 1662 and August 1663. Reports submitted by the St. Cyril Monastery to the authorities concerning the meteorites observed in Belozero." Added to this report one can also see, in italics, the note "The original text is in two columns written on two pages. The document comes from the files of the archaeographical research service." The authenticity of these files is unquestionable.

As for the truth of the details one can appreciate

the author's wisdom and scepticism in the document, since it seems from the end of the article that he had checked Levka Pedorov's statement: "and I, being your servant, sent a messenger to the priests in the district of Belozero and they wrote confirming what was alleged to have taken place at that time. . . ." Is it possible that Ivachko Rjevskoi could have imagined all this? This is virtually impossible as the report was recorded by a scribe of the Archimandrite Nikita's monastery and as is well known they were excessively strict in Russia in the seventeenth century and had unlimited power. Even a superficial check of the veracity of his words would have brought to light at once any possible enigma—with all the painful consequences. It is also quite probable that Rjevskoi would have had the story confirmed by the priests before telling their Eminences in the St. Cyril Monastery about it. Furthermore it is improbable that he was mentally disturbed in any way, since if that were so the authorities would have had nothing to do with him—certainly not in those days at least. Thus we have a document, the authenticity of which cannot be disputed, written in a style tending to obscure the issue because of its childlike, solemn tone, about a matter which is as mysterious as it is true. If we put it in twentieth-century language then it reads like this:

"On 15th August 1663 between 10 and 12 local time (that of the church services) an object emitting fire and a loud noise appeared in a clear sky. It had a diameter of around 40 metres (a twelve-storey building!) and was travelling from south to west. It stopped over the Robozero lake, which has a surface of about 2 km by 1. The object gave out blue smoke and had two streams of fire projecting from it in front. The object disappeared, in circumstances which are not quite clear, some distance above the lake but returned to the same spot an hour later. This occurred a third time but it was now larger, more dazzling and more impressive. After being visible for an hour and a half it vanished westwards. While it was there some fishermen tried to approach but were unsuccessful because of the scorching heat and they sustained burns on their bodies. The light emitted was so strong that the lake-bed was visible and one could see the fish flying away in all directions. There was a rust deposit on the water where the fire had been which spread out because of the wind."

What was this object's nature? One thinks of mirages, but these are not accompanied by thunderous noises; neither are they so hot that they scorch people, frighten fish away or cause rust. Was it a collective hallucination? The object was seen by two groups of people, the one in the church square, the other on the lake, hundreds of metres away. The evidence of the one confirms and completes the other, since the fishermen supplied details about the phenomenon which could not be seen from the land. The complexity of the whole matter is particularly striking: a collective hallucination cannot usually be heard at first, then visible three times and finally even palpable too.

Perhaps it was a meteorite, as D. O. Sviatskii asserts and as we read in Part IV of the *Historical Files*? We quote the following lines from Sviatskii's book *Astronomical Phenomena in Russian Chronicles* (Petrograd, 1915 page 190): "The explosion of the meteor on 15th August 1663 probably occurred in a south-westerly direction during the morning before 12 o'clock and in clear skies. Two fragments were projected in a southerly direction over the lake whilst a third and fourth came down in the west." We find it difficult to share this opinion since in the first place it seems to us from the document that it was one and the same object seen three times at intervals and fragments from meteorites are ejected simultaneously as a rule. Moreover Sviatskii mentions two fragments as being "projected" but the document contains no such reference to this and thus one is not in a position to infer any such interpretation or conclusion. On the other hand we do see from the article that the fishermen made some attempt to approach the object but were unable to do so because of the great heat. The velocity of the object may have been that of the boat itself, i.e. 4–6 km per hour or even lower, since we may assume that the men either went after it in their boats or were able to row away from it on its approach. In any case the velocity must have been very low. Unfortunately the document says nothing about the duration of each appearance, so we do not know if the "hour and a half" referred to covers the whole period of its manifestation or only the second or third. As for its first appearance this lasted long enough to allow people following the service to leave the church and follow the object to the lake (about 500 m further) which suggests a walk of about ten minutes. The second manifestation either lasted half an hour or one hour and a half. I am inclined to think that the whole event continued about one-and-a-half hours, thus leaving us to presuppose half an hour for each appearance. But as for meteorites it is known that they penetrate space with a velocity of 30–40 km per second, which is about the speed of the earth in its journey round the sun. So a meteorite's speed is dependent upon the velocity of these two heavenly bodies and the nature of their orbits. Whenever our planet comes across a meteorite travelling in the opposite direction, our relative velocity with regard to the meteorite is about 60–70 km per second. If both orbits run parallel and the latter overtakes the former then of course their relative speeds are virtually nil—yet because of our gravitational pull the meteorite's velocity is increased to 11 km per second. It penetrates the upper levels of the atmosphere where its velocity is decreased because of thick layers of air. The meteorite's fate then depends upon its mass; the larger it is the greater the velocity. Those weighing 10–100 grammes develop at the earth's surface a speed of several tens of metres per second, but larger ones weighing several hundred kilogrammes attain a velocity of up to 500 m per second. The one over Robozero must have had a weight of 30,000–250,000 tons, bearing in mind its composition and also any faults arising from wrong estimates of its size. (But the actual size given cannot be so very far from the truth; not just because in those days people were more used to estimating distances and dimensions but also because the object can be compared with known points of reference.) The speed of an object as big as that must have been enormous (in this connection consider what has been said about the "Tungus miracle"). One must point out here that whenever any astral body comes into our atmosphere with a speed of 5 km per second the thermic explosion immediately causes it to evaporate, the energy release being roughly equal to the amount resulting from an explosion of the same quantity of nitroglycerine. . . . Even if we suppose that the meteorite was made of ice its explosion would be 1.5 times greater than that of the atomic detonations over Hiroshima or Nagasaki. In that case there would not have been a single witness left alive in the neighbourhood of Robozero. Yet these witnesses certainly lived to tell the tale—and an explosion did not take place. From which it incontestably follows that the object must have had a speed of less than 5 km per second.

But its original velocity was *not* as low as this, and for good reasons. Seen from a purely theoretical angle, and thus making allowances for human error caused by not working under the best conditions, a body 40 m in diameter must have been visible at a distance of 130 km. In practice this reduces itself to a distance of 10 km however. The object's speed above the lake amounted to 5 km per hour at the most and if it had approached the lake at this speed it would have needed two hours to cover the distance of 10 km. So we conclude that its speed varied; a fairly high one on appearance, but reducing to 1.3–1.5 m per second. Yet there is no record of its falling, despite this slowness—it went off, in fact, gradually, and in a horizontal direction. Whatever its speed a meteorite must fall and the document makes no mention of this; whereas the plunging to earth of a similar object in like conditions would certainly never pass unnoticed. . . . The article only mentions its disappearance after its third and final visitation.

So was it perhaps a comet or rather the nucleus of one? The possibility of such a thing contacting our planet is so remote that the chance is hundreds of milliards of times less likely than that of a meteorite falling; it works out at a possibility of once every eighty million years. But leaving this aside it is clear that all arguments brought to bear against the meteorite hypothesis are equally valid when countering the comet theory.

Was it ball-lightning? Although not a great deal is known about what happens exactly when this takes place we do nevertheless have some idea of what the conditions must be like before it does so. The behavioural pattern is likewise known, as also the accompanying phenomena. It is certain that ball-lightning arises in the vicinity of stormy fronts, mostly in July and August and at the end of a storm. It is usually preceded by ordinary lightning and lasts between one and five minutes—seldom longer. The diameter is 10–20 cm although on several occasions it has been known to reach 2.7 m! Ball-lightning can either remain stationary or move with a speed of several hundred kilometres per hour—and in any direction, independently of the wind. R. A. Leonov asserts in his book *The Riddle of Ball-lightning* (Moscow, 1965) that it can attain a speed of 100 km per second. It is usually red or orange-yellow like a flame and an explosion may or may not occur when it appears.

The 1663 Robozero incident shows some affinities with ball-lightning traits as well as an equal number of non-affinities. But if it is to be classified as a case of ball-lightning despite this, then it must be one of history's exceptions: an extraordinarily large ball-lightning must have been involved and it defies and exceeds all that is known in this field, to such an extent that it should have a different classification. But what are the Robozero characteristics which render the ball-lightning hypothesis untenable? First and foremost the weather; it was a warm, sunny day in summer and the document stresses the fact that the object did not come out of a cloud but from clear sky. Besides it is unscientific, to say the least, to assert that the second and third appearances are typical of ball-lightning behaviour. The object's returns took place right before the witnesses' eyes and the two streams of projecting fire the document mentions are not traits of ball-lightning either, any more than the long duration of the whole event or the rust deposit on the water.

Neither mirage, nor collective hallucination, nor meteorite, comet or ball-lightning. What *was* it then?

About twenty years ago the radio-astronomer Bracewell, an Australian attached to Stanford University, was bold enough to formulate an hypothesis which he repeated at Byurakan in September 1971. He assumes that the civilizations which have developed in the centre of the Milky Way are able to send out automatic probes in all directions. The purpose would be to contact other civilizations, collect information or simply to draw the attention of inhabitants of space elsewhere. It seems an attractive idea to link the Robozero fire with such attempts but unfortunately we do not know how we are to do this. What does such a probe consist of and how does it behave? It may consist of anything our fantasy leads us to. Following this line of reasoning it is very easy to link the Robozero event with a "flying saucer" manifestation, but would our knowledge of the universe be increased thereby?

The solution to the Robozero "riddle" is not known to any mortal, but anybody can attempt to solve it. Does a solution exist? Whoever knows it let him speak....

THE KARELIA CASE, 1961

During a routine trip through the woods south of Karelia in February 1961 forester Vasili Bradski discovered on the banks of one of the many lakes (frozen at this season) of this region a fairly large crater which two days before had not been there. Unable to unravel the cause he hurried to the nearest control point and sent a telegram to Leningrad: "Inexplicable crater on the edge of a lake. Send specialists and divers." Although the following day was a Sunday it nonetheless saw the start of an enquiry by six specialists flown out from Leningrad who examined the lengthy gash on the lake's edge: a hole about 30 m long, 15 wide and 3 deep. The crater was narrower towards the bottom which itself was smooth, though around the edges there were chaotic heaps of grass and soil. But the bottom of the hole was as smooth as possible, as if someone had used a roller. As for the soil excavated by the object there was no trace of it. . . . The ice on the lake nearby was largely broken and at that battered spot there were ice-floes, but elsewhere the ice was undamaged. Black and crumbling pellets were found on the bank which resembled buckwheat grains—these could be crushed between the fingers.

On the bottom of the lake divers found a portion of the soil displaced which was stretched out like a "tongue" across the base for about 100 m.

The theory was that the object had first slid across the soil on landing and thence into the lake, yet there was no trace anywhere of any such object and even when a metal detector was used there was scarcely any reaction.

The divers dragged some of the ice-floes on to the bank and noted that the submerged parts were green. Samples of the pellets, the soil, the ice and some water were collected.

The possibility that the cause was ball-lightning was rejected outright since not only had there been no storm but there was also no trace of any scorching agent. That it might have been a meteorite was barely discussed at all since even sophisticated detectors could find nothing of the sort. Besides this any meteorite will make a crater five times its own girth and such a meteorite would not be small enough to escape the attention of sensitive apparatus, astronomers, meteorologists and other mortals.

Meanwhile the divers found roughly in the middle of the lake another gully along the bottom about 100 m long, which almost seemed as if it had been excavated for a piping system. At the end of the trench there was a hillock about 1.5 m high which looked as if it had been piled up when the trench was made. All around the "tongue" and the gully the ground was untouched and neither, once again, did the detector apparatus offer any clue. Who or what had dug the hole and where was the object lying?

It was gradually deduced that the object had skidded over the soil into the lake, ploughed up the bed and then by some complicated means or other had managed to resume its flight. So this must have been a special sort of machine indeed, to say nothing of its pilot (if there was one) who judged on our own criteria should have been considered a candidate for a gold medal in sheer presence of mind.

The case was studied at Leningrad University under Professor Vsevolod Charmov, in the course of which the meteorite and ball-lightning theories were rejected for the reasons given above. Nothing strange was found in the samples of ice, water and soil, and radioactivity was normal. The green colour of the ice, however, could not be explained. (In connection with UFO activities in similar areas one quite regularly hears of "green ice" or "green snow"—see for instance *The Saapunki UFO: Results of the Investigations. Flying Saucer Review* 1712 and 1713, 1972.) The pellets revealed under the microscope a metallic sheen which does not occur in any known organic material, and neither were they soluble in any acid. Chemists therefore concluded that they were an inorganic substance and probably not of natural origin. In general everybody concerned with what caused the crater shows scepticism about the existence of any apparatus capable of carrying out what is supposed to have happened and of surviving it. No cogent explanation of how the crater came to be has as yet been given. The scholar Viktor Demidov, who took part in the investigation, linked it with UFO's.

But the phenomenon of a hole in a frozen lake is not something peculiar to Russia, since seven years after the Karelia events, on 1st April 1968, two fishermen found a 500 sq m hole in the 90 cm-thick ice on the Upprämen Lake in Sweden. The hole was perfectly triangular in shape and blocks of ice over 1 m in diameter were scattered over the ice a long way from the hole. Here too the authorities set up an enquiry and divers were employed, since it was thought that some object or other had landed and caused the trouble. The divers were unsuccessful in finding such a thing though they did bring up the reddish skin or crust of some indeterminate material. In the ice on other lakes nearby several more triangular holes were seen, one of which was as big as the Upprämen crater and another smaller. In the 21st April 1968 edition of the daily newspaper *Dagens Nyheter* a meteorologist asked if the holes were not perhaps caused by a warm air-current bursting; this was naturally a theoretical question since such a thing had never been known.

Discoveries of craters in the ground where the dislodged soil is completely missing are things which quite often occur in UFO literature. A striking instance of this was published in the French UFO magazine *Lumières dans la nuit* in October 1970. The French police searched in vain for the soil dug out of a hole in a field at Rouillac (Charente) on 10th January 1970 and their quest for the object causing it was just as unsuccessful. It transpired in the course of a thorough investigation that a saucer-shaped object was seen flying near the field the previous day and the owner of the ground saw a huge light. The boulders at the bottom of the crater looked as if pulverized and the sand seemed like ash.

The English author Rex Dutta devotes a whole chapter of his *Flying Saucer Viewpoint* to a discussion of unexplained craters which, whether or not connected with UFO activity, disturbed the rural population in various places in England.

As for the facts of this particular case they belong, like the Karelia and Robozero ones, to the essence of UFOlogy. A very fascinating and serious investigation was undertaken by the French police and Air Force after the discovery of extremely odd-looking imprints in a clover field at Marliens (Cote d'or). A purple substance found there was analysed chemically by the Paris municipal laboratory and spectrographically by the university at Dijon. The conclusions of both institutions working independently of each other were in complete harmony: the substance consisted of small

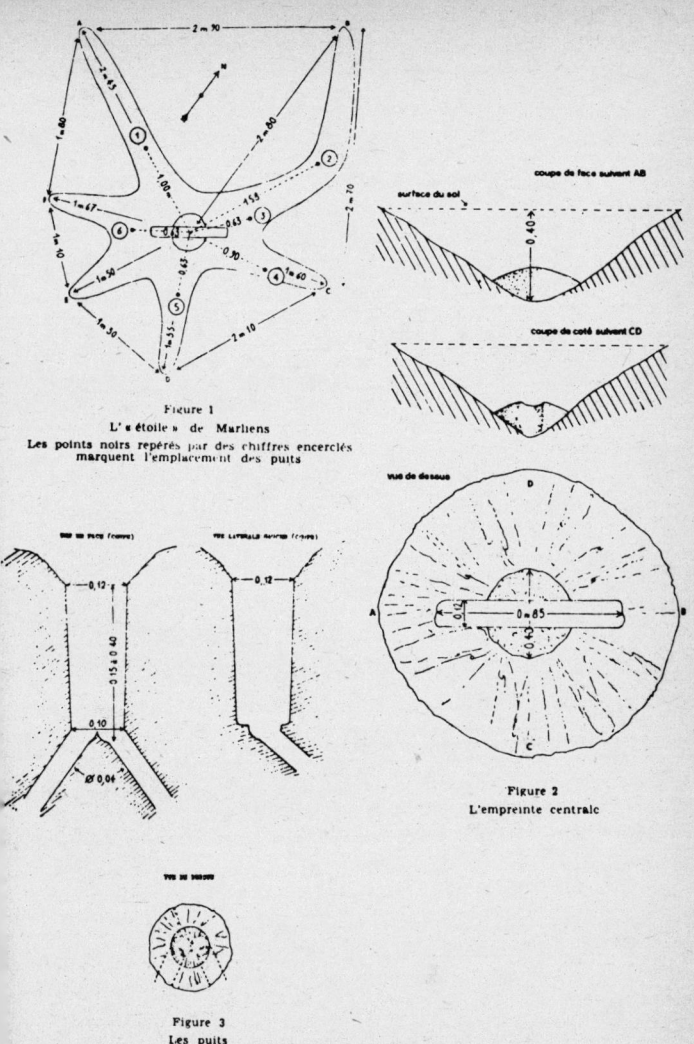

Figure 1
L'« étoile » de Marliens
Les points noirs repérés par des chiffres encerclés marquent l'emplacement des puits

Figure 2
L'empreinte centrale

Figure 3
Les puits

Odd imprints at Marliens (*Phenomenes Spatiaux*, September 1967)

crystals of quartz and aluminium oxide in the early stages of fusion. The fusion presupposes a heat of 1500 degrees (Centigrade) yet the clover leaves on the "landing strip" were not singed at all. . . .

4. UFOLOGY IN POLAND, CZECHOSLOVAKIA AND HUNGARY

A Polish weekly takes the initiative in a thorough study of the saucer question——The UFO photographed over Muszyn——The Ministry of Information issues a brochure——Janusz Thor plagiarizes Menzel——Dr. Hynek undertakes a lecturing tour in his native Czechoslovakia——The UFO Information Centre in Prague——Two Czechoslovakian books of UFO's——Bànky Robert is not allowed to demonstrate the non-existence of aeroplanes on Hungarian television channels.

POLAND

The history of Eastern European UFOlogy begins in Poland: ten years earlier than in the neighbouring countries but a decade later than in the West. It was a time of remarkable UFO activity. From 1957 to 1958 we find the first publications about the saucer phenomenon, in the sense in which this had developed in the West; it was likewise linked with ETI speculation. The same pattern of discussion suddenly emerged as everywhere else: a very large part of both the scientific establishment and what one terms the "serious press" were against accepting the idea of the existence of UFO's and they certainly rejected completely any notion that such things could originate anywhere in space. But gradually even quite a large number of cases of UFO's being seen in Poland was published and for a short time the subject was not taboo. Some quite serious newspapers busied themselves with the UFO "mystery" (now freely discussed) and even the *Dookola Swiata,* a highly esteemed monthly magazine for popular science, gave some space to the problem and taught its readers to take the matter seriously. It was this newspaper which defended in no uncertain terms the idea that the phenomena could be of extraterrestrial origin. Stories about future space-journeys, spacemen from elsewhere visiting our own planet, UFOnauts and little green men or fearsome creatures in black—all these uncritical, tongue-in-cheek tales were classed as space-fables by this journal, and the editorial board of *Dookola Swiata* set about undertaking serious research in the field. For this reason a number of journalists were sent in 1958 to the Carpathian Mountains, a region with much UFO activity at that time. Unfortunately the paper published only a small part of their findings and mostly without comment, or in a reserved and unenthusiastic spirit. Even the news of a UFO photographed on 22nd December 1958 at Muszyn was treated in lukewarm fashion. The account of this runs as follows:

> The witness states: When I looked out of the window at about 3 o'clock on 22nd December I saw a strange shimmering light coming from the clouds. Although I had no filter for my camera I took the photo through the window, thinking that the light-sensitive material would record the orange glow. From the window I could see the road to Zegiestowa, the railway, the Poprad river and the top of the mountain silhouetted against the clouds. The whole landscape was bathed in an orange light which was about 500 metres from my window. When I developed the film I saw a large grey lens-shaped object on the negative and at the same time one could make out the fairly clear outlines of trees and other details. The sun is in the background, on the extreme right, and the mysterious object is in the foreground. A number of specialists have examined the negative and found nothing suspicious about it, whilst other experts declared that it must be a genuine UFO.

As a result of *Dookola Swiata*'s UFO expedition officials from the information ministry decided that a small group of students at Warsaw University should study the Polish UFO's and try to find a solution. An unnamed professor of physics who seemed himself to have had a strange experience with a flying saucer was to be responsible for the students, but the plan never materialized. Polish scientific circles intervened, went to see the minister involved and pointed out the shame which would accrue in the eyes of the world if Polish science let itself be misled by "such nonsense." As the specialists of the physics and psychology faculties seemed to know everything about the UFO's the minister ordered them to give the Polish people proper instruction on the subject.

UFO photographed by Dr. Stanislaw Kowalezewski at Muszyn, Poland. 22nd December 1958.

In 1961 someone otherwise unknown to us, Janusz Thor, published a pamphlet of 123 pages entitled *Latajace Talerze* (Flying Saucers). This book was a concise account of discussions about UFO's as these had been conducted in the Polish press in recent years. The tone of the book is severely disapproving: those concerned with UFO's—their names are not mentioned—are reproached for having "occupied themselves uncritically with Western sensation-mongering," their chief fault being that "in the first place they have not been able to distinguish the essential in these Western stories from the things of minor importance." This is followed by a number of cases of UFO's being seen in Poland, but only to show how foolish the accounts of them are. Janusz Thor carefully refrains from explaining these misinterpretations, which indeed is not necessary in official instructional reading matter. Most of the book—a little less than 100 of the 123 pages—deals with all the possible and impossible meteorological phenomena the innocent observer is apt to take for UFO's. It is quite evident that Janusz Thor has not only very carefully read Menzel, but also diligently copied him.

After this one hears very little about UFO's in Poland: even the years 1967–8, which saw much UFO activity in the Balkans, are without any Polish references to the subject. The Polish Information Ministry and scientific circles in Poland have slowly come round to the view that the pamphlet copied from Menzel ought not to be withdrawn.

CZECHOSLOVAKIA

In this country little was published about UFO's until approximately 1965, although the second half of 1955 was a busy UFO year according to the magazine *Letectvi a Kosmonautika*, which specializes in aeronautical matters. Several spectacular observations were recorded in 1964 and, in particular, the year following. As a result the spread of information was permitted (see our remarks about press rumours concerning UFO's in the preface) and several sensational reports found their way into the big periodicals, and it is from these articles that we know that their character is perfectly in accord with UFO observations made elsewhere in Europe. An event like the following one could quite easily have come from an American air base and the wording of the account is surprisingly like one from the "Bluebook":

> The following took place during a nocturnal military exercise at Brno when I was doing my army service in 1960. During a pause in the operations we saw above the town a peculiarly coloured light. After remaining some time it suddenly vanished but turned up again elsewhere in the sky. Because this went on some time we drew the attention of our commanding officer to it, who told us to use binoculars and radar. We did so and headquarters sent up fighters to try to reach the light. We watched on our radar screens and every time a fighter neared the light it disappeared, only to re-appear elsewhere before the fighter even had time to turn around. This went on for about an hour, after which the light disappeared for good.

This story was published in the above-mentioned *Letectvi a Kosmonautika* in April 1966 and was not the first important UFO sighting to be mentioned by this paper: in 1965 (July) one of their editors had undertaken a random test by publishing a long article about an event to do with the Russian Tupolev 104 which took place on a flight from Central Asia to Moscow. In August that year there was actually a flicker of interest shown by several newspapers after a couple of sensational UFO sightings. Of these, the one which seemed to us the most important was recorded by Jaroslav Kalista in *Lidova Demokracie* on 20th August 1965. Several newspapers printed their views on UFOlogy and said that the Czech who saw strange things in space should either go as quickly as possible to the oculist or admit he saw a balloon or a star. Eastern Europeans seem to have developed the same ease at finding "explanations" as their comrades in Western Europe and the United States. *Letectvi a*

Kosmonautika printed the account without comment and added for good measure a letter they had received from someone in Ukerske Hrodiste.

Then Dr. Allen Hynek, an American with a Czech background, arrived on the scene. He is now considered to be the most important pawn in the UFOlogy debate. One can read his book *The UFO Experience; a Scientific Inquiry* which was published in 1972, a book which so far has produced the most important contribution to the UFO debate, and in the history of the science will be considered at least as a "by-blow."

In 1967 he held a lecturing tour in his native land on the UFO problem, during which many people originally sceptical listened to him and after reflection decided that the flying saucer phenomenon should be taken seriously. Numerous critical journalists and scientific people began to study the subject in Czechoslovakia when the American Condon team and the Russian Stoljarov Committee had strengthened scientific interest in it.

During 1968 the youth weekly *Veda a Technika Mladezi* published a number of unsigned articles about UFO's and their history, as we know from various editions. The final article was by Peter Michelmore (Boulder, Colorado, U.S.A.) who gave Condon's views even before the actual Condon research had been officially concluded. Number 24 expressed the opinions of several people, amongst whom were K. G. Henize of the Manned Space Centre, Houston, Texas; José Vaz Da Silva of Brazil; T. P. A. Angelic of Jugoslavia; P. Magno of Italy; Rudolph Pesek of Czechoslovakia; Ake Hjerstrand of Sweden; S. Aranguez of Spain; and J. Allen Hynek. As a result of the increasing interest in UFOlogy an independent group was set up in Czechoslovakia on the lines of foreign ones and *Mlada Fronta* issued the following report on 18th February 1969:

Prague. As from today Czechoslovakia has a centre for UFO's led by scientists such as Dr. Josef Dvorak of the Medical Centre of the Air Forces, Dr. Jaroslav Sychra of the Institute of Atmospheric

Physics, Dr. Svatopluk Kriz and Dr. Boris Valnicek of the Ondrejov Observatory. All information on the subject, whether from laymen or scientists, will be classified and analysed by the Centre—which unfortunately has very limited means at its disposal as yet—and the findings will be published. The Centre will work in close contact with the Czechoslovak Air Force and will have links with foreign UFO centres. The UFO Information Centre has been established at Panska 8, Prague 1.

Naturally this was responded to by foreign UFO publishers, especially after the French newspaper *Le Monde* had devoted a few paragraphs to it on 20th February 1969. The names of the Czech scientists connected with the Centre were important enough to make foreign headlines when it was set up; but the bulletin they promised did not appear and apart from the news of the establishment of the Centre nothing further was heard. On 5th July 1969 a journalist, Stanislas Bartl, wrote an extensive article in *Mlada Fronta* from which we quote the essentials:

> On 19th February last our paper published a report about the setting-up of a UFO Centre of Information in Prague; but five months have elapsed since then and what activity has it shown? It was unjustified anxiety on the part of one of our colleagues that the Centre would mean too much work for him. On the contrary there has been no wave of UFO sightings reported, as was the case in other countries for several years. Perhaps Czechs have something else on their minds, or is it that the UFO's have been avoiding our territory for five months? . . .
>
> To date the Centre has received only six reports of various atmospheric phenomena and these amount to "moving points of light in the night sky": phenomena which our correspondents couldn't explain. It is a pity that the facts are in general so vague and the evidence so incomplete that one is unable to say what it was. The most detailed observation,

that concerning a "strange star which suddenly became motionless, gave out a dazzling light and developed a carmine-red tail," was recorded by Otakar Crvcek of Sudnice near Nachod. His account was accompanied by a sketch and the case is being investigated.

The Centre was also informed of a case ten years ago of an object which someone saw land in the vicinity of Radotin. This object ejected a toadstool-shaped apparatus about five metres in diameter which then shot away. Mr. F. J. of Prague spoke personally about this observation but as he was 500 metres away he was not able to supply exact details.

Immediately after the setting-up of the Prague Centre we received letters from interested and enthusiastic readers including military people from Prague, Pilsen, Brno, Ceske Lipy and other places. The writers said that they had been interested in UFO's for many years for various reasons and some of them seemed to own extensive files on the subject; others had foreign contacts.

Mr. Georges Klinger, for instance, who is connected with the Prague Physics Institute, is studying the question of whether or not some details recorded throughout history do not show evidence of the possibility of visits from other planets; amongst the many things he sent to the Centre we found a plaster statue which was a memento of the Brno exhibition about the Great Moravian Kingdom (830–906). It appears to be an exact copy of an original on show at the exhibition, and represents someone who seems to be dressed in a diver's uniform and equipped with an antenna. Was this a cosmonaut seen at the time of the Great Moravian Kingdom? The Centre turned to Dr. Vincent Stana of the Brno Archaeology Museum, who is of the opinion that the statue (the original of course) must have been part of a buckle made of gilded bronze, itself part of a belt. The statuette shows a farmer holding a sceptre and a cornucopia. The buckle was found in 1957 on the site of a (now vanished) fortified Moravian castle. This was near Hodonin and the clasp, dating from the 9th century, was found there by Professor J. Poulika in the course of archaeological work.

The report about the Czech Centre created more interest abroad than it did at home, since the news of its foundation was spread around the world by international press-agencies, and shortly afterwards the Centre received reactions on a world-wide scale from UFO associations and from individual UFOlogists—the greatest interest exists or existed in the Centre's connection with UFO activities, since many foreign authorities and individuals are willing to exchange information and co-operate in this field.

As a result of our report having been wrongly interpreted people abroad got the impression that the Czech Centre was supported by the State. A rosy picture which we, also, envy! If one reads letters from abroad it is easy to understand that their associations can only carry on as a result of financial support from their own members. At home someone expressed his indignation that the Centre should waste money on trifles although well aware of the bad economic conditions still existing; and the same person even suggested that the Centre's building might be given over to the homeless or those in bad housing. So there is talk about an imaginary "waste of money" and a "building"—but what is the truth of the matter? The fact is that the Centre consists of a corner of a room allotted to *Mlada Fronta*, Panska 8, Prague 1, with a few bits of furniture. It has no proper office equipment and the Centre is grateful to the newspaper for the administrative help and accommodation offered; as well as for the use of telephone, typewriter, scissors, gluepot and wastepaper basket. The Centre gets nothing from the government and it does not ask for anything. The staff are entirely unpaid and work there in their spare time—not one of them is salaried. They do all their work out of interest in the UFO cause.

What are the aims of the Centre? With the very limited means at their disposal they hope to register and analyse the various problematic manifestations reported; also to eradicate the sensational aspects, which always accrue, so that the real facts can be studied freed of all distortion. One can doubt the existence of UFO's as technical and natural phenomena—but not as a social phenomenon; and for this reason alone they deserve to be taken seriously. The possibility of life on other planets is not excluded as long as there is no proof that Man is the only living being in the universe; and we can just as little reject the idea that any extraterrestrial life may be more advanced than our own. It is not difficult to suppose that our eventual contact with some other and superb civilization would be the most crucial moment in our history.

Even if the Prague Centre cannot rejoice in public interest in UFO's at home it is nonetheless thanks to the setting-up of the Centre that the ban on publishing articles dealing with space phenomena has been lifted at last in Czechoslovakia. Two books by Czech authors appeared at the end of 1969 and the beginning of 1970 which linked the UFO problem with ETI. The number printed was high by Western standards and every copy was quickly sold; so quickly in fact that we were unable to obtain our own order, which was placed straight after their publication. We therefore have to depend on critical reviews of these books to find the gist of their arguments. The Czech Henri Chaloupek, who lives in France, wrote an article about both the books for *Phénomènes Spatiaux*, the French UFO paper, the substance of which we reproduce here.

In 1969 there appeared *Zahady letajicich taliru* (Riddle of the Flying Saucers) by an engineer, Wenceslas Patrovsky. This was a popular work of 200 pages giving a general introduction to the UFO problem and from general observations in history to particular observations in Bohemian history he proceeds to American recordings during the years 1950–69. Patrovsky deals in turn with the physical side-effects of UFO manifestations, and writes about a number of them recorded in Latin America, Australia, Antarctica and Western Europe. He also disputes Menzel's explanations, writes about UFOnauts and photos of actual UFO's. He gives a chapter to UFOlogists and their congresses, then discusses in detail whether our planet ever had extraterrestrial visits. Patrovsky deals with UFO sightings in Central Europe and Russia and explains why information about them was ignored for a long time—at least until 1967, the year of Hynek's lecture tour in Czechoslovakia. The book ends with a thorough study of the UFO problem from logistical, chemical, physical, statistical and analytical viewpoints. The author further discusses the possibility of other dimensions existing or a parallel universe; similarly the possibility of interstellar or intergalactic journeys and the control or abolition of gravity by the manipulation of electromagnetic fields. In this he depends on the theories of Burkhard Heim which he feels may force us to seek and accept physical laws other than those we know at present.

From early in 1970 there is the 217-page book of Josef Fleissig (scientific journalist for the daily *Prace*) entitled *The Riddle of our Century*. This author maintains contacts with scholars the world over, especially those dealing with astronomy and astronautics in which he is very interested. He has first-hand information through these contacts, who may be either for or against the existence of UFO's; and for the sake of objectivity Fleissig puts both points of view, giving mainly the arguments put forward by American experts attending the 1968 International Astronautical Congress at New York's Waldorf Astoria. There was an exchange of ideas about UFO's on the edge, so to speak, of this conference, and from Fleissig's book one can learn the views of scholars like Allen Hynek, James McDonald, Carl Sagan, Robert Hall, Robert Baker, Donald Menzel, Garry Henderson, Roger Shepard and Frank Salisbury. Fleissig makes specific reference to the Condon Report which he believes is the most valuable study of the problem which has yet appeared. Like Condon, Fleissig rejects all stories about humanoids' visits (which are nonetheless mentioned by serious authors of good repute such as Vallée, Ruppelt and Michel). The book contains some very interesting theories from fourteen Czech scientists, only one of whom, the geophysicist J. Mrazek, supports the hypothesis that the UFO is extraterrestrial in origin. The last chapter is by Allen Hynek who deals with the end of Project Bluebook and here we see Hynek's grim determination to continue with UFO research.

During 1970-71 we attempted to contact the Czech Information Centre but unsuccessfully: our letters remained unanswered and we ourselves were unable to go to Prague. Other informal attempts to gain information likewise came to naught so we may assume the Centre has been discontinued, though why we do not know.

HUNGARY

Our placing of the beginnings of Eastern European UFOlogy in Poland was not quite correct. To begin with we find, in the U.S.A.F.'s famous files (ATIC, Bluebook) some fifty hitherto unpublished reports of UFO sightings on 10th July 1947 in Hungary. It was also in Hungary that a public, though very modest, debate was held about UFO's after a meteorite was seen in 1954 over Budapest and Györ. But the Urania Observatory then hushed up the discussion so it did not compare with the Polish trends during the UFO years 1957-8. We have to wait till the end of 1967 before the problem acquires its characteristics again —which it then does in a way only Rumania was to equal. The cause of this sudden interest in Hungary was definitely connected with the increased wave of UFO activity in Eastern Europe. After various reports in the dailies *Magyar Nemzet* (23.11.67) and *Nepszava* (24.11.67) about this activity the youth magazine for science and technology *Élet és Tudomàny* published on 1st December of the same year a general review of the UFO problem, which meant that the way ahead was now clear for further study of the "presumably unknown natural phenomenon." No other Eastern European country is as well provided with Western publications as Hungary is, and the whole press was swamped with the opinions (for and against) of eminent UFOlogists—with the same spitefulness familiar elsewhere, coming especially from the sceptical toward the "faithful." The years 1968 and 1969 were full of polemic in the field of the UFO, when the anti-UFO people clustered around the magazine *Tükör* whilst their opponents selected *Lobogo* as a base from which to sally forth. There were several authorities in favour of the existence of the UFO, like the biologist Horvàth Sàndor for instance, the doctor Böszörmeny Nagy Emil, the technician Horvàth Iànos and the well-known actor Bànky Robert. Their chief foe was Kulin György, director of the Urania Observatory, who went as far as to maintain that no astronomer or scientifically trained observer had ever seen a UFO. This assertion was naturally very quickly disproved by opponents and Dr. Kulin György was driven to showing on Hungarian television how UFO photos could be fabricated. Thereupon Bànky Robert wrote that he could demonstrate in the same way the non-existence of aircraft and publicly asked if he might be allowed to do this on Hungarian television too. But so far he has received no answer to his request.

5. THE AKADEMSKI ASTRONOMSKO—ASTRONAUTIKI KLUB AT SARAJEVO (JUGOSLAVIA) GIVE AN EXEMPLARY LESSON TO UFOMANIACS

UFO's over Golgotha?—AAAK's name is taken in vain—A conical object seen in Jugoslavian skies—Fixing the weight of a UFO—A stratosphere balloon "examines" Jugoslavia with a scientific purpose, or perhaps some other—Did the 1954 UFO wave reach the Balkans?—Orthothenic lines on Jugoslavian maps.

Flying Saucers are Real, by Donald E. Keyhoe, is the first book in which we read of Jugoslavian UFO's; and the widespread notion that they are of extraterrestrial origin is implied in his description of how a UFO, shaped like a disc, was sighted above Tito's land on 7th May 1949. Further details are unfortunately lacking, but as we now know for certain that Keyhoe obtained his information from the American Air Force directly, we may just as certainly assume that Jugoslavia took part in the "prehistoric" period of UFO activity. Since that time several strange objects have been seen in Jugoslavian skies: there were waves of UFO activity in 1954, 1967, 1969 and presumably in 1971.

Before describing these years let us first return to historical UFOlogy and pay some attention to a strange UFO analysis by AAAK—the Akademski Astronomsko–Astronautiki Klub at Sarajevo.

Here Jugoslavia has something peculiar to offer us. As we shall see in Chapter 9, there are drawings on the walls of various medieval monasteries which could be connected with UFO's. The oddest one of them all is to be found on a fresco in the Visoki Dečani monastery, one of Jugoslavia's most attractive and best-preserved. Since 1968 a number of specialists have been interested in this particular fresco, apart from art historians and students of religious history. Two details in the famous fresco—the "Crucifixion"—, which is in the highest dome of the monastery, have since that time been the subject of discussion amongst UFOlogists, engineers, space-travel experts, visionaries and sceptics. The well-known science journalist Trifun Mickovic described this fresco in the 26th July 1969 edition of *Borba*. The essence of his article amounts to the following:

Against a blue background in the upper left and right corners of the "Crucifixion," and behind the crucified figure of Christ, the old masters painted two objects which as far as their shape, size and apparent movement are concerned might well pass for present-day space-ships. It was formerly thought that these two figures represented the sun and moon, but recent studies have shown this hypothesis to be untenable or virtually so. It is true that many frescoes from this period do show the sun and/or the moon but none like those of the "Crucifixion" fresco at Visoki Dečani: the figures of the latter clearly show human traits and are half naked, pictured like cosmonauts piloting their spacecraft (see photos on pages 81 and 82). All drawings of the sun and moon executed in those times represent these bodies as if moving from east to west; and wind directions are easy to determine by means, for instance, of the iconographic material: chiefly the churches in which these drawings occur. Moreover the sun and moon are depicted sending their rays down to the earth. Thus they are not the sun and moon because first it has been shown that they are depicted as travelling from west to east; and second it is clear that the rays are not vertical but horizontal. Finally there are the "cosmonaut-like" figures apparently steering the "sun" and "moon." These three points lead inescapably to the conclusion that the fresco portrays

THE AKADEMSKI ASTRONOMSKO 81

two space-vehicles in flight. The one on the left has a blunt prow with six horizontal beams of unequal length; while the right "vehicle" has a pointed, triangular front with three rays projecting from it. The little man in the one on the right is sitting in the direction of travel. He is looking around towards the "vessel" shown on the left which seems to be following him at some distance.

Jugoslavia: "Astronauts" on the walls of one of the famous medieval Jugoslavian monasteries?

As we said, the sun and moon are often depicted on medieval frescoes, so that we have plenty of material to use as comparison; and we find that no other at all is drawn in the style these have. For instance, in the monastery at Pec—which is from the same period as the Dečani foundation and in all respects like it—there are large numbers of frescoes with portrayals of the sun and moon. These are very accurate and faithful representations of the "real" sun—the artists struggled to get every detail correct no matter how small—and the "suns" at Pec are all ringed with rays

82 THE EVIDENCE ASSESSED

of equal length, so that they look like sunflowers symbolizing that heavenly body. According to tradition an eclipse of the sun was supposed to have taken place on the day of Christ's crucifixion in the year 33; which is why the Pec crucifixion fresco shows the sun "lightless" i.e. in dark shades. By analogy one would expect the Dečani drawing to exhibit the same "lightless" sun therefore, assuming that the "space" objects on this fresco were also meant to show suns or the sun.

The Pec monastery collection contains a famous Jerusalem icon which likewise shows the Crucifixion, and here too we can see representations of the sun and moon above the figure of Christ. These are painfully naturalistic, however, as they usually are when perceived by the human eye. There is no trace of any human shape in the middle of these clear skies and the position of the sun and moon in relation to the cross is quite different. One is well aware of the conscientiousness with which the medieval painters of icons and frescoes respected the traditional patterns laid down once and for all time.

In discussions about space-craft possibly being linked with the Dečani "sun" and "moon" pictures, some devoted champions of this theory feel that certain details from the New Testament concerning the Crucifixion (which was accompanied not only by a darkening of the sun but also by an earthquake) may well be connected with a space-vehicle appearing at that time. . . .

The question is whether the artists responsible for the Dečani frescoes themselves were aware of this interpretation and for that reason drew cosmic vehicles above Christ's head; or whether during their lifetime they saw space-craft and so drew a faithful picture of them. Or did they copy them from material now lost? Or was it all a matter of sheer fantasy?

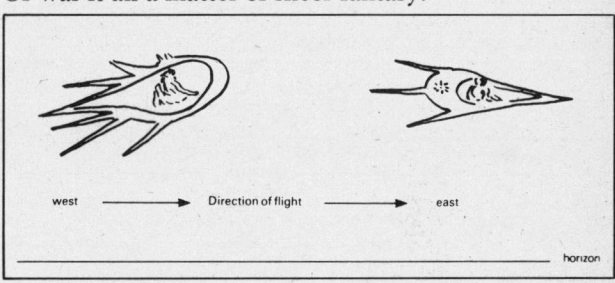

The New Testament details may be interpreted as one likes, but what is certain is that Christ's death was not accompanied by manifestations of human beings piloting space-vehicles. We would also refer to the monastery on Mount Athos, where there is also a picture, on a fresco, of a "vessel" something like the Dečani one. The Athos fresco depicts St. John in an unusual landscape busy dictating sacred texts to a young disciple. Above their heads there is an enormous egg-shaped object. Unlike the manned craft of the Dečani fresco this object has no "crew."

In a letter to the authors of this book dated 5th January 1972 the Akademski Astronomsko–Astronautiki Klub confirmed the existence of the Dečani frescoes, but as Muhamed Muminovici, the secretary, said: "I am of the opinion that these pictures can be interpreted just as one pleases."

We refer to AAAK here on purpose—they are often quoted in foreign articles about UFO sightings—but their name is ill-used, since more than once we have come across reports from UFOmaniacs about sightings over Jugoslavia, from which it would seem that AAAK had declared the phenomena to be "inexplicable" or "mysterious." The truth is that AAAK is not a "UFO circle"—there is no such thing in Jugoslavia—

and its function is therefore not to give triumphant reports about UFO's to the world. On the contrary the Klub is more than sceptical about the wild accounts so often met with in that land. AAAK is simply an association of amateur astronomers, university lecturers, mathematicians and students of physics who aim at popularizing rocketry and astronomy. If a UFO appears, then AAAK follows up the matter—but purely to try to explain the event.

In this regard their members did some remarkable work linked with an unknown object which was seen over Jugoslavia on 18th October 1968, a case registered as a UFO in nearly all international UFO magazines. The account of it runs as follows:

> Although it was daylight the object was very striking because of its brilliance; its light was at least a hundred times greater than that of Venus which appeared later on in the west. The object was travelling in the direction of the azimuth 200 degrees, about 40 degrees above the horizon. At first it was an intense blue, but turned whitish-blue and finally reddish, depending on the intensity of the radiance. There was a strong glimmer in the centre of the object but this later disappeared. When the first stars came out the greater part of the object, apart from its centre, seemed to be transparent. About 17:15 the object was south of the Sarajevo Observatory with an azimuth angle of 180 degrees, and it vanished from the telescopic field around 18:50. It was at about 17:30 that one could last make it out with the naked eye but while it was going away it did not change its shape.

Some of the AAAK people made a number of photos by means of a refraction telescope with a maximum magnifying power of 28.5. The film was an AGFA and the camera of the make known as "Zenith." Two of the photos came out beautifully and two others satisfactorily. The object was conical in shape and had ribbed elevations, with some areas brightly lit, others less so. In the course of the flight there were turning movements made which can easily be seen from the photos, which were taken in immediate succession.

This event aroused the curiosity of the Jugoslavian population since hundreds of thousands of people in Sarajevo, Mostar, Konic and many other places saw it. The press and radio reported it but nobody dared to speak out about its nature and the government refused to attempt any explanation. Even the photos failed in the end to give any more information about it than the drawings and descriptions. AAAK members decided on a thorough study and their first conclusion was that it was no known kind of balloon that could have been sent up in Jugoslavia. An advertisement was put in two provincial dailies by the Klub, asking for further and more precise details, preferably from experienced observers using optical instruments. AAAK formed a group whose purpose was to identify it, and six months later they issued a 42-page brochure *Identification of the Object seen on 18th October 1968.* After considering the general possibilities of measuring flying objects the group then set out a number of calculations for UFOlogists to draw upon. The results were as follows:

The object was 25.40 km above Sarajevo. The reconstruction of its route agreed with the data supplied by eye-witnesses (see map, page 87); the object moved with an average velocity of 8.8 m per second (i.e. 31.4 km per hour). Stratospheric air streams caused the lateral drift of the object so it did not have independent propulsion; the total weight was 800 kilos.

Therefore the thing seen on October 18th over Jugoslavia which caused such emotion and is still referred to in UFO literature as "mysterious" was a stratosphere balloon of unknown origin.

We quote the pamphlet:

The final question to be asked after all that has been brought to bear on the subject is what purpose the object served and what equipment it had. Everything suggests that its aim was to study the nature of the terrain over which it flew. This might have been: 1. a study of the atmospheric conditions like

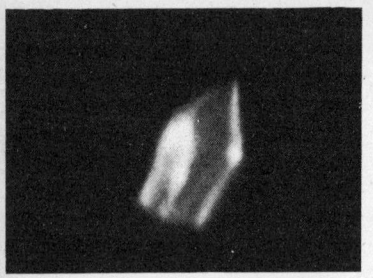 

Sarajevo, 18th October 1968. Photos taken by a member of the Akademski Astronomsko-Astronautiki Klub.

temperatures, moisture, air pressure, wind directions and speeds, the electric charge in the air, and so on.
2. a geographical study of details useful for both military and scientific purposes e.g. communication systems, buildings, contours, industrial areas, magnetic features, etc.
3. a radio-telecommunication investigation, including activities relating to radio-teleprinters, radio-telephonic and other functions based on electromagnetic waves.

The object would have needed technical equipment to carry out such functions properly but the nature of this cannot be ascertained, though it may safely be assumed that such equipment would consist chiefly of modern sophisticated machinery with the so-called "integral coils" which even radar is often powerless to detect. This type of balloon could have been released by a scientific group for purely scientific purposes but it could just as easily have been sent up by a military organization with very different aims in mind.

If one knows the height of the balloon—25.40 km —then one can determine the area of the zone from which it was visible. Based on assumptions about the technical equipment it had on board for photographing the area, it can be concluded that the

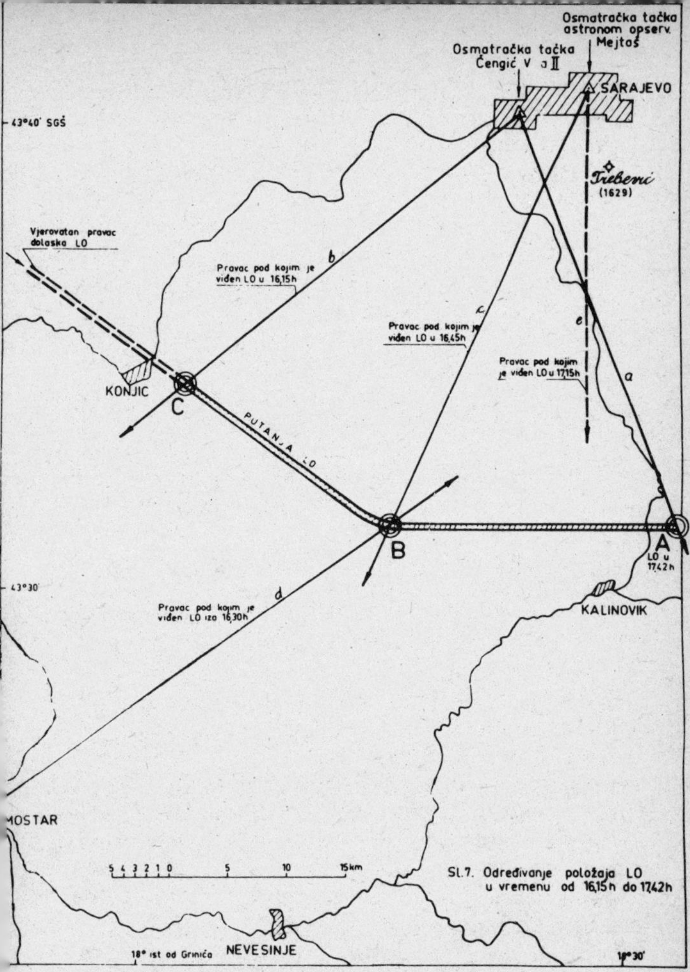

Jugoslavia, 18th October 1968. The route followed by the object.

Jugoslavia, 18th October 1968. Dimensions of the object identified by AAAK:

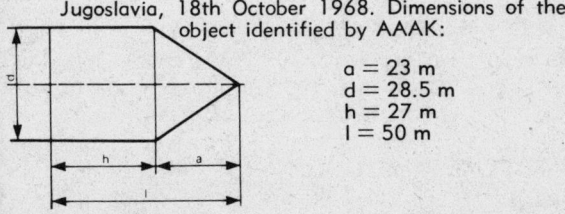

$a = 23$ m
$d = 28.5$ m
$h = 27$ m
$l = 50$ m

maximal angle of viewing was 120 degrees so that the width of the zone was 68 km (see map, page 89). It is worth noting that its flight was over the central areas of Jugoslavia. This fixing of the zone of theoretical visibility from the ground is important, significantly so, in so far as one assumes that the object carried equipment able to send back to base by high-frequency electromagnetic waves the information collected. With this in mind one can then speculate as to the whereabouts of the bases, the reception centres. The area of theoretical visibility is determined by the curvature of the earth and, to a lesser extent, by the nature of the relief. Areas where possible signals could be received are shown on the accompanying sketch, but their breadth is determined by their height above sea-level.

In the first zone the signals could be received at all points, but in the second area only at those points which are 1000 m above sea-level; and in the third zone districts over 2000 m above sea-level. The following map of Jugoslavia and neighbouring countries shows all these details (see map page 90).

The radii of these circles now appear as: 570 km, 680 km and 720 km. The circles cover the whole area containing each point at which possible high-frequency UFO signals might be received. The outermost circle, indicated by the figure of 2000 m, shows the zone in which only places 2000 m above sea-level could receive UFO signals. The other two circles closest to the centre indicate the same points which, however, are at a height of 1000 and 0 m respectively. As the sketch clearly shows, the signals sent out could be received in all the countries surrounding us. It was noted that, because of the balloon's direction of drift, it was most likely to have been released from somewhere in the West. If one now chooses a certain point ("M" on the map) in Italy say, which is over 2000 m above sea-level, and we extend an arc with radius r_2, then we realize that the arc includes the whole of our territory. From this it follows that signals could be received from an object flying at 25.40 km at that spot in Italy, regardless of where exactly over Jugoslavia the object might be. Point M was fixed in Italy because it was shown that the object came from the west; but it could nevertheless have been any point in any of our neighbouring countries. All these considerations about the possible uses the object was put to are only a part of a number of tentative conclusions drawn regarding its aims and destination.

After this precise and perhaps successful identification AAAK members saw further UFO's. These too were photographed and according to the Klub belong to the same category, viz. stratosphere balloons. These sightings were either in Sarajevo or in the immediate vicinity of that city. They took place on 16th May 1970, 29th September 1970 and 8th October 1971 (see photo on page 91).

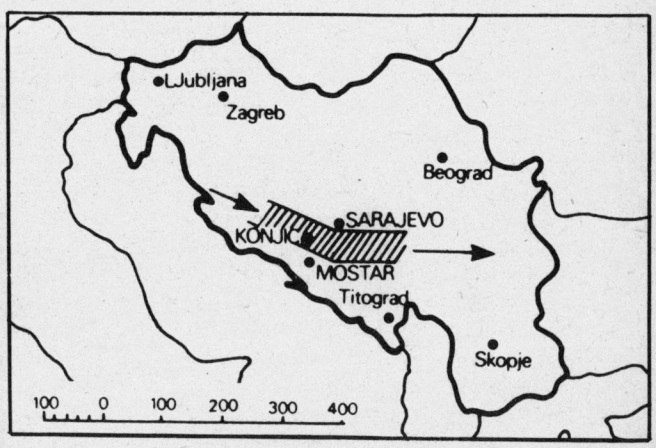

Observation area shaded

Zones in which any possible signals sent out by the vehicle could be picked up.

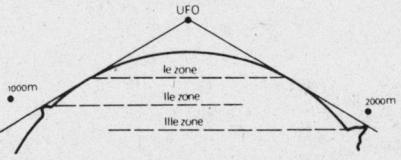

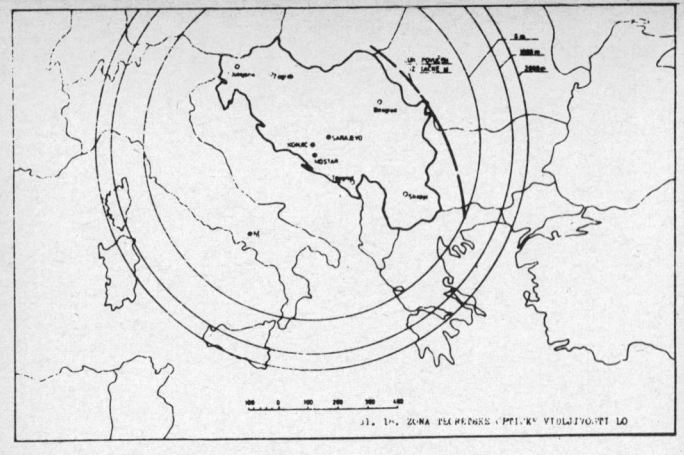

Extreme limits of area where radio signals could be heard.

There were two reasons for attaching such importance to AAAK; first because we think that this approach can be of value to serious UFO observers in all parts of the world, since reports about UFO sightings are worth more if the misunderstandings have been done away with—misunderstandings, that is, to do with objects which are actually easy to identify; and secondly because we wish to stress the skill of AAAK's members and the serious attitude they show towards the UFO problem. This will of course help them gain credibility when expressing their points of view about atmospheric or spatial objects. We certainly pay all due regard to their verdict about the four UFO waves in Jugoslavia already mentioned.

Flying saucers were seen all over that country between 15th October and 25th of that month in 1954. The most important witnesses (who mention low-flying saucers as well as large cigar-shaped objects sailing along at high altitudes) live in the districts around Lubljana, Sarajevo and Belgrade. Thousands of people were involved in the sightings and AAAK's opinion was that this wave had much in common with the French one which occurred in the same year—in October and November. But unlike the French wave the Jugoslavian one hardly reached the press at all. The cases which did attract attention were treated

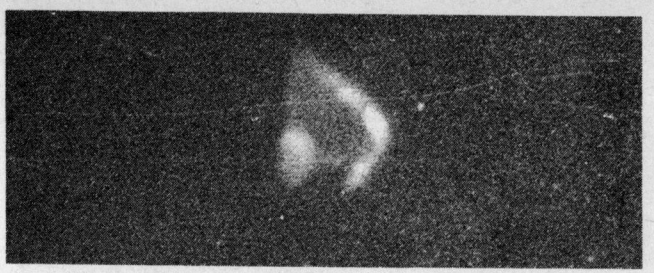

Photograph taken at Sarajevo, 29th September 1970.

ironically which unfortunately makes the reconstruction of the Jugoslavian wave of sightings impossible. Flying saucers were recorded, as in France, from the end of August 1954 until the end of the following November, which is also when the French wave ended. The peak of the latter must be placed in the first half of October 1954 but the Jugoslavian one in the second part of that month. In view of the lack of material the geographical location of the wave cannot be other than a matter of contention. In the following years the press likewise took no notice of the UFO problem, about which something was known in Jugoslavia, but only from foreign publications. But here too, as in all other Balkan countries, the silence surrounding UFO's seemed to be broken at the end of 1967. In November and December of that year inhabitants of Ivangrad claimed to have seen various UFO's which moved in symmetrical circles, constantly changing their altitude and then finally disappearing at an alarming speed.

Although the season was very damp an unexplained conflagration took place in the Komovi forest after low-flying objects had passed over it. Mysteriously damaged trees were found in the course of an investigation of the causes of the fire. The trees had snapped as if hit by a whirlwind, which was said to have spared others in the immediate vicinity. The Jugoslavian press did pay some attention to the whole matter, especially after it had been reported from Golubac that at about the same time a number of objects faster than jets had carried out some mysterious manoeuvres. Locating them by radar was possible, but not their explanation, and after Jugoslavian aircraft had vainly tried to

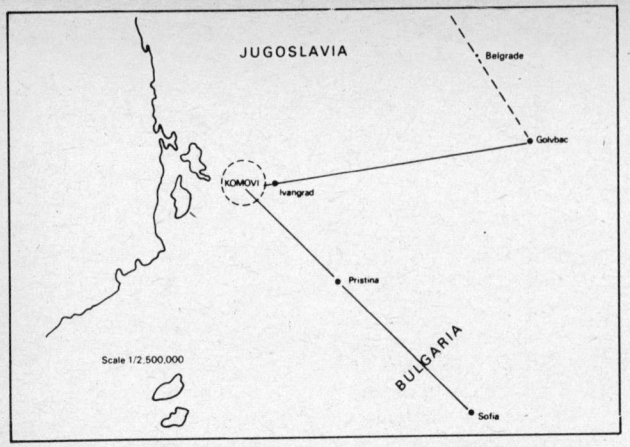

The burnt forest at Komovi. Luxemburg UFOlogists think the Sofia–Pristina–Komovi line is orthothenic.

pursue them they moved across to other cities and villages. About 100 inhabitants of Pristina, the capital of the province Kosmet, reported that they had followed a flying object with the naked eye and that the thing had seemed like an unusually bright star. A jet was in the sky at the same time but the object appeared to be both higher and faster.

During that same autumn dozens of people saw UFO's over Belgrade, Zagreb, Golubac, etc. (see list). Note that the Komovi forest and the cities of Sofia and Pristina lie along the same route, as also Komovi, Ivangrad and Golubac. It seems premature to conclude from this that all these places indicate the existence of an orthothenic net but it is certainly odd (see map). AAAK did not wish to say anything about this, as there were insufficient details about the matter and the ones available were too unusual for any study of them to be considered.

Finally, in 1971, Jugoslavia experienced the same panic as in 1967: research into the "UFO wave" of 1971 has not yet begun, but we feel that a number of plastic balloons are responsible for the "rumour" in spite of the frequently sensational reports and conclusions in foreign UFO magazines about the Jugoslavian wave (see inter alia APRO bulletin Sept.–Oct. 1971).

6. EMIL BARNEA FROM CLUJ (RUMANIA) OFFERS SOME IMPORTANT CLUES

25% of UFO photos are authentic—UFO photos by the American Rex Heflin—Dr. Hartmann hangs a "UFO" on an invisible thread—Police interrogation methods of sceptical and spiteful scientists who cherish prejudices—A picnic in Baciu Wood—The Rumanian Emil Barnea's photos are remarkably like Heflin's—Florin Gheorghiţa investigates the facts—The conclusions of the Belgian Delcorps.

In the lecture which he gave during the UFO symposium held by the American Association for the Advancement of Science in Boston on 26th, 27th and 28th December 1969 Dr. Allen Hynek described a class of UFO phenomena he called "daylight discs." To be more specific he meant objects seen at a reasonable distance (as a rule) and he added: "It is obvious that the existence of this category is confirmed by photos, more so perhaps than any other group." He wound up by recalling McMinnville: "I would not go so far as to say that *all* these photos are evidence of an authentic UFO. But I do say definitely that 25% of the cases thoroughly examined are genuine reports, so that we can say that to this extent probability of deception is nil."

We do not know for certain if Hynek has the Rex Heflin photos taken in the vicinity of Santa Ana in California on 3rd December 1965; but we do know quite definitely that he does not have those made by Emil Barnea on 18th August 1968 in the Baciu Forest near Cluj. Why do we bracket these two series to-

1. 2.

Heflin photo no. 1

Heflin photo no. 2

Heflin photo no. 3

3.

gether? Because we find the similarities between them particularly striking, bearing in mind the fact that there is an interval of three years between them and a distance of 16,000 km. Frank Edwards relates the history of the Santa Ana photos (*Flying Saucers: Serious Business*) and he also gives many pages to the Condon Report (pp. 437–55).

At the time of the sightings Rex Heflin was in the cabin of a lorry: "At this time, I became aware of the UFO, however I thought it was a conventional aircraft ... The UFO moved from my left to in front of me and momentarily hovered there. At this time I grabbed the camera (semi-automatic Model 101 Polaroid), from the seat of the truck and took the first photograph through the windshield of the truck.

"The object then moved slowly off to the north-east. I then snapped the second picture through the right door window (window closed). This is when I saw the rotating beam of light emitting from the center of the UFO on the bottom side.

"The UFO positioned itself to another angle of view and I snapped the third picture through the same side window as in picture two ...

Cluj: first photograph

"As the UFO traveled, it maintained a relatively level altitude (150 feet) in relation to the flat terrain, however the UFO acted similar to a gyroscope when losing its stability. The UFO continued moving away slowly gaining altitude, and tipped its top toward me slightly. It seemed to gain stability, then it increased its velocity and altitude more rapidly leaving a deposit of smoke-like vapor.

"The smoke-like vapor was blue-black in color and circular in shape as though it had emitted from the outer ring of the UFO. This doughnut shaped vapor ring remained in the area in excess of thirty seconds. The UFO disappeared in a northern direction toward Saddleback Mountain (this is known on the maps as Santiago Peak and Modjeska)."

Heflin estimated its diameter at 10 m, its depth about 3 and the distance from him approximately 50.

The UFO's colour was ash-grey, the top gleamed and the general outline was sharply delineated. It did not make a single sound during its rocking movements, but parts of the surface reflected the sunlight.

The Air Force described the UFO as sharply defined, with a reflecting surface "dull gray color, with the sun" reflecting from different portions of it as it wobbled. The staff of the G2 office at El Toro say that the light lines on the original photos were very clear. On 27th October Major Hector Quintanilla Jr., who at that time was Bluebook's director, told journalists from the daily *Santa Ana Register* that the Air Force had concluded after thorough study that the object was a photographic trick. The newspaper quoted on 9th December, however, a letter from E. Poe, an Air Force Colonel, to Alphonso Bell, member of the House of Representatives, as follows: "We have *not* classified the photograph as hoax." ... From the point of view of the Colorado study the principal question of concern is: *does a case have probative value in establishing the reality of unusual aircraft?* In a case like this, where both the observer and photographs *clearly* allege an extraordinary vehicle, a second question is, of course automatically implied: does the case represent a fabrication or was the object a true unknown? But it is not in general concerned only with establishing evidence as to whether or not there exist extraordinary flying objects.

In that context, this case is equivocal.

Hartmann tells us he was able to simulate the first three photos by hanging a model on an invisible thread; and he finds the strongest arguments for doubting the authenticity of the case in the fourth photo, which shows the presence of cloud (as well as the smoke-ring) which could not have been there *according to Dr. Hartmann* although the weather man in the *Los Angeles* wrote "We do not have an observational report from Santa Ana at 11:30 a.m. ... but from surrounding reports it would appear that the sky was hazy and the horizontal visibility was between 2½ and 5 miles ... reduced by haze and smoke. Earlier in the morning there had been low overcast conditions but these clouds had apparently dissipated leaving considerable haze." (Condon, page 437).

A new study was made by the aeronautical engineer John R. Gray (16 years with Aerospace Engineering, including 4 years with the Apollo programme and now Senior Associate Engineer for the Hughes Aircraft Co., Aerospace System Division) and this revealed that Heflin had left the lorry before taking his fourth photo. The camera's in-built light meter had used the light in the cabin, so that there was over-exposure and the clouds could not be photographed. Also it is quite likely that the UFO itself left a vapour-cloud as well as the black smoke-ring which might have caused it. There is a similar phenomenon about the fourth photo made at Cluj, of which we shall have more to say later....

Finally there is some recent evidence about the appearance of disc-like UFO's which strongly reminds one of events at Santa Ana and Cluj: in August 1971 at 3:00 p.m. an object was sighted on the Baraque Michel in Belgium, which according to witnesses was skimming above the ground at about 15 m. It was a round craft, metallic-grey in colour and had a dome (as also was seen after enlargement of the first Heflin photo and especially in the photo, published by the Belgian UFO magazine *Inforespace* No. 5, 1972, of a disc-shaped UFO disintegrating in 1953 at Bouffioux, Belgium). This object, likewise, left behind a black smoke when it disappeared.

The presence of cloud on the fourth photo made by Heflin cannot be taken as proof that the object was not authentic, since the cloud, smoke or fog could have been caused by the UFO itself before leaving— Heflin is certain that this was the case. It is strange that such an argument against the trustworthiness of the Heflin case should be put forward on the basis of doubtful meteorological data.

A further "argument" making Hartmann doubt the photos' validity is the confusion surrounding their treatment and the doubtful identity of the people concerned with them—people who often pretended to be "camp officers." Heflin himself had no idea what happened to the photos in all the confusion, and one can read about this complex matter in the Condon Report. Whatever the facts of the case, this "argument" is more that of a subtle legal ploy than a scientific conclusion.

Yet Hartmann cannot simply reject Heflin's photos out of hand; that it is possible to forge photos like these by means of an invisible thread does not necessarily prove that Heflin's are a hoax.... Furthermore Hartmann took no satisfactory account of other circumstances and indirect witnesses. Heflin, for instance, was not alone long enough in the place to hang up threads and take photos in various positions; and Hartmann himself does not tell us how long he needed for reconstructing the scene. Exactly one year after Heflin had taken the photos, and at just the same time of day, other researchers took photos of the terrain above which the UFO had appeared. Pictures of the electric cables, trees, poles and shadows on Heflin's photos were compared with those on the new series, and it was determined that Heflin had taken the photos within a very short space of time and in quick succession. It was shown quite irrefutably that the "Heflin UFO" was not just something hung up on a thread and then photographed. The authenticity of these pictures is virtually unquestioned and they are amongst the most famous of all UFO photos; even Hartmann said in the end that no conclusion could be arrived at in this case.

There is also the Cluj matter of 18th August 1968. We have learnt how little witnesses are really concerned about their sightings, and how used they must get to being frightened away by the almost police-like interrogation methods of sceptical men of science. Let us remember that for the average observer in a case like this the game is hardly worth the candle; the sensational stage is soon passed, and then he finds himself having to put up with the scorn and sarcasm of his neighbours. What particularly strikes one about the Cluj affair (which factor also runs like a thread through Hartmann's studies) is the doubt cast upon witnesses' veracity whenever the style of their accounts does not suit the person making the investigation—in this case the scientist. A witness, then, is a "man in the street," but the fact that he may not be scientifically trained does not imply that he is not in command of his own common sense. If he is treated as a person of no account because of this lack of skill he can become aggressive, nervous, indignant, uninterested and so on. For instance in the case of the photos taken near Cluj the director of the observatory there said straight after he had seen them in the paper that they were either a hoax or else a weather balloon photographed under special circumstances. In this case it was clear that the astronomer in question had seen neither the original photos, the negatives nor the witnesses, and thus had no idea of the circumstances under which the photos were taken. And although it was afterwards shown that no meteorological balloon (or any other balloon) had been released at that time, and that the photographed object looked about as much like a balloon as a piano on a plate of sprouts (so to speak), the chief witness was made out to be "drunk," "illiterate," "fraudulent" and a "layman" by the "scholar" in the case concerned. Who is right, as ordinary people see the matter, the "layman" or the "scholar"?

The Cluj photos were not published in the Rumanian press until 18th September that year, when they appeared with a short commentary. The Rumanian engineer Florin Gheorghiţa, a resident of Cluj and a dedicated UFOlogist, made a thorough study of the case and brought out a report. This we now give below, completed and/or corrected by us after meeting the witnesses in 1968 and 1970.

On Sunday morning, 18th August, the technician Emil Barnea and his girl-friend Zamfira Matea were making for Baciu Wood close to Cluj. They were with two other people—a man and a woman—whose identity for strictly personal reasons must not be divulged. These two were the reason for the absence of the fourth photo—because they are in it and did not want the embarrassment of its publication; it is unfortunate that we cannot print it. We stress this to show how often it comes about that important material may not be available because of trivia—material which could not only be valid proof of the existence of UFO's but also at the same time could shed light on their behaviour. We shall refer to this photo, which we have studied closely, again. The weather was excellent and the party decided to picnic in a light, open spot in the wood far from the Cluj–Bucharest road. Emil Barnea was looking for dry wood for a fire when he suddenly heard his girlfriend call out that she had seen something peculiar. He simply must come and see. Back at the spot they had chosen for the picnic he saw a large, round, metallic object shining silver in the sunlight. It was flying in a strange manner over the wood and quite soundlessly. Barnea hurried to his rucksack, took out his camera, measured the light and the distance and then took a photo. As the object was moving rather slowly he was able to take a second photo in less of a hurry. He noticed alterations in its course and degree of brightness. Two more photos were taken hurriedly because the object suddenly accelerated, shot upwards and disappeared. The time was 13:23. There was no breath of wind and the only sound was that of birds singing. The four witnesses remained quite silent as they watched the object's progress for two minutes—they were too amazed to talk. After some days the strong impression the object had made on them gradually grew weaker and after a week or two when the rest of the film had been used up Emil Barnea developed the negatives and made copies. Actually he did not know what to do with them and was afraid of being laughed at. Then the engineer Gheorghița came back to Cluj at the beginning of September when his holidays were over, so Barnea showed him the photos and gave him all the details. After further investigation, about which we shall have more to say later, one of the photos was published in many newspapers on 18th September 1968, together with a brief review of Barnea's evidence.

Emil Barnea is 45 and is generally respected for his integrity, though he is regarded as perhaps a shade egocentric. After serving some time as an army officer he has been employed as a technician with a building firm for some years. This was how Gheorghița had met

Cluj: Barnea's second paragraph

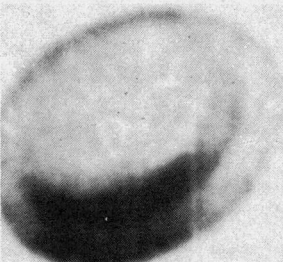

Cluj: detail photo 1

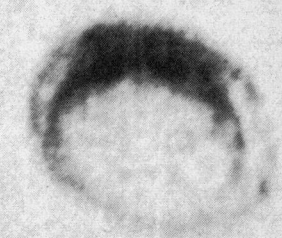

Detail photo 2 (see also drawing page 106)

him two years before—as a purely business acquaintance. Barnea told him that he was not interested in the UFO problem in the slightest and was apt to be sceptical about such rumours. We know for certain that there was no book at all anywhere in Cluj about

Barnea's third photograph

Detail photo 3

Heflin's photo no. 4

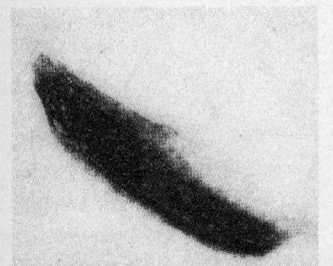
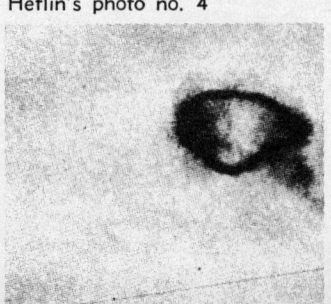

the subject at that time and that neither Barnea nor any of the other witnesses had ever seen such a book. Even the 34-year-old Zamfira Matea, a clerical worker, who is certainly not a flippant person, had scarcely ever heard people talk about UFO's. All this not only makes their account of the event more credible but also more important. After further research the following details about the photos and the event were recorded: (1) The place where the photos were taken lies 4.7 km west-south-west of Cluj. (2) The temperature in the sun was about 36°C. (3) The sky was cloudless but there was a strange sort of vapour at a great height which was only spotted when the object had flown very high and had disappeared; this "vapour" is visible on photo 4. (4) The camera was a FED 2 with an interstar of 2.8; the film was a normal 17 din, ORWO. (5) None of the witnesses had seen the object approach—it was only spotted when it was right above them. (6) The object flew straight at first from the north-east. (7) After changing from its south-westerly direction it seemed to fly gently towards the earth. (8) Its altitude was reckoned at 600 m and it was at an angle of 85 degrees above the horizon. (9) The object kept its course during its flight, both vertically and horizontally. (10) During the short initial flight the route and position constantly altered. (11) The object seemed made of metal, which appeared to shine more fiercely before the acceleration and increase in altitude (soon after photo 2). (12) The object could not be identified with any man-made machine connected with flying. (13) The "machine" (sic) had a diameter exceeding 30 m according to the witnesses.

The negatives were examined, to ensure that there was no hoax, first by Cluj's best-known photographic reporter and then by an eminent photography specialist from the Ager Press at Bucharest. Both men decided the negatives were genuine, and the one attached to the Ager Press made the peculiar psychological remark that if Barnea had intended any swindle he—being only an amateur after all—would have placed the UFO right in the middle of the photo. The fourth photo is odd, because here the object has become so small, as if lost in a sort of dark cloud so that it is no longer properly visible. This might well be compared with Heflin's fourth photo and the theories suggested about it. After professional photographers had studied the matter the film was examined by a public laboratory in Cluj and found to be normal; nobody had tampered with it. Gheorghița could now reconstruct what happened on the spot. Even a superficial glance at the photos shows that flowers and plants on the first three are all the same (we will forget the fourth one until further notice) so that a flight plan could be worked out (see drawings) by means of simple calculations, and the UFO's approximate height and dimensions obtained from its three positions. It is remarkable that Barnea's estimate of the UFO's diameter is so close to the truth.

The photos were sent to Ager Press with a request for their publication. In a country such as Rumania there is no question of any reimbursement for publication of this sort of material. Thus one may not accuse Barnea of any desire for gain or profit which could have encouraged him to tamper with the photos. Besides, one is likely to be careful there not to make a fool of the authorities by requesting them to publish false photos.

The UFO was a subject for discussion for quite a long time after the pictures finally appeared in the paper. Barnea and his girl-friend had lengthy interviews on Rumanian television, and Barnea himself was subjected to several tests by someone working for the magazine *Informația Bucureștiului* in order to demonstrate convincingly that he had excellent powers of perception.

We consider it inopportune to analyse Barnea's photos at the moment: there are shadow-lines on them which can scarcely be considered "natural" if one considers the position of the sun and the time they were taken. This matter caused a passionate discussion amongst Cluj University technicians who, after studying the pictures thoroughly, made models to examine

Flight pattern (drawing by Florin Gheorghița)

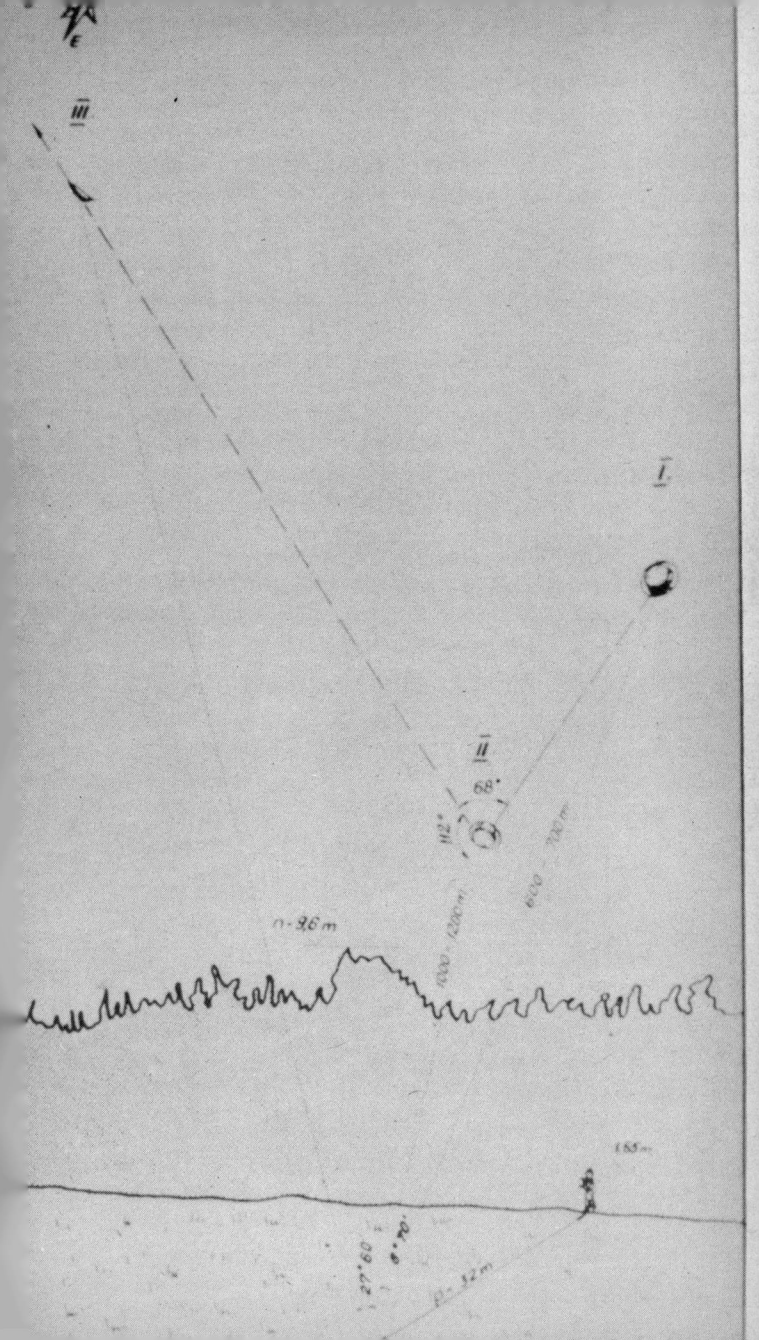

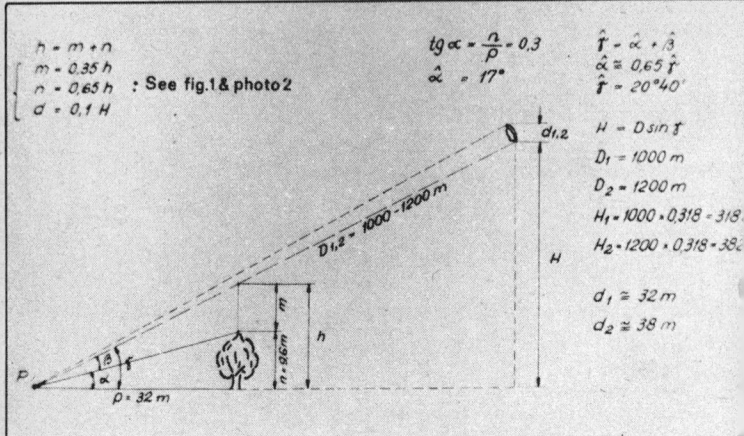

Calculation of the Cluj UFO's diameter
(F.S.R., Florin Georghiţa)

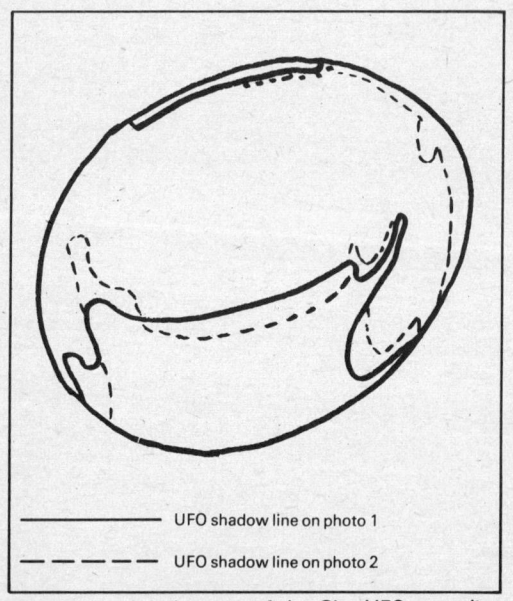

———— UFO shadow line on photo 1
- - - - - UFO shadow line on photo 2

The light and dark zones of the Cluj UFO according
to photos one and two (drawing by G. Delcorps)

the light reflection or illumination of the UFO and then concluded that the object lit up itself. Even the French UFO magazine *Lumières dans la Nuit* (October 1971) had the photos examined by two specialists before publishing them. The analysis by the Belgian G. Delcorps is especially noteworthy and instructive, not only for its conclusions but also for the attitude of seriousness and precision he shows. Unfortunately Delcorps examined only the first two photos and noted that the UFO on photo 2 cannot have been filmed 85 degrees above the horizon, as Barnea had estimated, but at 31. The object on the first photo was put at 19 degrees above the horizon, its diameter being reckoned 22.3 m—this figure was based on verifiable calculations as well as on the trees and plants shown. He proceeded on the assumption that the object as pictured on photo 2 was in fact 600 m from the camera. This is possible, since other calculations proved that it must have been moving at an altitude between 360 and 484 m. Delcorps was struck by the distribution of the light and dark areas which even to a layman can seem strange. Delcorps did not know what his Rumanian colleague's conclusions were but he came to the same ones, viz (1) that the object on photo 2 is not a reflected image of the one shown on photo 1 (see drawing); and (2) that the object carried its own lighting system. He considered it out of the question that there was any chance of trick photography.

We shall not undertake further technical discussions but we should like to stress that we consider ourselves to be "laymen," unqualified for explaining the nature of UFO's, which we feel is not our task. We merely assert that the UFO phenomenon *exists* and we think the Cluj and Heflin photos important evidence.

7. THE UFO PHENOMENON AND RUMANIAN MASS MEDIA

Swedes and Frenchmen show that they know all about UFO's in Rumanian newspapers—Some newspaper correspondence gets into trouble—A Rumanian professor hopes for an international UFO observation point—150 amateurs and professional astronomers are requested to keep a look-out for UFO's—In Bucharest a scientific UFO circle is established—Comparative drawings once again underline the universal character of the Rumanian sightings.

It is worth enquiring how the UFO phenomenon has been able to influence the information media, though in countries like ours, where the subject has been under public scrutiny since 1947, this is not possible because there are such an overwhelming number of publications in the West concerning them. It is no longer possible to say who the people chiefly influenced are or what the influences themselves are, whereas in Rumania such an analysis is certainly still possible.

Echoes of UFO discussion got through to the Rumanian press quite early, usually treated as "amusing stories" told in an ironical way. This attitude arose because the UFO was held to be adversely influenced by official American journalism—which was all lies and sensationalism. Under the title "Flying Saucers" the youth paper *Scînteia Pionierului* published on 28th July 1956 several famous cases (Kenneth Arnold, Thomas Mantell and others) which quoted the opinions of the Swedish savant Benediks that UFO's are nothing but examples of ball-lightning. In Rumania people have been used for years to limiting themselves to listening only to the "well-informed" specialists when these were foreign ones. Thus the weekly magazine *Lumea* published an article by Charles Dauzats of Agence France Presse on 29th July 1965 under the title "Flying Saucers, Illusion or Reality?" One can easily imagine what his answer was.

Meanwhile Rumanian men of science let themselves be influenced by the scepticism of their foreign colleagues amongst whom, of course, was Menzel. They tended to reject the problem and did not study the relevant documents. Answering questions put by the editor of *Informaţia Bucureştiului* Professor Călin Popovici (head of the astrophysics section of the Bucharest Observatory) said on 9th December 1967: "At the moment I do not know a single academic person who has seen a UFO. If there is in fact such a person then he classifies the object as an unknown but natural phenomenon like plasma clouds, which may or may not have arisen as the result of magnetic fields disturbed for instance by the presence of high tension cables. Only those hypotheses which are based on natural, terrestrial phenomena are put forward by scholars. Personally I think we are dealing here either with the testing of new forms of propulsion or atmospheric effects which have not yet been adequately studied."

The co-author of this book Ion Hobana, who has written a number of science-fiction books, originally followed this newspaper correspondence as an interested layman. But he made a couple of journeys abroad—visiting among other places Belgium and Holland—where he met people involved with the problem. As a result he began to keep files and then entered the debate himself. His first article appeared on 27th January 1968 in the weekly *Magazin* where he outlined the UFO problem in a subtler way than was usual in Rumania. The "UFO taboo" in neighbouring countries was already broken and in 1967 (see our preface and the graph on p. 120) there was an increasing number of UFO sightings, so Rumanian interest in the subject grew. Various readers responded to Hobana's article and reported sightings which he filed. Naturally not all the reactions were favourable. After one interview with Hobana on T.V., the television commentator of the newspaper *Flacăra* wrote that a "science-fiction writer had uncritically expressed the opinions of the high priests of the Saucer Cult." This led to further newspaper polemics in which other interested parties joined, but it died down after a few weeks of muddled debate. *Flacăra* sought the opinions of two scientists, one of whom, George Stănilă, doctor of physics, department chief at the Bucharest Observatory, opined that it was "absolutely necessary" to start "the study of the UFO problem in a scientific and systematic way." He then referred to James McDonald. The other savant, Dumitru Andreescu, a member of the astronautical commission of the Rumanian Academy, reluctantly acknowledged the reality of the UFO phenomenon but added: "I am no champion of the idea of extraterrestrial causes of UFO's, but on the other hand I cannot support those who reject *a priori* this possibility ... If we wish to analyse the cosmic hypothesis to some extent then we must ensure that we do not proceed to judge these unknown aerial phenomena from exclusively terrestrial bases and principles."

The summer of 1968 saw the discussion of this problem spread to nearly all Rumanian newspapers, especially since at that time there were many UFO sightings reported in the Balkans. The important daily newspaper *Scînteia*, with which Ion Hobana had editorial connections at that time, published in a supplement in August 1968 the results of a comprehensive survey of international character which included Dr. Menzel, James McDonald, Dr. Dobronravov and Gabriel Voisin, constructor of the first sea-plane. Nicolae Patraulea was the Rumanian who took part in this enterprise, a correspondent member of the Academy of the Rumanian Socialist Republic. He wrote: "I am of the opinion that the fairly well-documented reports, of which there are many, and the photos of UFO's are as yet insufficient material for establishing a sound UFO hypothesis. I would like to see UFO reports given wider publicity and more international cooperation in the study of this problem. So I now call for the establishment of as many UFO centres and observation stations as possible for the study of phenomena low in the atmosphere."

On 1st March 1968 the high-brow weekly *Contemporanul* published James McDonald's letter to U Thant (see Appendix C) beside UNO's acknowledgement of the latter's service connected with the Commission for Space Research. An influential student magazine, *Viața Studențească*, asked Hobana to explain the UFO problem in a series of articles, which he did from May to August 1968. Even the provincial newspapers began to show an interest in the "mystery." *Tomis*, of Constanza, published articles by various authors on the subject. Hobana was used to hitting out at these articles—regardless of whether they were for or against UFO's—when they contained errors, which so often in UFO literature seem to have to occur. On 18th August 1968 Emil Barnea took the photos already discussed in the previous chapter, which were published a month later in the Rumanian press and a couple of years later by foreign newspapers; thanks to Florin Gheorghița they appeared in *Flying Saucer Review*, *Lumières dans la Nuit* and *Phénomènes Spatiaux*. (A nice detail that flatters our own vanity is that the Dutch press was several days in advance of the English *Flying Saucer Review* in publishing a Rumanian UFO photo—the authors of this book issued them in *Vrij Nederland* on 10th January 1970, which meant that this Amsterdam weekly was the first non-Rumanian one in the world to print them.)

Seeing that foreign countries now also began to show some interest in the Rumanian UFO affair, the editor of *Rumania Today*—a newspaper specially intended for circulation abroad—requested Hobana to write an article about the present state of UFO research there. He wrote one for the August 1968 edition and on 21st August of that year it was reprinted in its entirety by *La Voix Ouvrière* at Geneva. *Panorama*, the Belgian weekly, did the same for Hobana's

OBSERVATORUL ASTRONOMIC POPULAR   Nr......... din.............
Astroclubul Central București
Serviciul "Atenție O.Z.N.!"
B-dul Ana Ipătescu nr.21
Sectorul 1, BUCUREȘTI 22.
   Telefon: 12.93.89

   C ă t r e
       tov..
      membru prin corespondență al Astroclubului Central.

   Cunoscînd pasiunea și preocupările Dv. ca astronom amator, precum și luînd în considerare faptul că sînteți membru al Astroclubului Central București, de pe lîngă Observatorul Astronomic Popular, vă rugăm să ne sprijiniți cu colaborarea voluntară a Dv. în cadrul noului nostru Serviciu "Atenție O.Z.N.!". Ca atare, solicităm din partea Dv. o alertă permanentă în privința posibilității apariției Obiectelor Zburătoare Neidentificate (O.Z.N.) deasupra teritoriului Republicii Socialiste România.

articles "Flying Saucers in the East" on 24th December 1968 and "The Object over the Carpathians" on 31st December 1968. In the coming years this spread of information should increase. UFO's were put on film at Cluj on 19th September 1968 (see page 140). The film was screened for a number of Rumanian scholars and it was seen by Ion Corvin Sîngeorzan, director of the People's Observatory in Bucharest. (One of the authors was present.) He gave a number of lectures that year about the UFO problem and he said to reporters from *Dobrogea* (Constanza): "There is no doubt at all: UFO's do exist." On 12th October 1968 he published an article entitled "Flying Saucers, Phenomenon of a Rational Activity" in *Informația Bucureștiului*—a title which speaks volumes. Thus the following statements cause no surprise: "The appearance of genuine UFO's over populated areas especially is sometimes coupled with sightings en masse which according to statistical laws shed light upon the most objective traits of the phenomenon. It is therefore very unfortunate that there are scientific people who belittle the observations, perhaps from a love of leisure or from scruples stemming from their entrenched and obdurate scientific views which make them dismiss the matter as something deriving from 'public ignorance' . . ." Finally the Observatory sent in the middle of December a letter to 150 amateur astronomers announcing the establishment of a liaison office ("Beware UFO's") and requesting their co-operation (see page 112 and Appendix B). On 24th December the press reported the setting up at Cluj of a scientific UFO circle which would collate sightings and attempt explanations of phenomena as accurately as possible.

Both the liaison office and the circle ceased their activities after publication of the Condon Report—a clear example of its influence, which is likely to be the same all over the world. Even the vigorous NICAP has done more than falter under the blow. But it is hardly likely to be a year before important scientists either as individuals or as groups will conclude after thorough study that the end result of this officially sponsored investigation is extremely unsatisfactory. (What we see as the most important viewpoint is that expressed by the subcommittee for UFO research of the American Institute for space research—the AIAA —which concluded as follows in November 1970: "Our committee sees no evidence to support the opinions put forward by D. Condon that extended studies of the UFO phenomenon would produce no further scientific facts." The AIAA is now busy on a project which aims to deal with the UFO problem in as technical and exact a way as possible. The magazine *Industrial Research* ascertained in January 1971 from an enquiry amongst its specialized readers that 76% of them held the Condon conclusions to be inaccurate.)

The magazine *Lumea* paid great attention to the Condon conclusions and in 1969 published six extracts of a detailed nature, and these of course were the negative aspect of the UFO problem *entirely*—as they occur in the Report. As for *The Condon Report* itself (published by Bantam Books, New York) this was not available in Rumanian bookshops so that readers there, whether or not scientifically trained, were unable to form their own opinions about its real content.

However, Hobana did study the Report and on 28th

March he published an article about it in *Contemporanul*. The article was actually by James McDonald who, it seemed, could not share the views contained in the Report. McDonald showed (1) that certain details were wrongly interpreted by the Condon workers and thus had no scientific basis; (2) that unexplained cases were not reported in all their details; (3) that no investigations were put in hand after a number of cases had occurred (McDonald himself did some research again); (4) that in certain instances some essential facts which were definitely in the Condon files had not been brought out.

Informaţia Bucureştiului published on 9th April 1969 a review of the Condon Report by Roscoe Drummond called "The UFO's are still around" which has become well-known and was previously printed by *The Christian Science Monitor* on 1st February 1969. The *Bulletin of the Atomic Scientist* published a contribution by Dr. Allen Hynek in its 1969 April number, and this was worked up into the form of an interview with the scholar and as such was printed in *Scînteia Tineretului* in December 1969. Meanwhile Hobana had expressed his dissatisfaction with the Report in an interview published in *România Literară* (3rd April 1969)—as also in two articles in the popular *Cutezătorii* (22nd May 1969 and 18th September of that year). He also did this in a number of radio broadcasts and by taking part in several international enquiries. The press was teeming with explanations put forward by people who were no doubt well-respected and learned, but who appeared to be very ill-informed on the subject. Hobana used precise factual material to invalidate their contentions where necessary—which was often enough.

The Rumanian UFO War intensified on 28th November 1969 in the course of a popular television series, "Any Questions?" Viewers were able to ring up the studio and question a panel of experts about UFO's—the team itself consisting of two scientists, a journalist, a science fiction writer and Hobana himself. Unfortunately this broadcast had little success, largely because of the prejudices of the two scholars

The weekly *Cutezătorii* was a solid Rumanian bulwark for the idea of UFO reality. Cartoon here reads: "Mum! Dad! They have been writing about us in *Cutezătorii!*"

Professor D. Menzel claims that unusual cloud formations are often taken for UFO's, but the authors do not agree. Lenticular clouds, such as the one photographed here by J. Weverbergh on 12th October 1970 at Mărăşeşti (Rumania), are always identified as such without any shadow of doubt.

taking part, who constantly reiterated their view that "the whole UFO business" was impossible because of the state of present-day knowledge. Hobana countered their arguments effectively by using impressive documentation and by quoting from the Condon Report... to the astonishment of both gentlemen who had not even read the book whose views they had come to defend.

But not all Rumanian academics shared the views put forward by their colleagues on the "box." The world-famous Henri Coandă, inventor of the jet and the Coandă-effect, said on 15th October 1969 in *Apărarea Patriei* that he had reservations concerning the extraterrestrial origin of the UFO's. When asked if they were objects created on our planet by an unknown power he said: "They could also be something else. I am not used to denying any scientific theory *a priori*. We must think that it is possible that somewhere in the universe another form of life has evolved from principles clearly different from our own."

In 1970 Hobana took up this idea in *Almanahul Scriitorilor* where he tried to imagine why UFO's take so long to make contact with us. 1969 was noted for still further Rumanian UFO sightings and their publication in foreign newspapers like the NICAP *Bulletin*, the *Flying Saucer Review* and *Phénomènes Spatiaux*.

At the beginning of 1971 both authors of *UFO's from Behind the Iron Curtain* published a book in Rumania entitled *UFO's: A Challenge to the Human Spirit*. In particular the Condon Report was dealt with and the scientific press reviewed the book favourably. The engineer Liviu Macoveanu wrote in *Informația Bucureștiului:* "This book is a felicitous combination of serious scientific information and literary gifts, which makes it more fascinating than a novel or a piece of science-fiction" (16th March 1971). Macoveanu went on to say that especially young people with imaginative gifts and an appetite for the new should pay attention to the material collected by us. He thought the title of our book—*UFO's: A Challenge to the Human Spirit* might be altered by the coming scientific generation to *UFO's: A Revelation for the Human Spirit*.

Rumanian UFO discussions thus began again. The above-mentioned Dumitru Andreescu said in a radio debate about UFO's on 1st May that he was "more interested than ever before" in the problem. The psychologist Professor Paul Popescu-Neveanu hinted that the proofs of the existence of UFO's are "overwhelming." When asked what he thought about the psychic condition of the observers he answered that one would be better off subjecting some members of the Condon team to psychological tests. . . . The questionnaire attached to our Rumanian book certainly provoked responses but these were mainly to do with the volume —not with the UFO itself. Also there were sightings reported after its publication, though unfortunately not as many as we had hoped and expected. But the fact that some were sent in to us shows once again that discussion of the problem does not necessarily have as an automatic consequence that "people suddenly see UFO's." No, people see them when the objects really are there.

On 20th March 1971 Hobana met a large number of students, which was the starting-point for a wave of intense activity which now is still building up. Based upon this student interest in activity a "scientific UFO circle" was founded in Bucharest a month later. They put on a monthly meeting for public debate and interested parties are kept informed about the results of the circle's efforts to clear up the problems of Rumania's most enigmatic sightings. Scientific research workers, university professors and engineers are members of the circle, as well as students. A monthly bulletin is circulated.

At the beginning of 1972 there was an important interview with Hobana in the weekly *Tribuna*. At the same time, unfortunately, the popular *Săptămîna* started to publish a series of sensational articles about dubious "facts" and "rumours" concerning "the men in black" who had honoured our planet with a visit from outer space. Besides this, Rumanian Television bought the well-known serial *The Invaders* and certain evil spirits seemed to forget that the serial is based on science-fiction. In any case the concept OZN (Objecte Zburatoare Neidentificate—Rumanian for UFO) has become a marketable one in daily life there. In general, scientific circles are less aggressive about the matter and gradually Rumanians have become aware that behind the letters OZN a phenomenon lurks which one day *will* be studied.

More than 90% of the 162 cases selected and reported by us from Romania remained unpublished hitherto; so there is no question of mutual influencing of the witnesses. Most of the UFO sightings were reported to us freely and afterwards we contacted the people concerned with the most interesting phenomena. The authors do not claim that all 162 are inexplicable manifestations, but neither have they wanted to draw obvious conclusions pointing to the existence of an IFO or UFO. We would stress once again what we think is our sole purpose: publishing reports of things hundreds of thousands of ordinary citizens have seen and found strange or inexplicable. We also thought that in the process of including a number of cases in our list we would have to be somewhat less critical than we appear to have been from our earlier publications, because the *totality* of these 162 examples afford an excellent picture of the way in which an East European country reports the who, what and how involved in UFO sightings. So far, there is not a single UFOlogist who has at his disposal as comprehensive a view as this of UFO manifestations in Eastern Europe. From all the cases examined by us, of which naturally only a small part will be published, we can clearly see a pattern emerging which has internal structural features exactly like other evidence from all over the world. We have already dealt with this in more detail in our foreword. The Rumanian pattern differs from the international one only as regards the "quality" of the witnesses, the Rumanian observers being for the most part qualified people: more than 50% of the reports come from (graduate) engineers or students reading exact sciences. The characteristic features of Rumanian UFO sightings are dealt with in more detail in Chapter 9. Here we append an outline and summary:

ONE Concerning the Witnesses:
1. The best sightings of UFO's which can almost certainly be regarded as genuinely Unknown Flying Objects come from the people best qualified for this work. Hynek, McDonald and Vallée also came to this conclusion.

2. 99% of the witnesses do not desire to remain anonymous.
3. A great deal of reporting is done by one person on behalf of a group of witnesses.
4. Apart from the high percentage of "qualified" observers, the Rumanian stories cover the spectrum of social life there, since we find amongst the witnesses university readers and professors, meteorologists, army and navy officers, journalists, publishers, doctors, pilots, engineers, technicians, students, practitioners of science, farmers, workers, housewives, judges . . .

TWO   Concerning the Phenomena:
1. The UFO phenomenon appears to have a historical character.
2. Most of the sightings take place in July, August, September and October: see graph on page 122.

One can ask if the summer weather, which is what brings observers out into the open for longer periods, is responsible for the higher number of sightings in these months. It is easy to come to this conclusion and other research workers have dealt with it as well. For instance, the well-known collector of cases of UFO sightings Vuillequez published a short study of this problem in the French UFO magazine *Lumières dans la Nuit* Number 102 in October 1969: a short review, but one which came to positive conclusions. Vuillequez made graphs of 1965 UFO sightings occurring in both the northern and the southern hemispheres. We reproduce this graph (p. 121) from the magazine in question so that one can see what emerges.

It is clear that all over the world UFO's are seen in the same months regardless of whether or not it is summer or winter in any particular place. The similarities are striking if we put next to each other Vuillequez's graph and those of the Rumanian sightings in 1968 and 1969. This once again underlines the universal character of the Rumanian UFO behavioural pattern.

3. The international nature is likewise shown if we compare the times of the Rumanian sightings with the times of those elsewhere. For this purpose we can use Vallée's graphs and one may compare the observation

	J	F	M	A	M	J	J	A	S	O	N	D	Tot.
1517											1		1
17th C.		1											1
1709		1											1
1737											1	1	1
1793											1		1
1812													1
1837				1									1
1843			1										1
1904							1						1
1905							1						1
1914									1				1
1914-1915									1				1
1926							1						1
1927							1						1
1927-1928							1						1
1932-1933							1						1
1944				1					1				2
1945							1	1					2
1947					1								1
1953						1	1						2
1955							1						1
1957								1					1
1957-1958							1						1
1958				1									1
1958-1959				1									1
1960												1	1
1961									1				1
1963					1			1	1				3
1966						1	(1)	1		1		1	4
1967							2	1	1		2	4	10
1968			3	4	4	3	3	12	19	5 (+1)	3	4	60 (+1)
1969	3	1			3	6	7	3	3				26
1970			1	1	1	4	3				1	1	12
1971	2	1		1		1	2	3					10

Graph of recorded sightings in Rumania, 1517–1971

times of various types like those confirmed by Vallée with our own graphs of Rumanian observation times recorded in 1968.

4. Peak year was 1968, when 60 cases were reported to us, so we think Rumania had a UFO wave that year. The American Air Force had 1,112 cases reported in 1966—the peak year for them. We are of course aware

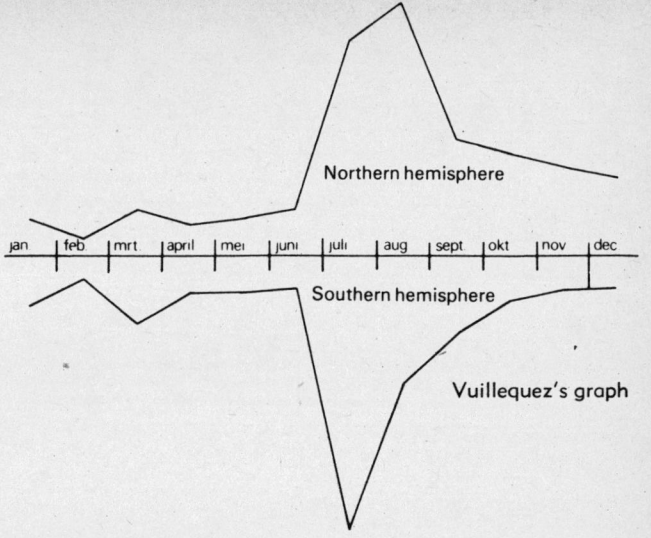

Vuillequez's graph

of the completely speculative nature of this comparison since América's population on 1st January 1969 was ten times as large as that of Rumania (202 million as compared with 20 million). The number of UFO cases in 1968 in Rumania would have to be 111 if we wanted to be able to say that in Rumania the level of activity was the same as that of the U.S.A. On the other hand if we bear in mind that America has 30 times the area of Rumania then we arrive at a figure of 37. So is the number of 1968 Rumanian sightings enormous? No, because the population density in Europe is considerably greater than it is in America.

It can further be pointed out that America in 1966 had the Bluebook—an *official* centre for the reporting of observations by civilians, the military or the police; whereas with us it was a matter of sheer chance whether or not anybody reported a sighting. But regarded in this light 1969 is also a fairly important UFO year, as we are still receiving information about manifestations occurring in those two years. Are all these reports accounts of genuine UFO's? Once again we refer to our foreword, especially regarding what was said about "rumours." In our estimation—and in this we are helped by the UFO study circle in Bucha-

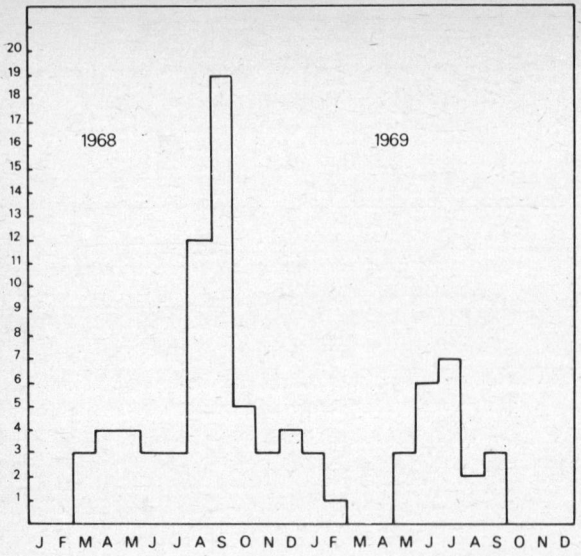

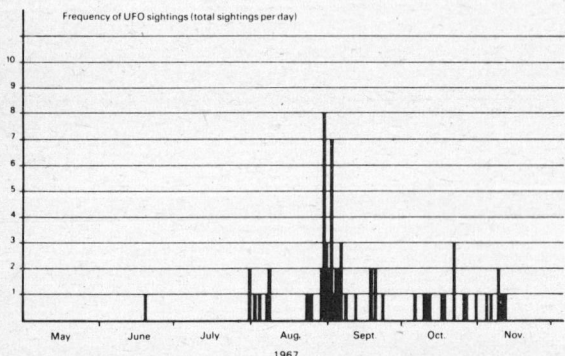

Stoke-on-Trent, Summer 1967. Highest points reached by the wave in the vicinity of this town. The wave was thoroughly analysed by two amateur astronomers. Compare this graph with the international one and the 1968–69 Rumanian wave. (p. 120 and above).

rest—49% of cases published by us occurring in 1968 have to do with genuine UFO's. The other 51% can presumably be dismissed as sightings of balloons

(12%) or as various other atmospheric phenomena (39%). It is striking that our prognosis differs so very little from that of the American Air Force when analysing sightings in the United States: the balloon pattern, in particular, is very similar. We conclude with a larger number of genuine UFO's than they do, yet we have been fairly critical in judging them; and if we feel that our figures are not high but that the American ones are low then this is so because we *know* they are low: we know it from astrophysicist Allen Hynek, who has demonstrated this to be the case often enough. If we add up the percentage of unsatisfactory details from the American Air Force's statistics then we arrive at 44.5% for the unknown American ones against 49% of the 1968 Rumanian cases—which come pleasantly close to each other.

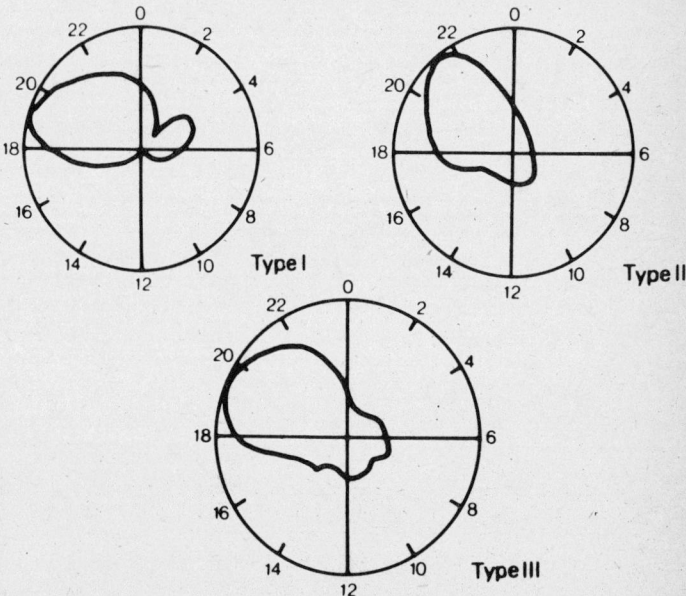

Times of the sightings as published by J. Vallée after an analysis of 6000 cases.
Type I: just above the ground, or landings.
Type II: abnormal movement with at least one stationary.
Type III: unusual object.

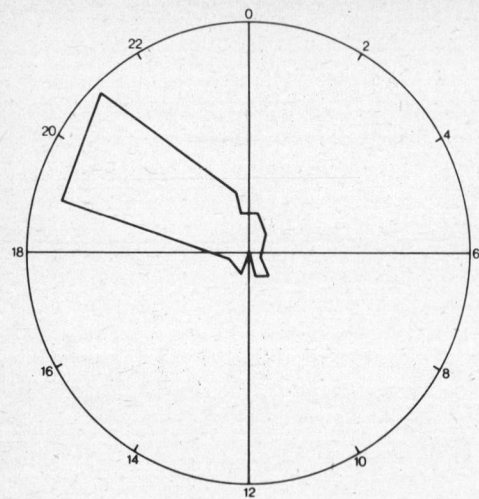

Rumania, 1968 wave. Period of the sightings; all types.

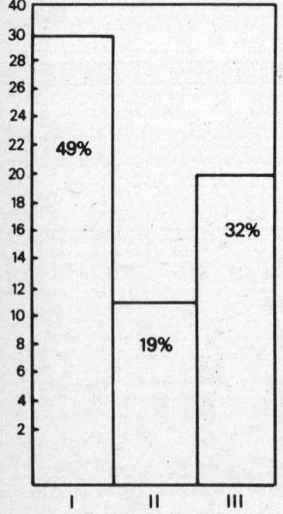

Rumania, 1968 wave; presumed identification.
Group I: UFO
Group II: balloon
Group III: various (inadequate data, astronomical, aeronautical phenomena)

But what is more important than this comparison is the following statistic (see graph below).

We put together the graph showing all the sightings with that of the cases we presumed had been identified, from which it appears that the "identified" reveal a peak similar to that of the unidentified. This could show that people came too quickly to the conclusion that what they saw was "known"—a fact which McDonald has often used in reproaching those he thought were too critical as UFO investigators. Thus an answer could be given here to what we feel to be the oddest problem connected with UFO's and their "rumours," as we have said in our preface. Why, in a busy UFO time, are there so many faultily interpreted phenomena reported, why so very many more than in "normal" times? Does the presence of a UFO unconsciously make everybody look up into the sky more often? If this is the case then the champions of the paranormal hypotheses certainly have something to get their teeth into! Or is an unexpectedly large number of manifestions simply a known/unknown natural phenomenon?

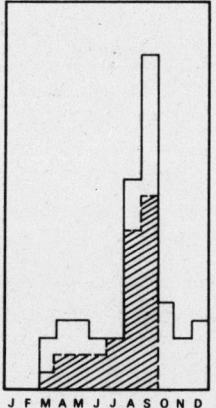

Rumania, 1968 wave. Presumably identified as UFO (49%) in respect of the total number of sightings for that year. The pattern is noticeably the same.

8. SILVER DISCS, SATELLITES, BALLOONS AND OTHER DISPUTED FLYING OBJECTS

UFO reports collected like stamps—A strange manifestation over the Carpathians—Movements untypical of balloons—During accelerations orange changes to red—Dr. Ion Xantus hangs a satellite on a thread—Producer Nacu sees a silver disc—Broadcasting station YO–5–TZ is disturbed—A student of physics sees a UFO for two minutes.

The above-mentioned 49% of genuine UFO's over Rumania in 1968 is a high level but it is of course caused by the highly trained quality of Rumanian observers. Scanning the world as a whole we see that the figures are different. One can only safely assume that an average of 20–30% of all categories reported internationally are inexplicable; in other words 70–80% can be checked and found to be misinterpretations of less familiar natural phenomena, or the side effects of machines sent up from the ground. This figure of 20–30% is not only proposed by authorities like Professor Hynek, but the Condon Report too agrees that it has to classify as "unknown" or "unsolvable" 23.70% of the cases it investigated. Other scientific people who are very busy with the problem put the figure of "genuine" UFO's even higher: James McDonald, for instance, considers it to be around 40%, and he shows that good lay associations like NICAP tend to be hypercritical about the reports sent in. McDonald supported his contention by using scientific methods like the calculations of angles, differences in temperatures recorded, inversions and so on. But most UFO circles are less critical about the reports they get, and one sometimes has the impression that their aim is like that of a dedicated stamp collector—to gather as many different samples as possible. Yet even for lay people it is possible to approach the material in such a way that only those cases remain for publication which a team of scientifically trained workers thinks can be definitely explained or classified as UFO's.

In this chapter we print two cases we examined—two sightings which thoroughly stirred public opinion in Rumania. At least a million people were involved in this affair and hundreds of reports were made of these two events: the Banat case of 29th, 30th and 31st March 1968, and that of Cluj in September the same year. The reactions these sightings caused were very great, especially after the Oravița Bistrița photo had been published in two papers (see photo page 130); and after the filming of the second case had been seen by many Rumanian scholars. Even sceptics thought it to be a case of a genuine UFO. We too thought so until after a couple of hours of work done on some reliable observations—especially those of meteorologists—we felt we had to draw different conclusions. Although . . . and yet . . . In connection with the sightings above Banat there is a number of unsolved and strange features still left which we did not wish to lay aside as simply faulty interpretations of natural phenomena, especially as these odd goings-on were witnessed by entirely reliable observers. If the "UFO" over Cluj and numerous other places is or was almost certainly a balloon not released anywhere in Rumania then it is possible that there is still another element in the Banat case. UFO's quite often seem to have a weakness for balloons and are frequently perceived by meteorologists through the theodolite near them (the balloons).

A STRANGE OBJECT OVER THE CARPATHIANS

On 29th, 30th and 31st March 1968 thousands of people saw an object over Banat—in the northern

Carpathians between Hungary, Jugoslavia and Bulgaria—which has up till now remained unidentified. It is worth the trouble to analyse this case in detail, both because of the abundant material we have on the subject (photos, sketches, maps, etc.) and because of the high degree of the witnesses' reliability. There is a mass of evidence about the case described here, some of which was voluntarily sent to the authors of this book whilst other pieces were sent on request. Although it is confusing in detail and conflicting at times, it is never so where essential points are at stake. By detailed and precise study of the many pieces of evidence the authors were able to reconstruct the "route" taken by the object with a fair degree of chronological accuracy. The first reports we had of the UFO were through letters and at first it seemed to us to be an "ordinary" and "average" sighting. On 11th May 1968 a popular Bucharest weekly published a brief statement that a group of technicians had taken photos of an UFO over Banat, Oravița. The object was also recorded at some meteorological centres including those in the Semenic Mountains. A series of telephone calls to Oravița then produced the following evidence.

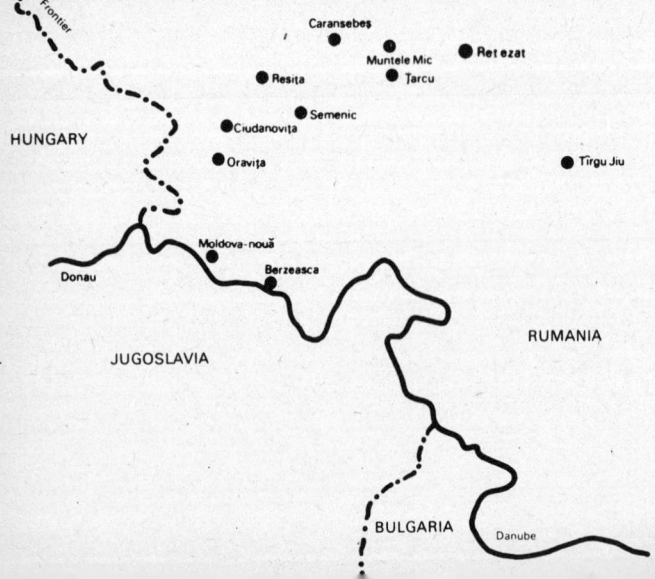

ORAVIȚA

A group of friends, Sipețean Ion, Opriș Vasile and Iorga Teofil, employees at the Banat mine, reported:

> On 29th March 1968 at 06:10 we saw north-east of Oravița a triangular, shining object at a height of over 7000 m at an angle of 35–40 degrees. (More than 120 people saw the object with the naked eye.) It was strongly illuminated with a yellowish-white light and we followed it without any optical aid until 8 o'clock. At 8:15 we used a theodolite and saw by this means that its shape was that of a truncated cone, both sides of which were illuminated, the eastern stronger than the western. Opriș Vasile photographed the object and we are sending you the negatives. At about 9 o'clock the object began to move away from us, but from 6 to 9 it had remained motionless in the air. The sightings lasted until 15:00 and around 16:30 the object was photographed again at an angle of 80–85 degrees, this time at Oravița and with a Smena camera. We also enclose the negatives of those photos and you will see from them that the object has a double ring with two different light centres. The impression we had was that this was the small base of the truncated cone. The object was watched by Sipețean Ion until the first stars came out. It is worth noting that some of our colleagues had seen the object already during the night 29–30 March at 02:30. As for the photos we would stress that they have been made by amateurs.
>
> Ing. Ilie T. Ioan, geologist
> Sipețean Ion, technician, geologist
> Zaha Gheorghe, technical topographer
> Mălinescu Adrian, technician, geophysicist
> (Many other names could be added to the list)
> The enclosed negatives comprise three photos, one of which was usable.

CIUDANOVIȚA

Letter from an observer of the same phenomenon:

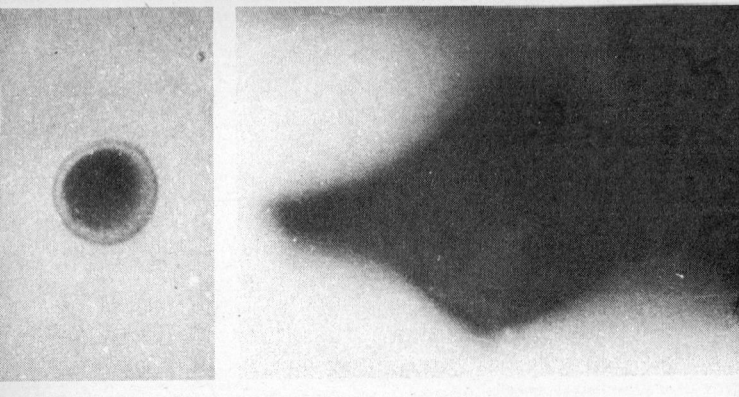

1. UFO photographed at Oraviţa on 29th March 1968.
2. UFO photographed by meteorologists at Ţarcu weather station 30th March 1968 at 18:00.

Drawing by the surveyor Lazăr of a UFO seen through a theodolite.
Fig. 1: commonest form
Fig. 2: less common
Fig. 3: seen very rarely like this
  A. darkest zone
  B. lightest zone
  d. diameter of about 15 m.
  D. large diameter of ca. 25–30 m.
  C. zone with its own lighting apparently
Angle of inclination of the central axis 5°–10°

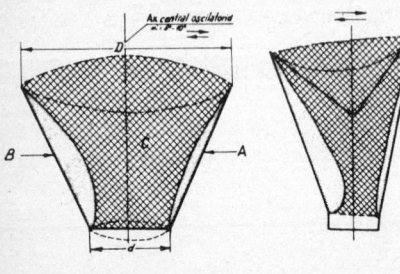 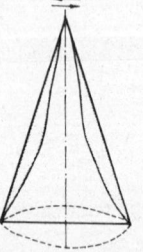

"We herewith enclose some facts regarding a phenomenon definitely seen by us on 29th and 30th March on the horizon of the Ciudanoviţa parish, Judeţul Caraş-Severin."

An illuminated object was seen on 29th March around 22:00 at 30 degrees above the horizon south of the parish, and it stayed until the following day, time 16:00 hours. On the evening of the 29th it was seen by a limited number of people but on the next day it was seen by all those going to work for the company between 6:30 and 7:00 that morning before sunrise. We enlisted the aid of the topographic service people so that by means of a theodolite we were able to get three different positions and shapes of the object and at the same time field glasses were used, which produced the same picture. Seen with the naked eye the object looked like a truncated cone with the apex pointing downwards and about the size of the half-moon, which was now on the horizon. Its light power was about that of Venus and even with the naked eye it could clearly be seen that one side of the object was lit up more strongly. This was side B and its position was variable, likewise its shape. Even the movements could be watched without optical aid, caused by the changing of the central axis vertical to the ground as well as the absolute movement of the whole object. The frequency of the change of axis was about once per second and the zig-zag movement southwards lasted approximately five hours. As already said, its geometrical form changed in time and place, the longest-lasting was Figure 1; this shape occurring more than any other. During the sightings several photos were made which because of the strong sunlight and great distance of the object did not turn out well.

Ing. Gh. Tănase
Ing. Ion Didicescu
Tech. topographer Sala Lazăr
Chef P. C. I. Bodea Constantin

ȚARCU

The meteorological station based in the Semenic Mountains was also said to have seen the object, one of the meteorologists there confirming on the telephone that the UFO had been sighted around 10:00 on 29th March. However, members of the weather-station in the Țarcu Mountains had been able to follow the object more closely. Our letter to Ţarcu was answered as follows:

> I enclose herewith the film (which I have not yet developed) together with two sketches and the necessary explanations prepared by my colleague Vitye Ingeborg and myself about the sightings. The object was observed at 16:00 on 29th March as my colleague at the Semenic weather station (Bălaşa Ştefan) has already told you. At 08:00 the next day it was again reported by Semenic, when I saw it in conjunction with colleagues from Cuntu and Caransebeş weather stations. The UFO's outlines were clearly visible and looked at first like an ordinary weather balloon. The object's shape was conical, with rounded corners, so not altogether unlike an egg. It was a dull-white colour and the side facing the sun glittered strongly. As a result of the strong reflections, the chaotic movements with slight vertical displacements and a motion almost contrary to the wind direction—things which are not typical of a weather balloon—we decided to look at it more closely as our suspicions were aroused. I did this for 2½ hours until its increased distance and position of the sun made it disappear. The object's movements were slow; sometimes the speed increased and occasionally it remained motionless. The sketch will show you the approximate horizontal distance and route.
>
> About 30 minutes after it had disappeared it was reported at roughly 13:00 by our colleague at the Berzeasca weather-station. Between 13:00 and 15:00 it was no longer to be seen in our sector but at 16:00 it appeared again, considerably closer and brighter and sharply outlined. It was like an isosceles triangle, with the base facing away from the direction of travel. Although the altitude did not seem at first to be more than 7000 m the acceleration rate was much smaller than at present. Its speed was now constant and it was soon at a height of about 30,000 m—a figure we arrived at with the help of two jet aircraft passing across between 16:00 and 18:00.

The object passed the zenith at 18:10 and at that moment we made several photos, both with an ordinary camera with yellow-green filter and without filter.

First sketch by Vasile Coțoi. UFO on 30th March 1968, 10:00—12:30 hrs.

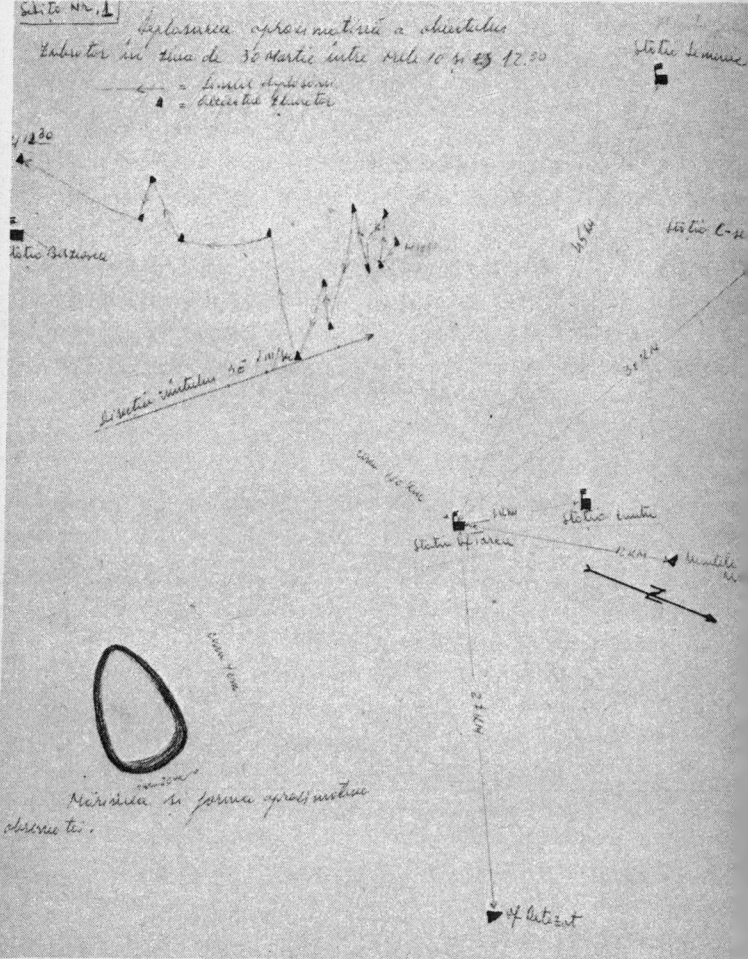

This time the movement was roughly linear but with a broad drift, the object keeping almost the same direction as that shown on sketch 2, where one can see its very big dimensions. Although it was five or six times higher than the aircraft the measurements were about the same. The object stopped glittering at sunset and the white colour dulled, which made me think the machine did not have any illumination of its own. But later it did begin to reflect some light again, though this might have been the last rays of the sun. When the stars came out the object turned a deep red, scarcely visible, but a triangular shape could just be seen. When complete darkness came the UFO seemed to take on a round shape and it began to shed a strong light—like Venus or Jupiter seen through a telescope but with a still more intense illumination. From this we concluded that the object had, after all, its own lighting, and the following morning the same phases of change of illumination took place. The movement was almost identical with the previous one but in the opposite direction (see sketch 2). Vasile Coțoi.

TÎRGU JIU

Was this object, which was recorded by various highly qualified observers, a balloon unknown to meteorologists? One suspects this to be the case because it was such a long time over the same region. But there are two facts which do not support this theory: (a) the movement against the prevailing wind —clearly seen by the Țarcu meteorologists—and the object's great height and (b) the UFO's self-lighting power which was confirmed by the same meteorologists and by other independent witnesses. A third fact working against the theory is the later sighting by a group of students and academics, which had all the marks of a genuine UFO observation (assuming a direct link between this and the three-day appearance of the odd object over Banat).

The students and academics reported that on 29th March between 18:30 and 19:00 a whitish-blue object

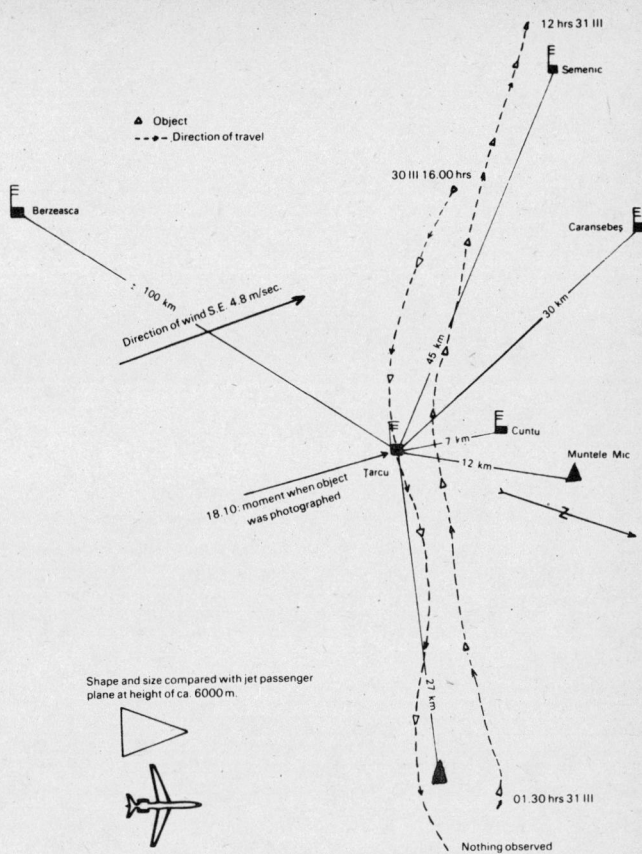

Second sketch by Vasile Coțoi, from 10:00 to 12:30 (at Țarcu weather station), showing:
UFO on 30th March 1968 from 16:00 to 24:00
UFO on 31st March 1968 from 01:00 to 12:00

came from an easterly direction, that is, from Oravița, Țarcu and other observation posts (with all of which the authors of this book have been in contact). It came at a great speed and with a zigzag movement, the colour changing from orange to red in the course of manoeuvres (accelerations in particular) which were difficult to follow exactly.

136 THE EVIDENCE ASSESSED

At first the object seemed to be about the size of a nut but the triangular shape became evident as it got bigger and clearer. After a sudden motionlessness the object went off at a very high speed, zigzagging again, in the direction from which it had come.

RECONSTRUCTION OF THE BANAT SIGHTING

As already pointed out we were able to reconstruct the route taken by the object—UFO or not as the case may be—from the best fourteen fairly detailed reports we received. Appendix D was based on the evidence of the following fourteen groups of witnesses, and the groups of observers given below are referred to by a number in the fifth column of that table:

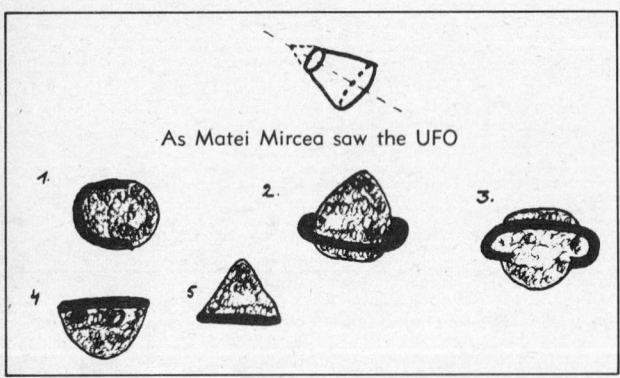

Arnăutu Ion: the thicker lines are not rings but areas of stronger illumination. Successive phases.

1. Muntele Mic: ski-centre
Matei Mircea, pupil, Class X1
Streian Virgil, id.
Lăzărel Ştefan, id.
Balatescu Mircea, radio-technician
+ many other skiers

2. Anina: private house
Bachici Mihai and wife, servants
Arnăutu Ion, pensioner

3. Tarcu Meteorological Centre
Vasile Coţoi

As seen at Oraviţa, 30th March 1968, 16:30 hrs.

From the Semenic Mountain. Dotted lines show stronger lighting.

Vitye Ingeborg, meteorologists

4. Berzeasca: Meteorological Institute
Ştefan Mircea, meteorologist

5. Oraviţa: colliery
Opriş Vasile
Ing. Ilie T. Ioan, geologist
Sipeţean Ion, engineering geologist
Zaha Gheorghe, technical topographer
Mălinescu Adrian, geophysicist
Iorga Teofil
+ a large number of farmers (see statements)

6. Caransebeş: meteorological observation post
Director of the above

7. Berzeasca: meteorological centre
Ienciu Ilie, meteorologist

As an engineer saw the UFO at Reşita.

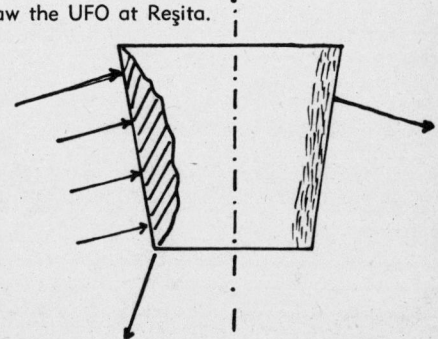

8. Semenic: meteorological station
Bălaka Ștefan, meteorologist

9. Orăvița: private house
Mădescu Ion, servant

10. Moldova-Nouă: private house
Berbecar Nicolae, pensioner (evidence unreliable)

11. Tîrgu Jiu: private house
Oprița Mihai
Oprița Virgil
Bușoi Virgil
Busoi Rodica, students

12. Tîrgu Jiu: school-building
Rovența Antoaneta
Natalia Lițoiu
Rovența Elena, teachers

13. Reșița: industrial steelworks
group of engineers

14. Steelworks
Ing. Gh. Tănase
Ing. Ion Didicescu
Sala Lazăr, tech. topographer
Sef P. C. I. Bodea Constantin
+ a large number of workers attached to this steel factory

THE SAUCER ON THE THREAD

The 19th September 1968 was a busy UFO day in Rumania, like the end of March that year. The long UFO sighting over Cluj, Sibiu and many other places reminds one not only of Banat (29th–30th March 1968) but also of the one above Bucharest on 10th September 1969 (see page 262).

As with these sightings the Cluj case has a number of details which do not support the balloon and satellite theory of Dr. Ion Xantus. In particular there is the fact that the best-equipped meteorologists announced that the UFO flew *against* the wind prevailing at the height where the object was located. One of the meteorologists even mentioned a "sharp acceleration." Some of the people under Dr. Ion Xantus reject his theory outright and the two authors of this book are equally at odds with each other about it. Ion Hobana thinks the question must be left open whereas Julien Weverbergh is inclined to agree with Dr. Xantus. Hobana's conviction stems from the fact that on the same day at least four other reports came in from fairly highly qualified observers (in Bistriţa, Bîrlad, Jucu and Bucharest-Braşov) of "objects" which must probably be counted as genuine UFO's.

19TH SEPTEMBER 1968, CLUJ

Emil Barnea's story and the publication of his photos in all the evening newspapers of 19th September 1968 created a sensation in Cluj—in Rumanian papers one seldom sees accounts of spectacular events. One can thus imagine the excitement when the very next day an unusual object hung above the town for hours! Everybody in Cluj stared at it. Amateur and professional photographers went to work on it, as also astronomers, Rumanian television men and people from the national film industry. We received scores of accounts, all describing the same phenomenon, roughly: that is, a shining, multi-cornered object had moved slowly across the whole of South-East Rumania and made thousands of people stare at it for hours—pilots, meteorologists, radar specialists, astronomers, farmers and judges and housewives all told what they saw of its shapes, colours and light-phenomena with very little variation in the telling. Only its speeds caused disagreements—the likenesses to the Banat, March 1968 case are striking. The papers published (once again) the sightings but an official explanation was never given.

We now give some very interesting photographic evidence (with elucidation) from Professor Xantus of Cluj; and a list of 24 reliable witnesses from a number of different places far away from each other—what they say confirms opinions held by Xantus, that the

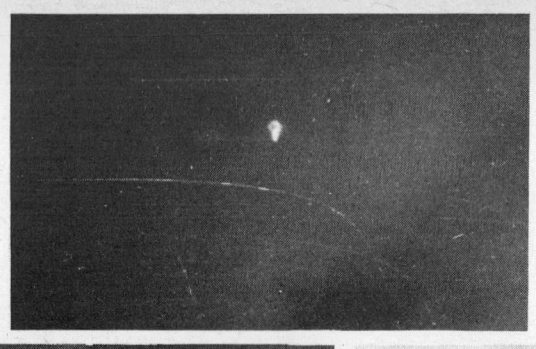
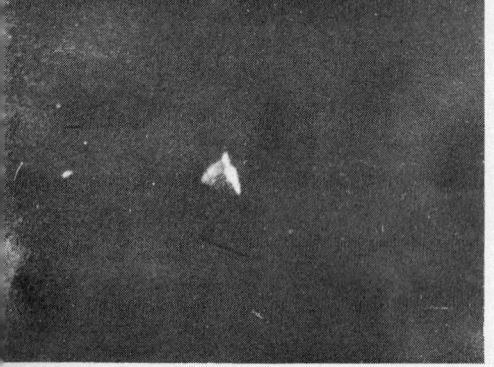

Photos by Dr. Xantus, taken on 10th September 1968 at Cluj. In the bottom right can be seen the model hanging from a wire.

phenomena were probably two balloons or satellites, since the object was seen at about the same time from several localities remote from each other. The whole case is typical enough to describe in detail and the following conclusions are, we think, of great importance (1) that people report exactly what they have seen—more or less; (2) UFO's or the rarer types of natural phenomena are certainly identified. The genuine UFO's have quite a different appearance and behavioural pattern, described as "odd" by both lay people and trained observers, and we also have more difficulty in reporting them. Consider for instance the evidence of the most important observer, Dr. Ion Xantus:

I saw the object with the aid of a telescope which

magnifies about 100 times; and watched it from its appearance at 16:30 until its final disappearance behind clouds which obscured it completely. My son and Dr. Dunky Alexandru also saw it (through prism binoculars) and we recorded our findings immediately. I made about 20 photos with a Weltaflex 6 x 6 and a Beiretta camera (Leica type) but having no diapositive for my telescope I can only send you a photo showing a point of light clearly outlined in the sky. With the aid of sketches and diagrams I have also made a model of the object we studied, which I hung on a nylon thread and photographed. I am enclosing this photo too, which clearly shows that the object was pyramidal in shape, with three sides. The corners and ribs of this "sky crystal" gleamed more than the sides did, a very white shine which to me would suggest a metal structure—duraluminium perhaps? My model shows very clearly how its white transparent plastic reflects the sun (see photos) without having any light source of its own. The farther the sun went down the more intense the reflection grew, so that around 18:00 the object shone more brightly than Venus or Sirius—I estimate a candle-power of 6–7 degrees. An exceptionally interesting fact was its slow speed —it seemed to stand still in the sky, but through the telescope a slow displacement in a south-southeasterly direction was discernible. The object was seen in so many other places at the same time— Timişoara, Baişara, Gilău mountains, Cluj, Sighişoara, Tîrgu Mureş and Dumbrăveni—which proves it must have been at a great height; people have suggested a figure of 12,000–13,000 metres. Was the reddish-yellow glow on the sides due to reflected light? Perhaps reflected from the clouds.

The next day, 20th September, at about 12:00 other shining objects were spotted above the town but I did not see them through my telescope because of cloud cover. However, I possess some interesting data about these objects, provided by a colleague who noticed they had the same shape as the one seen on the previous day. The model I made is about 10 cm long and was photographed at a certain distance, which made the picture a fair copy of what had actually been seen of the object through the telescope. Thin wires could be seen underneath the object.

Answering our reactions to the above Professor Xantus said, inter alia:

1. My studies showed that the object was undoubtedly a satellite for measuring radiation or, to be more specific, for tracking atomic experiments of the OV (orbiting vehicle) type. I was able to identify what I saw with the aid of a photo of this satellite which appeared in an excellent book in Hungary viz. Nagy Ernest, *10 Years of Astronautics* (page 72). I am sending you a negative, but it is unfortunate that there is only a point of light on it.
2. The amateur astronomer Cigiran Vasile saw the object during the morning of 20th September. I think it is a twin satellite because according to the literature on the subject only two like this were ever launched.
3. I know nothing about the thin wires seen.

The list we print below gives a good insight into the "who" "what" and "how" of UFO reporting in Rumania. Most if not all the accounts, which we naturally do not reproduce here in every detail, differ scarcely at all from that supplied by Dr. Ion Xantus after watching the object through his telescope.

CLUJ	15:15		Mircea Radu, designer
			Marton Zoltan, chief clerk
CLUJ	15:30–19:15	theodolite	Dumitru Peligrad, meteorologist (see cutting)
CLUJ	16:30–18:10	photos, telescope	Professor Ion Xantus, Dr. Dunky Alexandru,

SILVER DISCS

			Xantus Gabriel (student)
CLUJ	16:45–18:20	binoculars	Alexandru Keleti, journalist
TURDA	17:00	binoculars	Dr. Rusu Coriolan, legal adviser
CLUJ	17:10–18:20	diagram	Costin Nicolae
CLUJ	17:15	binoculars	Viorel Lupu, from aircraft Bucharest—
CLUJ	17:15–19:00	binoculars	Cluj Doru Stoica, student
OCNA MURES	17:25–17:27		Mihai Popovici (geologist) and many others
MEDIAŞ	17:30	sketches	Muszka Arpad, electrician Hajdu Francisc Schuster Peter
BĂZNA	17:45	diagram	N. Muşat
FĂGĂRAŞ	18:00	sketches	Chirovici Radu
CLUJ	18:00	sketches	Aniţa G. Juca
TURDA	18:00	photo	Bajun Gheorghe
BĂILE MAI	18–19:00	theodolite	Meteorological centre, Sibiu
MEDIAŞ	18:05–18:35	sketch	Ilie Barbu, geologist
SIGHIŞOARA	18:10–19:15		Liseanu Leonard, technician
MEDIAŞ	18:20–18:50	sketch	Ing. A. Abuşean
CLUJ	18:30		Parutiu Gheorghe, economist
FĂGARĂŞ	18:30–19:10	theodolite	Meteorological centre
FĂGARĂŞ	18:50	small telescope	Ciambur Dan
CLUJ	19:05		F. Gheorghiţa, engineer
CLUJ	—	film, photos	Rumanian television cameramen
CLUJ	—	film, photos	Rumanian film cameraman

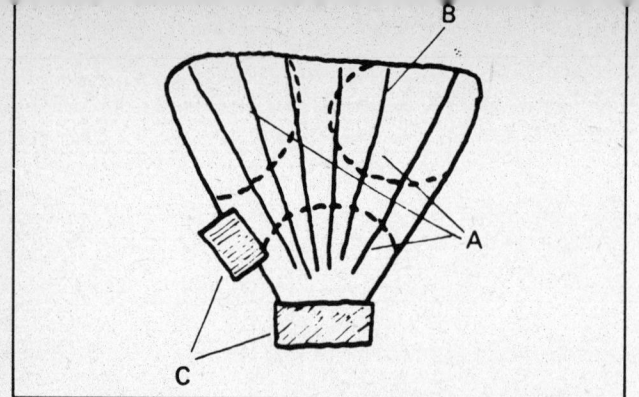

A. Lit-up zones like 3 spheres placed against each other.
B. Dark lines.
C. Two capsule-like objects, parallelepipeds, larger at the base.
Drawing by Ilie Barbu (Mediaş sighting)

As already stated the Rumanian author of this book wishes to link the other UFO sightings over Rumania on 19th September with the object photographed above Cluj. We were still receiving reports from such diverse places as Bîrlad, Bistriţa, Jucu and the train-route Bucharest–Braşov (see map, page 146) concerning observations of objects; but let us first deal with the one at Bîrlad. Cristian Nacu, producer in a local theatrical company, wrote to us as follows:

> At 08:05 I happened to look through the window of my flat on the fifth floor at Marx Avenue 51, Bîrlad, when suddenly I noticed an object moving over the town from left to right. It looked like a disc with a diameter of about 60 cm and it had a silver gleam. At the time the sky was heavily overcast and there had been some rain. I watched the silver disc against the dark sky for about 10–12 seconds when it suddenly disappeared. I was alone when it happened and I had no opportunity to draw other people's attention to it. C. Nacu, producer.

The sighting at Bistriţa was more interesting. A group of townspeople, amongst whom was Nicolae Rusu, an office worker, saw the object flying at an estimated height of 200 m at 18:10. Ten minutes later the same object was sighted over Tekendorf by pupils and headmaster of the local school, Nicolae Szekely. The object was also seen over Galațü-Bistriței, Archiub, Orosfaia and Ocnița. At the latter place it was observed by, among others, the agronomist Michael Hector.

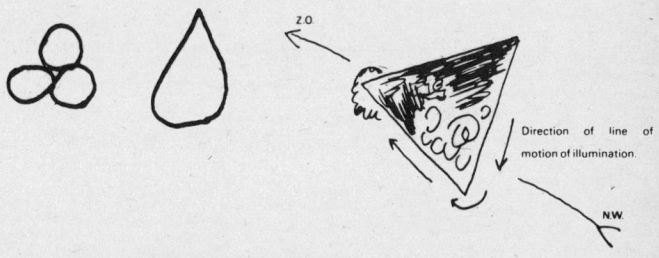

Bazna, around 17:45, "like three conjoined and illuminated balls." Sketch by Costin Nicolae, Cluj sighting.

How Liseanu saw the UFO at Sighișoara.

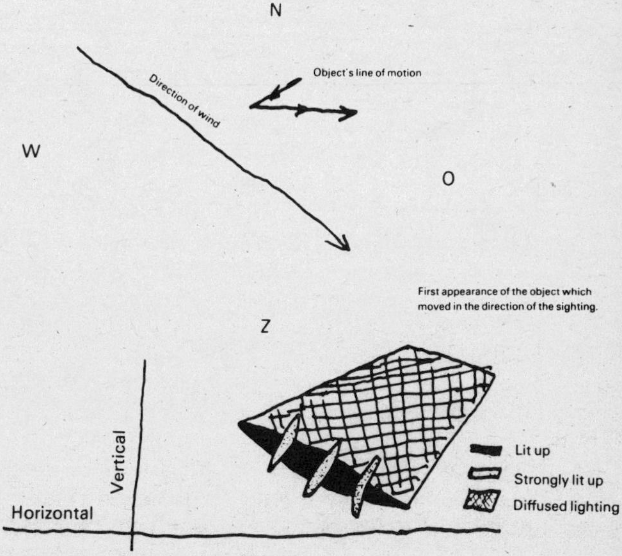

The thing seen briefly over Bistriṭa before vanishing in a southerly direction was saucer-shaped with three points in the centre like clover-leaves which emitted a strong white light. Over other places the light was said to have been of different colours. It is worth noting that when the object appeared the amateur radio station YO–5–TZ had serious transmission disturbances—something which television viewers also experienced. These disturbances were not caused by any equipment in the Bistriṭa meteorological centre, which recorded no atmospheric changes at the time of that sighting. Simion Ardelean, the director of the centre, did note at the time, however, some strong northerly air currents: the object must have stayed motionless in the sky for a while before suddenly disappearing to the south.

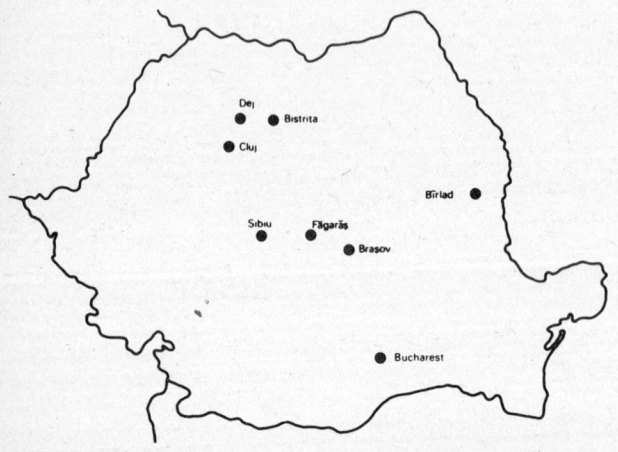

The Jucu sighting, between Cluj and Dej, is almost certainly directly connected with the "balloon" seen over Cluj, etc.

A geodetical engineer used a theodolite for twenty minutes to study a triangular object in the sky east of the Jucu station at a zenith of 55°03ᶜ degrees, which was 8–10 times larger than Venus. It attracted general attention. Through the theodolite the object revealed four triangular bulging surfaces which seemed to emit light at the edges. The aluminium-like body could be clearly seen shining against the still cloudy sky and witnesses became more and more convinced that it possessed its own light source, since it began to send out rays when it was just a point of light against a cloud. Deep yellow spots could be seen on its upper surface whilst moving very slowly in a north-north-easterly direction—45 degrees in relation to magnetic north. The altitude was 20 km and the size of the object must have been 180–200 m. It was hidden from the view by clouds.

A physics student sent us the following report and concluded: "I must have seen a UFO for two minutes."

I was in the Bucharest–Braşov train 20–25 km from the former and at 19:14 happened to be in the corridor. Several degrees above the horizon I saw a strange object which I began to study more closely. For 15–20 seconds it emitted a regular light pulse and at first it seemed to stay motionless in the air, with its orange-red colour changing to yellow and later to green. Around 19:15 a small object broke away from the larger one but suddenly vanished after emanating a constant beam. The bigger object stayed in situ about 30–35 seconds till it disappeared about 19:16 as if swallowed up, after having made a short sweep to the right. No other passengers saw it.

A. Approximate localization.

UFO: position

Horizon

The train had left Bucharest at 18:50 and had been underway 24 minutes when I made the sighting. The train was travelling north and might have covered

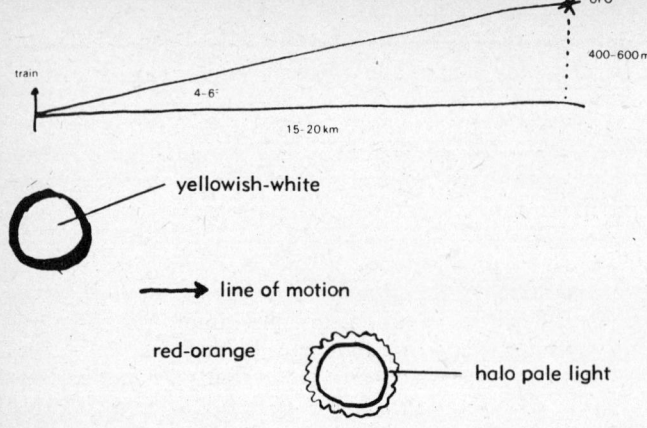

about 20–25 km. I saw the UFO in the east—from the right side of the train.

B. From the window I saw the following:
1. 19:13 The object may have appeared at a distance of about 15–20 km from the railway, horizontally on my right and 400–600 m above me.
2. Form, colour, candle-power, pulsations
Form: possibly spherical. Colour: whitish yellow and orange-red. Without becoming romantic I described it as a cosmic fairy as it shone so strongly. After 10–15 seconds I noted that the whitish-yellow part became more intense while the orange-red grew weaker.
3. 19:15 A small body, which was perhaps spherical or in the shape of a disc, detached itself from the UFO. Its colour was whitish-yellow but it disappeared immediately.
4. 19:16 UFO 1 described a small arc and disappeared momentarily and whilst it did so I noticed that there was a greenish light coming from the part of the UFO which previously had been the whitish-yellow colour.

The question arising is of course whether there were several UFO's over Rumanian soil then, or only one. If only one then it cannot possibly have been a balloon. In fact nine minutes after the last sighting at Cluj it was already 480 km further on between Bucharest and Brașov; and furthermore, as it was seen over Bîrlad at 8:05 in the morning and was clearly the same one that had hovered over central Rumania for the whole afternoon then it cannot possibly have traversed almost the whole of the country without having been detected. In conclusion we might say that the radio disturbances over Bistrița could certainly have been caused by the object which at about the same time was reported from central Rumania, but why in that case were the disturbances noticed only there and nowhere else? Note also that the weather station there recorded the object as hanging motionless in the air against strong wind-pressure.

Finally we would like to refer to a detail supplied by Dr. Ion Xantus, who studied the object over Cluj very closely with the aid of his assistants: the "something" which moved in the centre of the object's surface, or inside it. This action strongly reminds one of what was so accurately observed and described by the Naval Officer Cogut Marian (see page 178).

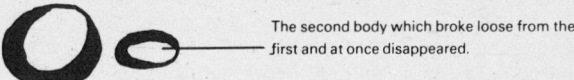

The second body which broke loose from the first and at once disappeared.

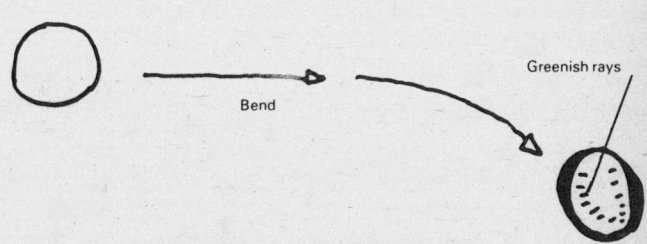

9. THE RUMANIAN SIGHTINGS UNDERLINE THE UNIVERSAL CHARACTER OF UFO PHENOMENA

The many-sidedness of UFO manifestations—Did the angel's glad tidings take place by means of the Montgolfier Balloon?—UFO-formations, flight manoeuvres, landings—"A square face with odd eyes"—Domes, cylinders, triangles, cones, deltas, satellites—The cowboy hat over the chicken shed—A UFO in the monastery garden—Six photos of a UFO over Colibița—UFO's are sighted by people from all walks of life.

One of the basic traits of the UFO is its versatility. In our previous book we described the various forms of the UFO, its speeds, dimensions, lighting etc., without proving the existence of any logical connection between them; and critical people are not persuaded of their existence by odd activities like the UFO splitting up or fusing together, shape-changing or vanishing from radar screens. This absence of firm data has led people to suggest that UFO's do not exist. But that is a rash conclusion to draw—UFO's are UFO's for precisely this reason, that they are alien to any other natural and logical phenomena we know! Accepting their "illogical" behaviour would be the first step towards building a methodology for scientifically approaching (i.e. *measuring*) the problem. We also said above that in spite of the apparent chaos a pattern was revealed, betraying the presence of "genuine" UFO's by its fixed data, regardless of whether or not the reports were sent in by people of limited vocabulary and intellect. The same pattern of behaviour—which we with our sober approach call "unreasonable"—can be seen in UFO sightings in East European lands. We have given space to several Rumanian sightings in order to stress once again the global, universal nature of UFO's and to show the universal factors again and again by means of examples.

THE HISTORICAL NATURE OF RUMANIAN UFO OBSERVATIONS

"Modern" UFOlogy begins after the Second World War but we all know that history records many sightings of things which with a little generosity on our part we could often classify as UFO's. Here we describe two examples from Rumanian history.

Monastery Lainici, seventeenth century. In the chapter about Jugoslavian UFO's we dealt with the question of whether medieval painters depicted space-vehicles on the monastery walls. The Decani frescoes are in any case more convincing than Rumanian drawings of presumed space-ships such as one sees everywhere in Rumanian monastery chapels. Every wall is a vast picture, so to speak, because the paintings are found in hundreds on both inner and outer walls; there are innumerable discs and spheres which of course do not have to be taken as space-ships but rather as a means of sending saints to heaven or bringing the angels down to earth. But it is also possible that some of these pictures represent the sun, moon and stars.

The Rumanian author Victor Kernbach gives us a different opinion in his book *Enigmele miturilor astrale* which appeared in Bucharest in 1970; he not only finds striking similarities between the murals in the church at Zagorsk in Russia, the Rumanian Biserica Domnească and the famous Mount Athos–Karay Protaton (see drawing, page 84) but he also has no doubt that these portray space capsules. He strengthens his argument by showing certain "impossible"—and in fact at that time unknown—factors linked with the masonry of the icons and murals.

However that may be, there is one drawing we must deal with and it occurs on an outer wall of the Lainici monastery. At the beginning of the seventeenth century the chapel walls of this monastery were covered with all sorts of religious art in order to instruct the illiterate faithful in the ways of God. These paintings have suffered more from vandals and weather than those in the famous monastery chapels in the north of the country, such as the one at Voroneţ. The scene in the porch there, however, "The Angel Gabriel brings the Glad Tidings to Mary," has remained virtually untouched. Furthermore it is an independent picture so that the odd "vehicle" above the heads of the two main figures definitely forms a part of it. The object in question—which is not a cloud—looks very much like a double Montgolfier balloon hanging over the two chief persons. The "balloons" end in a sort of pipe of narrow bore, from which red dots are being absorbed by a red, cloud-like strip. We asked a medieval historian who has specialized in utensils of the seventeenth century and earlier to identify the object but he was unable to do so. It is not possible that this can be an abstract arbitrary drawing because such things do not occur on monastery walls. Besides, the first Montgolfier balloon was not sent up until about 150 years after the drawing had been done.... If one compares this picture with the object seen over Bujoreanca in 1914–15 (see page 224) then the similarity seems quite striking. And note here the "large vertical cigar," thirty years before the classical French observation in 1954, to which Aimé Michel (in *A Propos des soucoupes volantes*) attaches so much importance:

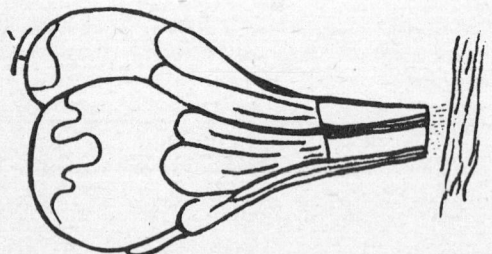

Drawing on the outer wall of the Lainici monastery, Rumania, after chalk copy made on site by J. Weverbergh.

Nicolae Bălcescu, July 1927. Gheorghe Achimescu, an

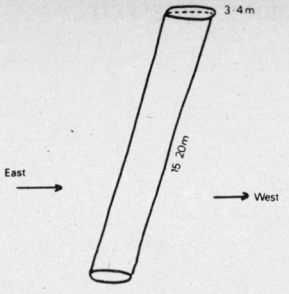

Drawing by Gheorghe Achimescu.

agricultural engineer, said that the weather was good on the day concerned and that there was little wind. Visibility was excellent. A cylindrical object flew over the village at an altitude of 200–300 m from west to east. It must have been 15–20 m in length and have had a diameter of 3–4 m. The colour of the object was a smoke-grey, there was no illumination and it functioned without making a sound. A group of children minding some sheep near the village looked up and saw it, convinced that it was God!

THE VARIOUS PATTERNS AND CONSTANT FACTORS RELATING TO RUMANIAN UFO SIGHTINGS AND THEIR BEHAVIOUR

FORMATIONS. On 24th June 1947 Kenneth Arnold saw nine saucers flying over the Rainier Mountains (Washington). This is the start of the modern period of UFO sightings, when they were observed flying in formation. Since then several similar observations have become almost famous: we need recall only the discussions about the Utah and Montana films. Rumania supplied several sightings of different kinds of formation-flying. It is remarkable that at about the time of the Kenneth Arnold sighting in June 1947 there were seen similarly six objects flying in formation over Oradea (see Rumanian catalogue No. 21, page 224). On 22nd May 1968, 19:40 at Băileşti, three cylindrical objects—followed by a fourth of similar shape—flew towards Bulgaria at high speed over the village, leaving white smoke-trails and emitting a strong light. The fourth object caught the others up and suddenly disappeared (Popescu Marin, engineer).

This sighting is interesting because of the sudden disappearance, which can suggest both dematerialization and the swallowing up of one object by another. On 23rd May 1969 a triangular formation was seen at Brașov by Ion Neagu, an engineer, and his friend:

> At about 21:55 I noticed at an angle of 40 degrees to the horizon a formation of five illuminated objects travelling at great speed. They were considerably larger than jet aircraft. I was in the Brașov park when the five came right over me and headed northeast. The objects were almost round—a typical feature—and seemed to have a diameter of about half that of the full moon. One of them flew ahead, the others following in V-formation. They shone brightly, like neon lights, and the sky was partly overcast by thin cloud which of course prevented the objects from gleaming as strongly as when they were crossing clear sections. It was noteworthy that after they had passed me two of them did not appear to keep the same distance from the others as previously, but started a zigzag movement. The paths of these two sometimes crossed and their zigzagging speed was not in accordance with the known laws of inertia and not related to the velocity of the others.

We often see in standard works on the subject this sort of meeting of two or more objects and flying off together—as for instance on 20th August 1968 at Ploiești: the orchestral conductor Leonida Brezeanu (conductor of "Flacăra Prahovei") witnessed this, together with his wife and Florin Iatan, administrator of the Ploiesti state orchestra.

Leonida Brezeanu: At about 21:50 we were sitting talking in the garden when a disc, deep-red in colour, flew over us from west to east. Its quick zigzagging movement was what surprised me and when the object had passed what I thought was a point of light like a star of the first magnitude such as Sirius or Venus (much smaller than the red disc), I suddenly noticed that the point moved quickly towards the object. They then flew off together in zigzag fashion, the "star" following the disc. Then the disc disappeared but the "star" remained until the disc started to shine again, after which they moved off together in an easterly direction. I was just too late to take any films of this and during the whole sighting there was not a single sound.

Florin Iatan: The red disc's zigzag motion was interesting. After it had approached the small, yellow object waiting there, as it were, they went off in parallel flight, the disc seeming to draw the smaller object along. The red colour of the disc changed into a neon-type white. After a few seconds the light went out and when it reappeared it was much weaker, looking like a headlamp in the fog. Both disappeared in a south-easterly direction.

FLIGHT MANOEUVRES. A normal type of movement amongst saucer-shaped objects is the one described by witnesses all over the world as that of a "falling leaf." Student Ion Cocheci, thanks to whom we have the following report, did not seem after a check we made to be acquainted with extant UFO literature, so that the classical terminology used by him is striking (24.06.68)

> I am a second-year economics student at Craiova University. I was standing at a window in the Students' Union, Bucharest Street 5, in order to get a breath of air when I saw a strange object perhaps 2–2.5 km high which resembled a disc with a diameter of 10–12 cm. It was emitting a dazzling light and was moving fairly slowly from north-east to the west, carrying out movements like those of a falling leaf; showing, as it did so, first its whole surface and then only one of its sides. It disappeared below the horizon after about two minutes. My friends Ion Jumote and Gheorghe Micuț also saw the object since they were there with me.

Sudden changes in direction and height, quite often

at angles of 90 degrees, are things the reader can find in almost all the reports of light phenomena collected by us. Frequently it is the description of these movements, defying the laws of inertia, which make us include the evidence in our list of Rumanian sightings. Take for instance a report sent in by a particularly well-qualified observer—45-year-old Bota Octavian, a professor of civil engineering at Cluj Polytechnic Institute. His scientific training and accurate account of the matter dispel all doubt about the movements; and just as little can we doubt the analysis he made of what he saw. This sighting took place on 4th August 1967 at Sîngeorz-Băi:

> I was on holiday at Sîngeorz-Băi and at 22:30 was peering out at the completely clear sky when I observed an unusual spectacle. An object, gleaming with a bluish-yellow light, was approaching from the east or north-east. It looked like a falling star and I was convinced that it was a meteorite about to land on earth but to my surprise it slowed down and then suddenly changed direction, climbing steeply and altering colour from a bluish to a whitish yellow. It was then that I thought it might be an artificial satellite at a low altitude. But the object changed direction right at the last moment again and went off at a totally unexpected angle of about 90 degrees without any perceptible increase or decrease of speed. It crossed about half my field of vision at a speed I estimated at 4–5 times that of ordinary satellites, then changed direction again at an angle of 90 degrees. During this last part of its route the colour varied from yellowish-white to yellow and rose-yellow. In cross-section it grew smaller as it became more distant. In the course of its first and second trajectories, and at the start of its third, the object had an (apparent) diameter of 5–6 times that of a normal satellite. It was perfectly dummy-shaped, the circumference boldly outlined and fully coloured—there was no trace of smoke and the complete flight lasted about one minute.

Analysing the situation afterwards I was unable to conclude that it was like any other known phenomenon such as an ordinary satellite, jet aircraft or ball-lightning etc. On the one hand it seemed to be bodiless and yet on the other the sky was perfectly clear. Its lack of linear motion was particularly unusual.

The following account of zigzag movement by a UFO comes from a schoolboy and is interesting for a number of other fixed factors. The witness was lying in some grass at 23:25 on the right hand side of the road between Mureşenii Bîrgăului and Ticuţa with mountains all around the spot. The sky was perfectly clear, there being neither wind nor cloud and all the usual stellar constellations were visible. Suddenly there was an "object" right above the witness and about the size of a star. It made no noise and its lighting was uniform. It then started up at a fantastic speed and carried out a zigzagging manoeuvre after travelling in a straight line for a short while. It traversed several straight stretches of equal length as if describing a geometrical figure. After returning to its original position its light went out but came on again after a short pause. This happened three times at regular intervals and then it disappeared for good. These and other unusual movements seem of course more spectacular when seen during the daytime, especially when the object carrying out the movements is saucer-shaped. A sighting of this sort took place on 24th July 1968 at Piatra Neamţ. At 16:35 a number of people spotted a metallic and saucer-shaped object with a sort of dome which moved and remained still several times in succession. When it was stationary the colour round the edges was the same as in the centre—a matt aluminium shine—but when it began to move the edges turned a light-green while the dome kept its aluminium colour.

LANDINGS. Ruppelt tells us how the U.S.A.F. at one time used to throw into the wastepaper basket all reports concerning UFO landings because they came from "unbalanced people." Once again it is thanks to the aggressive stance adopted by James McDonald and Allen Hynek that the views of serious UFOlogists have changed on this point. The turning of the tide was in 1969 when Jacques Vallée's *Passport to Magonia* with its 923 accounts of landings was published. Landings are now more systematically studied over the whole world. These landings not infrequently leave behind traces and thus positive measurements can be effected. The number of landings is indeed much higher than many lay people seem to think and appear to be increasing in the last year or two (1971 and 1972). It must also be mentioned in this connection that the American Ted Phillips checked 257 cases with clear evidence of landings and in eight of them UFOnauts were seen. (*Lumières dans la Nuit*, December 1972). From Rumania we have a dozen or so similar sightings but so far only one report of UFOnauts being seen to land and that in rather doubtful circumstances. However, we would prefer not to withhold it from the reader:

Summer 1953, Slobozia. Gabriela Dima, at present an economics student at Bucharest, saw on a sunny morning at about 10:00 an odd object hanging over the fields. In the middle of it there was a small green window and behind it a square face with strange eyes. This window then disappeared, and the object flew away without making a sound. Although the witness was only six years old at the time the memory of it is quite unforgettable.

Anybody who ever saw a UFO or spoke to a witness of one can confirm the vivid and long-lasting qualities of the impressions of their experiences. The age of six seems very young at which to be able to make detailed observations—yet this topic seems likely to be remembered in Rumania, which is remarkable.

One of the landings which could have been particularly interesting to Rumanians was that which took place in the Bucegi Mountains in 1957. However, we heard about this only indirectly because the witness, Mizof Pantelimon, an engineer attached to the Rumanian Land Registry, died of cancer in 1963, and his surveyor friend, Dumitru Banciu, was not present at the time. However he recorded Pantelimon's experience in 1957 and this was long before the very concept of "UFO" was known in Rumania. At that time Dumitru Banciu was convinced that his friend had seen a type of "helicopter" although the chief witness himself thought rather along the lines of a new and secret vehicle meant for carrying out espionage tasks. Dumitru Banciu provided us with the following account from his 1957 documents after he had read our Rumanian book:

> While we were carrying out work for the Registry a machine soundlessly approached our four-man team from about 200 metres over our heads. It was green and oval, with a particularly bright surface. When we approached to within 40–50 metres it took off soundlessly again and began to do a dance, so to speak, over us with an incredible agility, after which it disappeared.

The most important landing, however, took place on 28th September 1972; not only were strange and inexplicable marks left on the ground but in addition a twelve-man team from the UFO circle· thoroughly examined the site. This is further discussed in our Rumanian section.

DOMES. The following report describes an event of very standard type with effects like those of a hallucination. The witness's reliability is beyond all doubt but she asked us not to publish her name and address "because people so easily laugh at you." The witness was on holiday in June 1958 or 1959—she thinks 1958—in Sinaia, a well-known mountain holiday-centre:

> I am an abdominal specialist, now (1971) 50 years old and on the occasion concerned my perceptive

faculties were just as good as they are at the moment. At 04:00 in the morning I saw from my hotel window on the second floor the following event which lasted about a quarter of an hour: The sun came up into a cloudless calm sky and it began to get warm. An object appeared from behind the mountains, travelling east at an altitude of about 500 metres. Its size (apparent) was that of an Opel-Record with a dome on its top looking rather like a flat cap or hat. Underneath the object I saw a smaller triangular section protruding with rounded points on it. The machine itself had a silvery gleam and the sections protruding were bluish but on the top there were two more small domes coloured like the rest of the UFO. Its strong lighting made me think it was reflection from the sun. I did not hear a single sound so it could not have been an aeroplane or helicopter—otherwise it would have necessarily been audible. Neither was there any trace of smoke or dust. As for physical effects upon me, there were none, although the object came right over the hotel. It travelled slowly, like a cable-car, and made no other type of movement. I estimated that the thing approached to within 300 metres, after which it went over the mountains to villages lower down, such as Valea Largă and Comarnic. My husband, who died in 1962, was also a witness. It simply never occurred to me to photograph the object.

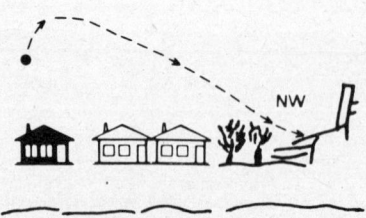

Reconstruction of the jump made by the Poenarii-Burchii UFO. A point of light shooting through the clouds. (page 161)

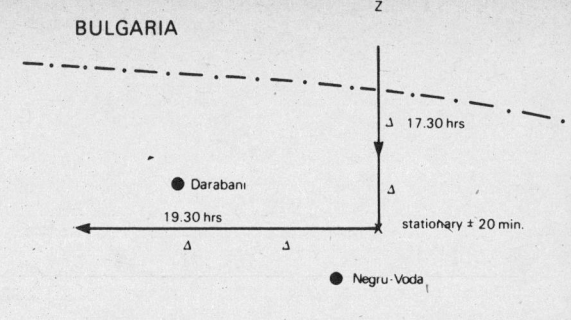

Flight of a triangular UFO in May 1969 near Negru-Vodă.

CYLINDRICAL OR TORPEDO-LIKE OBJECTS.

These are not recorded as often as saucers—American and Russian astronauts' accounts are famous in this connection. Most objects of this sort have high velocity and as far as we know never stand still. The following Rumanian sighting is a standard for this type. It was made by Marin V. David on 27th November 1967 at Poenarii-Burchii in Prahova province and publicised in the Rumanian press to some extent.

> On 21st November at 16:40 I saw an object, two metres long, which was cylindrical and flame-coloured. It was at a very high altitude and was motionless in the sky. After ten minutes it began to move straight up, leaving behind a trail about 7–8 metres long and of a white colour. When it moved off in a north-westerly direction the tail increased in length till it was about 12–15 metres. The top of the object was of a darker colour. As for the shape I could not make it out any more because it went off at the speed of an aeroplane.

TRIANGULAR OBJECTS: Ilie Dobre from Negru-Vodă told us about a typical triangular UFO which deserves to be classified as such because of additional details—especially the movement (1st May 1969).

At 17:30 an illuminated triangular object moved soundlessly and at a fixed speed from south to north. After 20 minutes of hanging motionless it disappeared at an angle of 90 degrees eastwards, just as fast as it had appeared. Many witnesses. See sketch (page 161).

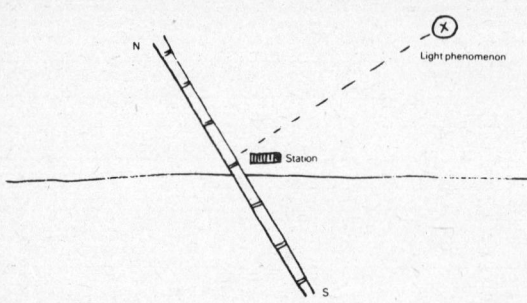

Sketch of the site of the Episcopia Bihorului sighting.
(page 164)

CONICAL OBJECTS. This is a common shape and one often identified as balloons, especially if the object stays for a long time in one place. Its behaviour frequently seems "odd" because it gets caught in various air-currents, as we have shown elsewhere in detail in this book. The following report, however, deals with an object definitely unconnected with balloons—the latter do not emit light at night. The authors do not doubt the authenticity of what Nicolae Dumitraş, a 62-year-old painter, says about UFO's. He saw one at Arad around 01:30 travelling through clear sky at a constant speed—"like a soaring bird"—from a north-north-east direction. He drew the object thus:

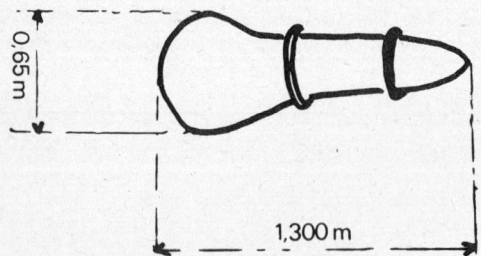

The "thing" had sharp outlines, was white in colour, like strongly heated metal, and it lit up the neighbourhood as if there were a full moon. It skimmed over

the tree-tops at a height of about 25 to 30 metres.
After three minutes of linear motion it disappeared
behind some bushes. Unfortunately Nicolae Dumitraş
could not give us the exact date of the sighting but it
was definitely at the end of May or the beginning of
June 1969. Why it is that the authors are sorry the
precise date cannot be given by the painter and his
friend as the night 31st May–1st June will become
clear to the reader later (see page 184).

DELTA-WINGED OBJECTS. The authors do not
doubt that the welder Mircea Dănilă saw a "genuine"
UFO in 1968 at Tîrgul-Ocna, near Bacău:

For two nights in succession a strange object flew
over the village. The first night, 5–6 May, it zoomed
from north to south at 20:35 and was seen by several
witnesses, one of whom wrote about it as follows: "It
gave off a brilliant light and many red sparks. The
chief part of the object (fuselage if it were an aircraft) seemed cylindrical, with the back tapering to a
point. There were little wings on either side which
ended in antennae. The whole thing resembled an
arrow somewhat, but one flying backwards."

SATELLITE-TYPE OBJECTS. Objects revolving
around each other belong to the best documented of
all phenomena unmistakably UFO in character. An
instructive example of this is the sighting by Vitolniek
and his colleagues in the Ogre Observatory (see page
286). The following observation of this type was made
by Lucian Rădulescu on 25th August 1968 in Rîmnicu-
Sărat:

At about 21:30 two objects flew soundlessly but
at fantastic speed over the town, each being approximately the same size as Venus when this planet is
nearest to earth. Both objects were a glaring yellow
colour and travelled north. Suddenly, at an angle
of 90 degrees they changed course without altering
speed and started to go north-west. The sighting
lasted about ten seconds and the two objects flew
around each other like moths round a lamp.

MATERIALIZATION AND DEMATERIALIZATION.

In our catalogue of Rumanian sightings there are many examples of objects suddenly disappearing and one of the witnesses says it is "as though it changed abruptly into a different dimension." In our previous writings we have stressed this aspect of UFO behaviour because we were convinced that once such mysterious happenings are fully understood then others will become explicable at the same time—including the origin of the UFO. The following account illustrates this materialization and dematerialization in slow-motion as it were: the witness Mihai Georgescu is especially reliable.

In the night of 9th–10th July 1969 I was in the international express Berlin–Prague–Budapest–Bucharest and at 01:30 it stopped at Episcopia Bihorului. The train was ten minutes behind schedule. Most of the passengers in my compartment were dozing or sleeping and as it was very warm I opened the window. After some time my attention was drawn to a bright cloud on the horizon—at an angle of about 30 degrees to the earth. For about 1.5–2 minutes the cloud increased in brightness and in the middle two special points of light were seen.

> These points of light jumped about in the cloud nervously, going both left to right and up and down. Then the object grew slowly hazier; the points of light disappeared and immediately afterwards the cloud also vanished. See sketches. I was unable to estimate the distance between me and the object, though I have the impression that it all took place very far away. I thought it might have been caused by some military manoeuvre in which searchlights were reflected by clouds. Over Hungary and Czechoslovakia the weather had been unsettled the day before but on this night, although it was dark as there was no moon, the sky was perfectly clear. The stars were very clear and there was no trace of the mist or fog always necessary for the diffusion of light. The phenomenon made no noise at all and did not occur again. Electrical discharges were re-

ported from the area of the object concerned as well as from other areas.

CHANGES OF SHAPE.   This is a phenomenon also found in sightings in the west. The changes are probably connected with materialization and dematerialization—features which seem to be closely connected with each other in the account submitted by Ion Popescu, a physics student in Bucharest who saw the following on 6th July 1969:

> It was a very hot night with a clear but moonless sky and a weak wind. A lighted object the size of a star came from the south-southwest, vanished momentarily and then reappeared three or four minutes later. It was now round and seemed to be the size of a football. The colour was blue or whitish. (It is possible that there was no connection between the first manifestation and the second.) The object remained stationary about 1.5 seconds and changed its shape to that of an ellipse. The colour altered too—from white to yellow—and the height varied. All this took place very suddenly. Its distance could have been about 2500 to 3000 metres.

REACTIONS OF ANIMALS.   Although Rumania is partially an agricultural country and many people keep animals, reactions from these to UFO manifestations

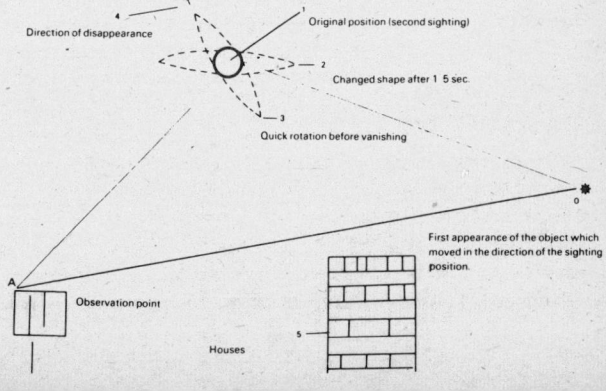

Physical presence of Rumanian UFO's: an empirical proof of their existence and the universality of the phenomenon. Sketch by A. Popescu.

are seldom reported. The authors think this is due to the fact that most sightings are made by the non-agricultural part of the community: as already pointed out, the number of engineers who report sightings is considerably higher than that of any other class of citizen. The following report from Petrila Petroşani was published in the Rumanian weekly *Magazin* (No. 545, 1968). The type of UFO recorded here is one found in many places all over the world since the start of the modern period of UFO manifestations, and has repeatedly been photographed. The panic caused amongst animals is a frequently reported phenomenon (and sometimes photographed) and these reactions are in our opinion connected with electromagnetic disturbances to do with the UFO.

On 22nd November 1967 I was in the kitchen with the door open when I was suddenly surrounded by excited chickens which I had not provoked with corn or any other food. My wife and I chased them out but they came back again still more disturbed and tried to hide. Once again I shooed them outside and left the house myself to see what the trouble was, thinking that maybe they were threatened by a hawk. I looked for the cause and saw, sharply outlined against the sky, an object gleaming like silver or aluminium, with small protuberances underneath, and on the top a much larger dome with antenna-like projections. I called my wife and we ran into the street together to follow the object's course, which seemed to be at an altitude of 5000 metres. The thing was about the size of a cowboy's hat. When I first saw it it was motionless but when we ran into the street it rotated and went off, twisting like a turnpike, until it was the size of a ping-pong ball. I drew the attention of several other people to it who were in the street at the time, including Gyorgy Iuliana and other building workers who were repairing the roof of a shop opposite my house. The weather was lovely that day and there was no wind. I enclose a sketch I made of the object." (Schmidt Ladislau, mining industry; see page 167.)

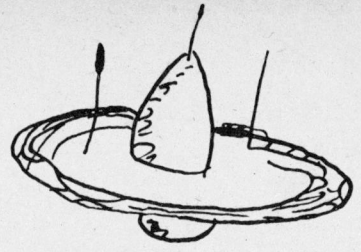

The UFO over Petrila Petroşani is one of the world's most commonly reported types (original drawing by chief witness).

FRAGMENTS, ASH, TRACES. These occur as little in the Rumanian UFO story as does angels' hair ... or any other remains of UFO activities. We have expressed our scepticism about such things in the past, and we feel convinced we are right because Rumania, although supplying much evidence of UFO activities, has no sensational material of that sort to offer—the press there reacts more soberly to such things than it does in Western countries. Sometimes traces were in fact found after a landing like that of the following typical one at Neamţ monastery in 1961. The question remains, of course, whether the boat imprint seen was not the result of a light-flash playing tricks on the retina. The marks confirm the landing, however, and one can only regret the fact that the witness took no photos at the time or at least did not do some drawings and measurements. Still, one should not forget that in 1961 the concept of "UFO" was still unknown in Rumania. (The witness Emanoil Manoliu, one might note in passing, is the son-in-law of the very famous Rumanian writer Mihail Sadoveanu).

In the autumn of 1961 I was in the Neamţ monastery; and going one fine evening towards the summer house in the garden where I lived during my holiday I was suddenly dazzled by a multicoloured light which, however, at once went out again. As a result of the blinding light I had difficulty in distinguishing something like an upturned boat above the little hill by the lake. After a few seconds this object suddenly raised itself vertically, like a helicopter but very quickly. The object looked like a disc over the mountains—a disc with a concave base, an estimated length of 6–7 metres and a breadth of about 3 metres. It vanished like a tornado in the air and I noticed the rush of wind it caused by its enormously fast takeoff from the earth. Otherwise there was not a sound. After a rather restless night I returned to look at the supposed landing-site with a priest who was very sceptical about it all, and to the amazement of us both we found that the grass had been singed and there was a light imprint in the soil, as if made by a hard object.

ELECTROMAGNETIC EFFECTS. These have never been connected in Rumania with UFO phenomena, or at least not reported as such. And engine-failure just as little, unless perhaps in one case well-known to the authors which happened on 14th December 1970. But no enquiry was made—the car in question could not be identified and there is no proof that the ball of fire over the road where the car was caused the trouble. But plenty of radio and television disturbances are reported from Rumania linked with UFO's, such as the one on 19th September 1968 at Bistriţa (see page 146).

PHOTOS, FILMS. The best UFO films were the Cluj two, made on 19th September 1968 by Rumanian Television and by the Buftea film company.

There is a special chapter in this book dealing with the best photos taken during the 1968 Rumanian UFO wave, and the authors think that the Cluj photos are amongst the best UFO documents in the world. There can be no question of falsification in this case (see Chapter 6) and the triangulation method of measuring adopted meant an almost exact figure was obtainable for the object's circumference.

Another series is the Rumanian one made on 4th January 1969 at Colibiţa, between 19:35 and 20:20. The authors consider this as one of the key documents of their book, though one which at first sight is much less spectacular than others showing a clear UFO outline. But here, too, there is no question of any falsification in view of the circumstances, and one can make the following firm conclusions from the fir-trees, stars and lit-up hotel shown on the negatives: (1) the object had a candle-power much greater than the stars, planets or artificial light sources; (2) the route taken by the UFO was not straight, which completely excludes the possibility that it was a meteorite or comet. Neither could the photographer have seen a helicopter or any other type of aircraft or powered balloon because of the total absence of noise and the presence of a strong light. So there is only one conclusion, and it is as objective and sober as the documents—it was a UFO. The following report about it was put together by the several witnesses concerned:

> A group of university lecturers, engineers and convalescents on holiday in the mountains saw an oval, yellowish-red object between 19:35 and 20:20 moving slowly west-north-west and traversing one-sixth of the sky till its disappearance over the horizon. Its diameter was estimated to be a quarter to one fifth of that of the moon and the unusual light power could be compared with that of a 500-watt lamp at a distance of 200 metres. Its height and speed seemed to change repeatedly and quickly but without altering direction. Sometimes it went a little back on the way it had gone, and after vanishing over the horizon it was visible for a few seconds again before its final disappearance.

The route taken by the Colibița UFO
(based on the photos).

The group, trustworthy and competent, rejected the idea that they had seen any known machine, planet or light phenomenon. A balloon lit up by the dying sun is also not possible as the sun set at 16:48.

One of the witnesses, an amateur photographer, used a 400 mm telelens (a Practica on tripod, Tamroi lens) to take six photos of the object with varying exposure times. The camera was not moved for the first four, but for the fifth and sixth the lens was re-adjusted. Exposure times: first photo, 5 seconds, second photo, 10 seconds, third, 10 seconds, fourth, 15 seconds, fifth, 5 minutes (from 20:03 to 20:08) sixth—time not stated. Average time between each photo was 2 minutes (see page 171).

The object's movement and relative candle-power can be fixed by the presence of a nearby star and an electric light in the wood which the observers presumed to be that of an hotel. The distance the object travelled between 20:03 and 20:08 excluded any possibility of its being a planet.

Ing. Iustian Schmidt Eric,
Professor Wagner Alexandru,
Professor Onițiu Viorel,
Chemist Dunca Șever (photographer),
Ing. Veturia Schmidt,
Tîrnăveanu (director of weather station),
Lawyer Pop Ștefan,
Ing. Mulea Bobica

Still another interesting UFO photo was taken on 12th June 1971 at Bușteni, a tourist centre in the mountains. The photographer was the 15-year-old Daniel Mateescu who used a Smena 8 with a 27 Din-film (opening 4 and B time). The witness confirms the statement that he did not use a lengthy exposure but that he moved, which meant that the photo did not exactly reproduce the somewhat elongated, spherical form he and the others saw. It was a bright evening and there was a light north-easterly wind when a "fireball" descended from the west, but after 10 seconds it disappeared. The witness is unable to say if the object "dematerialized" or just disappeared from view behind the mountains. A little later, at 21:11, the same object, or one identical to it, appeared in the west suddenly once more and this time it seemed to be much nearer, with a diameter one quarter that of

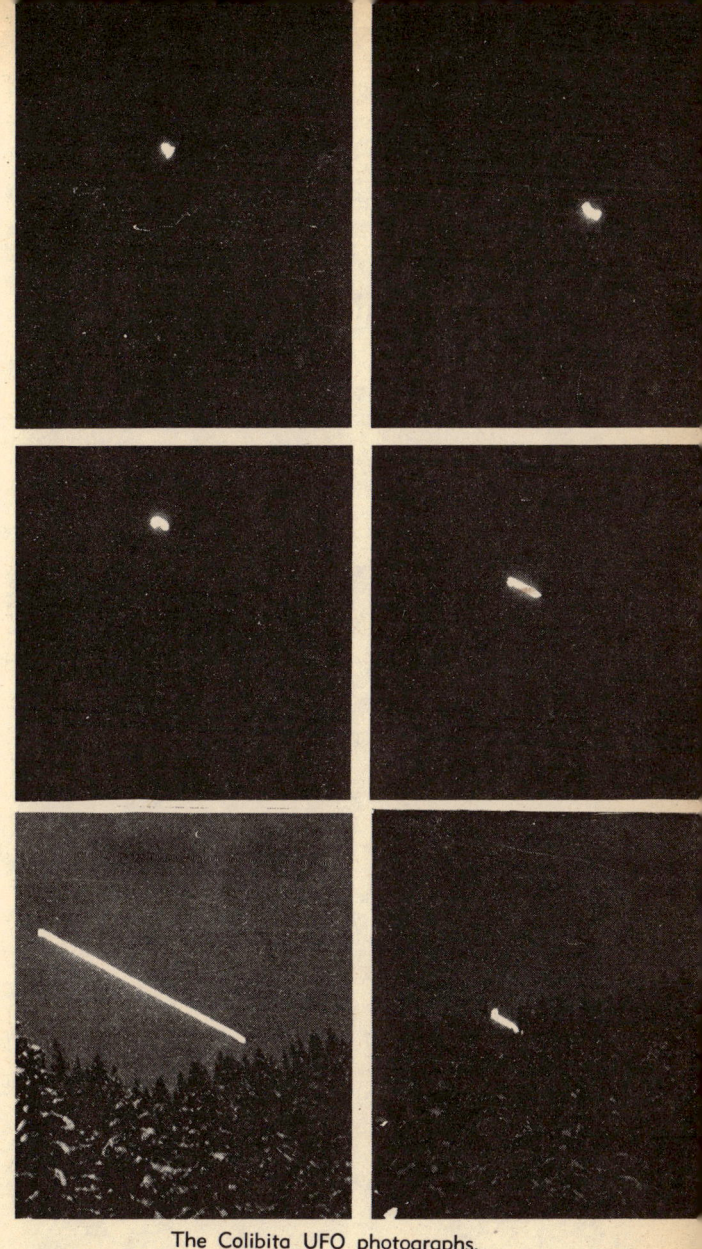

The Colibița UFO photographs.

the moon. Then it stood still in the sky over the witness at an angle of 30 degrees to him. It was at this moment that he took his photo, after which the object suddenly went out. It had been a reddish colour and self-luminous but it cannot have been a weather-balloon lit up by the last sunlight because on the 12th June the sun set at 20:00. Its light when compared with the town-lights (see photo 1, below) suggests that the object did not emit rays as strong as the one photographed over Colibița.

RUMANIAN UFO OBSERVERS AND REPORTERS: SPECTRUM OF RUMANIAN SOCIETY

UNIVERSITY TEACHERS, PROFESSORS. Teachers take a large part in Rumanian UFO sightings, as they do all over the world. Is this due to the fact that such people tend to write more than others? Knabe Richalda, mistress at a lyceum in Căpățâneni, gave us an acount of the "cowboy hat" she saw on 8th June 1968.

I live in a district near the hydro-electric powerstation at Gheorghe Gheorghiu-Dej and there is a heavily-wooded mountain slope in front of my house. I was sitting on the veranda under a clear sky between 16:30 and 17:00 when I noticed an object which reminded me of a cowboy hat, flying soundlessly over the valley from north to west. The right side of the object shone but the left was duller. It flew at a very high altitude and its diameter was about 50 cm. My neighbour sitting next to me, Corina Dumitrescu, immediately jumped up to fetch my husband who was on the first floor at the back, but the object had already disappeared over the horizon when he came on to the veranda; thus it was, unfortunately, that we did not take any photographs. (See sketch p. 175.)

Some other excellent work was done by a group of teachers in the case of the event on 28th March 1968

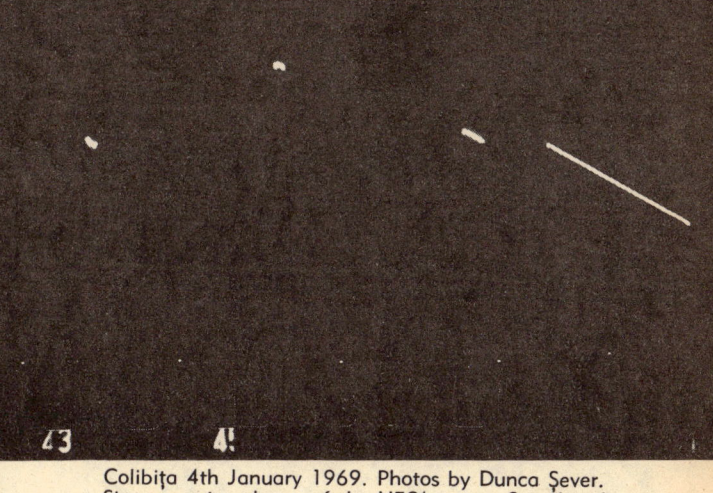

Colibița 4th January 1969. Photos by Dunca Șever.
Six successive phases of the UFO's route. Speed and altitude seemed to vary very suddenly without alteration in general direction.

in Tismana (see page 237) when radio disturbances were also mentioned.

METEOROLOGISTS. In our work on UFOlogy in the west we have paid considerable attention to sightings by meteorologists who use weather balloons a great deal, and use the special theodolite which can calculate the angles of sightings. Specialists such as these are particularly accurate and reliable in their reports of objects seen, as they are well acquainted with aerodynamics and astronomy as well as being experienced in all sorts of atmospheric phenomena and light effects. Ruppelt (see bibliography 8 but also 3, 4 and 5) who set up an enquiry into General Mills' meteorologists asserts that these people saw so many UFO's that they lost interest—we shall later see a similar situation in Rumania.

Photos by 15-year-old Daniel Mateescu, Bușteni (Sinaia, Rumania), 12th June 1971 at 21:11. Below, first photo: lights of the town.

The next report is from Vasile Voicu, director of the Sibiu meteorological station. One might well compare it with cases reported by American meteorologists. In all such cases the UFO seems to exercise a form of control before vanishing. This behaviour reminds us of the way in which UFO's are inclined to approach cars and sometimes follow them. It is a pity that one cannot speak of "logical" behaviour where UFO's are concerned, at least not in the sense in which we speak of logic. It would of course be a great temptation to classify all the side-effects and as yet unexplained problems to do with UFO's (such as those classified as "balloons" e.g. Cluj, 19th September 1968 or Banat, March '68) as phenomena brought about by "inquisitive" UFO's.

The most noteworthy thing about the following observation, in the last analysis a routine one like those made by meteorologists everywhere, is the witness's sentence that *he thought going on with his work more important than following UFO's*. This brings us to the tragic vicious circle again that meteorologists think their sightings unimportant so do not bother to report them, knowing that the establishment treats them with equally little regard; and thus the establishment shows no interest because they find that the reports come only from unreliable witnesses.

On 11th January 1969 at 08:20 I was outside measuring wind speed and direction with the aid of a hydrogen balloon and theodolite. The sky was perfectly clear and temperature −24° on the surface. The wind was calm. When my balloon reached 5400 metres, coloured red by the sun just rising, I saw a round silver object near it through the theodolite and I followed them both for 40 seconds. The object then disappeared after moving from 175 degrees to 200 degrees. In any case if I had watched it further I would have lost sight of the

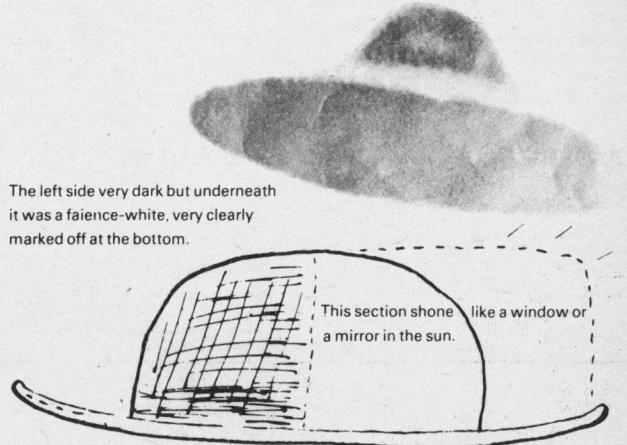

The left side very dark but underneath it was a faience-white, very clearly marked off at the bottom.

This section shone like a window or a mirror in the sun.

Knabe Richalda's "cowboy hat" (original drawing by witness). Compare with the Stock photo of the same object at Passaic (U.S.A.) on 2nd June 1952.

balloon—and I considered my work too important for that to happen. My first thought was that it was the moon, reflected through the theodolite lens, but after checking I found it was half-moon at that stage: moreover it was a very great distance away. The object could not be seen with the naked eye as it was so high up, and as far as I could judge the size seemed to be about that of a 3-florin piece—or a guilder either way. The movement was quick and straight and at right angles to the wind direction: thus, in relation to wind direction 360 degrees to 070 degrees the object moved from 270 degrees to 320 degrees.

ARMY PERSONNEL. The following case needs little in the way of further comment. It was a sighting made at the Baneasa airfield near Bucharest by officers with the rank of Lt.-Major—not by recruits or ordinary soldiers.

On 2nd December 1967 I was on duty in the radar station and at 21:30 I went outside to watch an aircraft about to land, only to find to my amazement that the said aircraft seemed to be standing still in the air. What struck me particularly was the dimensions of the plane and its strong lighting, though the latter was unstable. The object was 30–40 degrees over the northern horizon and it started to fall quickly towards the ground as if diving angrily on something; but then it recovered height, went from left to right, paused, and then shot towards the ground again. I drew the attention of several other people to the interesting phenomenon and dozens of us watched it until its disappearance over the northern horizon at about 23:30. I used the means at my disposal for observing it and after determining that it was conical in shape I contacted the local astronomical service who, however, were unable to see it because of some trees in the way. I am certain that what I saw was neither a natural phenomenon nor any known flying object. Neither was there any question of hallucination or optical

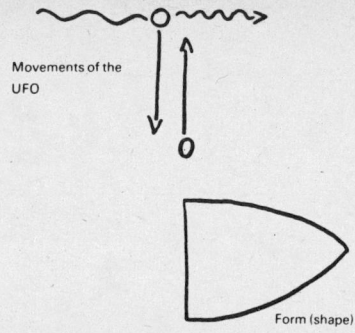

UFO seen by dozens of soldiers at Bucharest. (Sketch by Lt.-Major C. N.) Apparent diameter: 15 cm. When stationary the object was brighter. Apparent lateral movement: 40 m.

illusion; the object we saw had its own lighting and propulsion. It is interesting that one of my colleagues (Lt.-Major S. G.) saw a similar object when he was with another group of people at 04:00 at the same spot on 4th December 1967. (Lt.-Major C. N.)

In his written statement Lt.-Major C. N. regrets in somewhat sarcastic manner that scientific people pay so little attention to such phenomena, since he is convinced now that UFO's exist.

NAVAL PERSONNEL.

July 1964, Atlantic Ocean. At the beginning of July 1964 at 23:20 I was on board the MIN *Craiova* halfway between Matapan (Cape) and Sicily when I saw the following at 10 degrees to starboard in an arc of about 280 degrees.

10–15 metres above the horizon I saw a greenish "disc" quite a bit larger than the moon and in less than a minute the object acquired a "halo," its height and diameter meanwhile increasing very quickly. The apparent diameter was 1.5 metres and its colour a yellowish-orange. The object stayed 45–50 degrees above the horizon and in the middle of the halo there was a chaotically moving object which had the shape of a long radish and was emitting a brilliant glow. Seen through field-glasses this seemed like a strongly-illuminated metal object which appeared to be searching for something in its middle and doing so in an ever more frantic manner. But at a certain moment all its convulsive movements died down, giving place to an eruption of tongues of fire and dazzling sparks. After this one could see the "halo" only, just for a few minutes sharply outlined against the sky. These facts were witnessed by two others, one being Captain Daniel Nistorescu, whom I had called from the bridge and who saw the last phase of the object's manifestation. The exact details about it were recorded in the log-book under the title "Unknown Phenomenon" and personally I feel that it had to do with a UFO. I would say that the route taken by the object (and I base it on its height above the horizon—about 10 degrees—and its direction) was the southern side of the Bay of Biscay, Spain and Sicily. I did not think of checking it with the magnetic compass (I have since found no deviation on it) as we use gyro-compass (Naval Officer Cogut Marian, navigator).

This sighting is particularly interesting because of the great reliability and keen-sightedness of the witnesses; there was a similar observation at Warminster (England) in 1970 (28th March). One of the 30 or so people involved was the professional painter Terence Collins, who studied the object with a telescope and immediately afterwards painted what he had seen (see *Flying Saucer Review*, Vol. 16, No. 4). An interesting facet of the case is the photo: this was made at the same time but differs considerably from what was seen with the naked eye by many witnesses.

The final phase of the phenomenon seen by Cogut Marian was also described by a French biologist whose evidence as recorded by Aimé Michel can be read in the special edition "UFO percipients" of *Flying Saucer Review*.

JOURNALISTS AND PUBLISHERS. On 27th February 1972 there was a television discussion in Holland about the UFO problem in which the Belgian author of this book took part. The chairman, Mr. J. van Belle, asked him and the astronomer Ch. Titulaer if it was necessary to have seen a UFO "in order to believe they exist." Mr. Titulaer thought this to be the case, but Julien Weverbergh (the Belgian author) took the opposite point of view since although he had in fact seen a UFO, he felt he had known they existed ever since he read the Condon Report. By chance the Rumanian author of this book holds the same point of view—and he, too, saw a UFO at Bucharest on 30th

UFO as seen by Ion Hobana on 30th August 1969 at Bucharest (reconstruction, our own photo).

August 1969. At about 19:30 Ion Hobana was near North Station (not far from his residence) when he saw a triangular object arise from behind the station building. At 20 degrees above the horizon it travelled to the right and disappeared after a few seconds behind the houses (see the reconstruction). The object was a dull orange colour and it moved with one of its sides to the front, the opposite corner having three small globules behind it. Hobana estimated its size as being about a quarter that of the moon, but has no idea how far away it was, though feels it was fairly low and close in view of its large dimensions. He concludes it was a UFO.

DOCTORS. The Sinaia stomach specialist has already provided us with an interesting example of a sighting, but the one following is, seeing the qualifications of the witness, even more interesting. Adina Păun is a psychologist and this is what she has to say:

What I saw took place on 10th December 1967 at 07:30. I live in Magnet Street in Bucharest and was on my way home. It was a wet morning with low cloud-cover but very high up there were quickly-moving clouds. While I was passing the Republic factories I saw a bluish-green object right above them at an angle of 45 degrees. The thing had spines projecting which were almost equal to half its diameter. The spines tapered, so that the whole object looked like an illuminated hedgehog, or sea-urchin. The spines were definitely not beams of light since I could see their outlines quite clearly. I am unable to estimate the height of the object but in any case it was lower than the high clouds I mentioned and higher than the rain-clouds which sometimes hid it from view. It was neither the sun (which rose that day at 07:41) nor the moon nor any star. I carried on walking yet I saw it for fifteen minutes; it was only when I turned into my own street that I lost sight of it but I had the impression it was going slowly in my own direction. There is no question of its having been an optical illusion or hallucination as I know only too well what these are from my professional studies. The object was clearly visible for fifteen minutes and from various places so any such theory is excluded.

PILOTS.
17th August 1968. We were flying our Ilyushin at an altitude of 7600 metres over the fields of Oradea near the Hungarian border when I suddenly saw an

oval object scarcely a kilometre away from us 300 metres higher up on our right. It emitted a strong greenish light and was travelling fast in the opposite direction to us; my only professional reaction was to glance at the instrument panel and my watch—it was 20:21. After 10–15 seconds the object accelerated and disappeared westwards. Although the sighting did not last long it was sufficient for me and my crew to estimate the object's size: its diameter was about 2.5–3 metres. The passengers did not see the object because it was above our plane. I radioed our base, Vienna, immediately, to find out if any aircraft or other machine was in our vicinity at 20:21, yet not a single one had been recorded in an area around us of radius 400 km. I asked myself if it could have been a meteorite but these tend to fall vertically whereas what we saw continued on a horizontal path, and in any case meteorites do not suddenly change their velocity. Besides, there was no "tail" such as comets usually have. The bright, greenish light derived from its own lighting-system and could be compared to the colour of electric flashes. It was not an optical illusion. A few moments after we had contacted Vienna Budapest radioed to us that the crew of a Hungarian plane had seen a similar object 2½ minutes after we had done so. In view of the place at which it was observed for the second time it was possible to calculate that the object had a speed of at least 12,000–13,000 km per hour. That is a velocity which no earthly machine can as yet attain if it is moving through the atmosphere. (Benjamin Gabrian, Captain).

In an interview with Rumanian journalists the witness said "I believe that what we saw is usually described in the international papers as a 'UFO.' The fact that I saw it for 10–15 seconds—because the object lessened its speed until it was roughly the same as ours—is perhaps due to the object's extraterrestrial crew being very interested in us and our plane."

The object cannot possibly have been a natural

phenomenon as it flew parallel with the Ilyushin for a short time. So the authors have little to add to the commentary given by Flight Capt. Benjamin Gabrian. The sighting was very much like the classical one made on 5th December 1948 by the crew of a C-47 east of Albuquerque in New Mexico (see Ruppelt pp. 71–81); or like the even better-known case (if that is possible) discussed by Clarence S. Chiles and John B. Whitted and as reported in many UFO periodicals till finally published by James McDonald in Hearing Report.

ENGINEERS AND TECHNICIANS. The reader will have noticed that most of the cases we mention come from engineers and it is a fact that everywhere in the world it is the engineers and technicians who show the most interest in the UFO problem. The pure scientists, more inclined to abstract ways of thought, pay less attention to it. As an example we might give the sighting experienced by Adrian Brinzei, an electronics engineer and automation specialist at Ploieşti. It was a strange sighting he made with his family at Iaşi on 16th or 17th August 1968 and what he saw was probably a landing.

"At about 20:00 I was in my car close to the Bucium motel, not far from the Ţesătura factory on the mountain slope. The sky was overcast and when I looked up through the wind-screen I saw above the wood—about 20–30 metres—a large, shining object which seemed to be about 5 km distant. Its outline was quite clear and it had the shape of a truncated cone. Both ends were emitting light but the top one did so more strongly than the lower. I stopped at once and got out of the car with my son in order to have a better look. There was not a sound coming from the object which was a dazzling white. There were three of us altogether—my wife had stayed in the car—and all of us watched as it drifted down vertically, either in or behind the wood where it disappeared after a few seconds. We reckon its diameter to have been 10 metres."

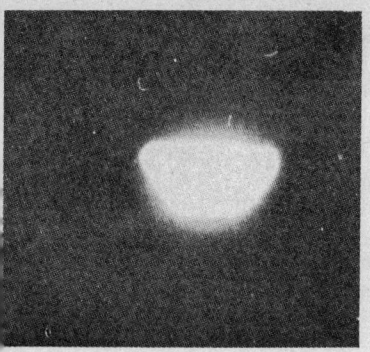 

Two successive photos of the same object on 30th November 1968 at 06:20 at Seattle, U.S.A. Hundreds of people saw the lights for three weeks near the Kent Space Research Laboratories of the Boeing Company. The UFO's which landed at Iaşi on 16th or 17th August and at Ploieşti (Rumania) on 15th September 1968 were identical with this object photographed in the U.S.A. (Photos: *F.S.R.*).

Illuminated objects of this nature, whether they land or not, are legion in UFO literature all over the world. Light-emitting truncated conical objects are well-documented, especially in 1968 when they were seen and photographed by hundreds of observers near the factories of the Boeing Company at Seattle, U.S.A. These latter UFO's behaved very much like the one thought to have landed at Iaşi. In fact the witnesses thought when confronted with the Seattle photos (not published until 1969) that someone else had been taking photos of "their" UFO.

SCIENTISTS. Miron Oprea is a professor of higher mathematics at the Institute of Petroleum and Gas at Ploieşti. The witness is also chairman of the Prahova Society for Mathematical Sciences. This sighting at Ploieşti took place on 15th September 1968 immediately after the preceding one and the reader will see why.

At 22:00 I was travelling from Vălenii de Munte in the direction of Ploieşti and was accompanied by my wife and two nephews aged 12 and 14. Just before the Blejoi frontier my wife saw a bright object south-east of us which was slowly drifting eastwards from the Vega petrol refinery. It seemed to have an altitude of about 100 metres and as we got nearer the refinery its outlines became clearer and clearer. It was cylindrical and had a brilliant ring underneath. The height was 2–3 metres and the diameter likewise 3 metres. There was strong bluish light coming from it. For 40 seconds I had the impression that the object was standing still in front of us 700–800 metres up, but it seemed to be descending slowly. When we reached the refinery the object had vanished behind the buildings—perhaps it had landed near the installation. I wanted to stop again but my wife and nephews were so afraid they persuaded me not to. That evening and at the same time and place another person witnessed the identical phenomenon.

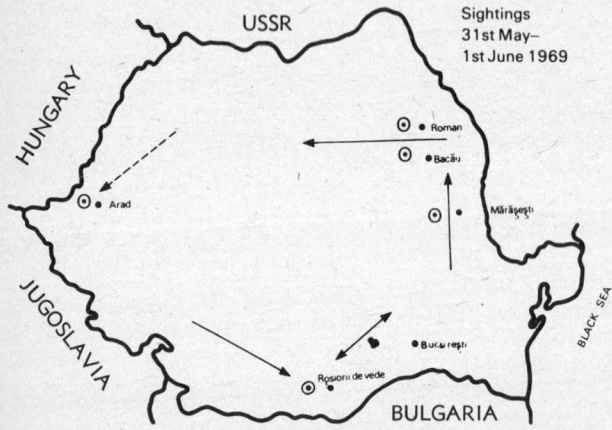

CITIZENS. An object flew over South Rumania in the night of 31st May–1st June 1969 and it is an excellent example of what is recorded by townsfolk of varying intellectual levels—judges, architects, chauffeurs, students, working-people etc. All the reports suggest that one and the same object was involved throughout. This Rumanian sighting is important for that reason as well as others—such as the fact that they all without exception stress the unusualness of the object which was seen in five different places (or four at least) by 20 or so people in the early morning of 1st June. The sightings at Mărăşeşti and Călugăra might suggest it was a fireball, whether or not it changed direction suddenly or exploded in Roşiorii de Vede in unusual circumstances; and one may well assume that it was one and the same object that appeared over all three places. At the same time an object appeared over Bucharest which could not be classed as a natural phenomenon because of its slowness and ability to change direction suddenly. We would stress that similar manifestations happened over the capital at different times, at 01:25 and at 02:30. These times were checked and verified as correct. The authors do not consider it impossible that this phenomenon belongs in the same category as the one seen at Arad at the end of May (see page 162)— but that is speculation only. The direction from which Nicolae Dumitraş saw the Arad object approaching and then vanishing seems to fit into a "flight-scheme" (see map), except for the time. But we do not know whether the time stated by Nicolae Dumitraş is correct, as we have not been able to check. Certainly the times given by him and by Zaharescu at Bucharest very nearly coincide (01:25 and 01:30). We do not wish to draw any conclusions from this—there is no point in doing so as long as we do not know what UFO's are; nor do we wish to comment on flight schemes (always assuming that UFO's can be fitted into such schemes) for objects able to travel 900 km in five seconds!

The following accounts of sightings were submitted from various cities:

1st June 1969, Mărăşeşti. Three witnesses: Ernest Gavrilovici, vice-president of the Culture and Arts Committee in Bacău province; C. Th. Ciobanu, Rumanian teacher; and the chauffeur of the car in which the two men went from Bucharest to Bacău. At 02:00 about 10 km from Mărăşeşti a bright phosphorescent

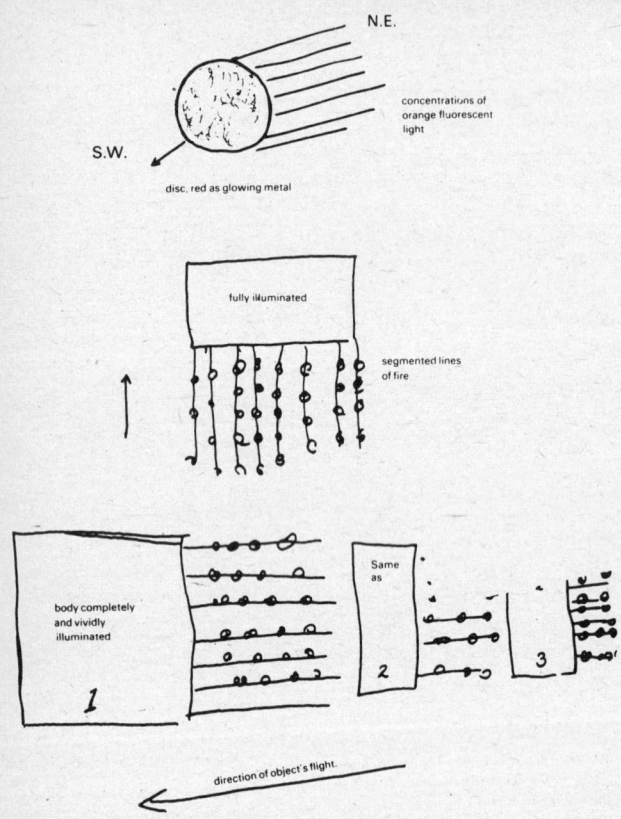

Three successive phases of the object seen at Roșiorii de Vede.

green object was seen travelling at enormous speed horizontally north-south over the horizon. Its size was compared with that of a basket-ball and its candle-power with that of a star of the first magnitude. The centre of the sphere was a deeper colour and the outer edges had a fiercer light of the pulsating sort. Ernest Gavrilovici used triangulation methods when estimating size, using certain points in the Vrancea Mountains when the object was 40 kilometres over them. The phenomenon vanished after a few seconds—behind some clouds, one of the observers said.

1st June 1969, 02:20, Călugăra. M. Țugurlan, legal consultant, reported:

On 1st June 1969 at 02:20 I was in my lorry between Bacău and Sănduleni when I saw a UFO flying northwards (Bacău–Roman) at first but then it began to travel to the west (Bacău–Sănduleni). It was 500–600 metres high and distant 7–8 km. Its size was about that of a football and it emitted a neon-type light with a yellowish-red "tail" of sparks, or so it seemed. The object disappeared behind trees after about one minute. The distance between the object and its "tail" of sparks was about 3 metres, the "tail" itself approximately 2–3 metres in length. The manifestation occurred while I was on my way up to the village of Călugăra. Other witnesses were the driver of the lorry and Professor Mihalcea Radu, resident at Livezile, Bacău.

1st June 1969, 02:30, Roșiorii de Vede. Isar Paraschiv, worker at the Roșiorii oil factory, reported:

During the night 31st May–1st June I was with my friend Mareș in the factory yard when he suddenly and with much anxiety pointed excitedly to an object flying amazingly fast—first from north to east and then from the south to the west. On approaching it seemed to be the size and shape of a football emitting a very strong light reminiscent of the streak of sparks given out during welding. But it changed shape suddenly whilst approaching, becoming a right angle with an illuminated surface of 6–7 sq m. The object was about 600–700 metres up and the whole fantastic spectacle lasted about 30 seconds. It flew horizontally, trailing a "wake" of seven or eight parallel lines which were segmented and fluorescent orange in colour. Later on the object divided into three, the first part having a surface of 2–3 sq m and the others smaller. The three sections flew behind each other and the tail remained in place. Others who saw the phenomenon were my colleagues Călinescu Alexandru, Urîtu Lazăr and several more who happened to be there at the time. People on night-duty at the Roşiorii North Station also saw it. The object made no noise at all during its flight. I would ask you to turn to specialized authorities in this field for an explanation of the phenomenon herein described.

1st June, 1969, 01:25, Bucharest. Radu Zaharescu, chief engineer at the Planning Department, sees in Salcîmilor Street for one second a brilliant ship glowing intensely white like heated metal (ultraviolet). Weak pulsations and a "tail" of the same colour but less strong. Size of a basket-ball, positioned between two blocks of five storey apartments and flying noise-

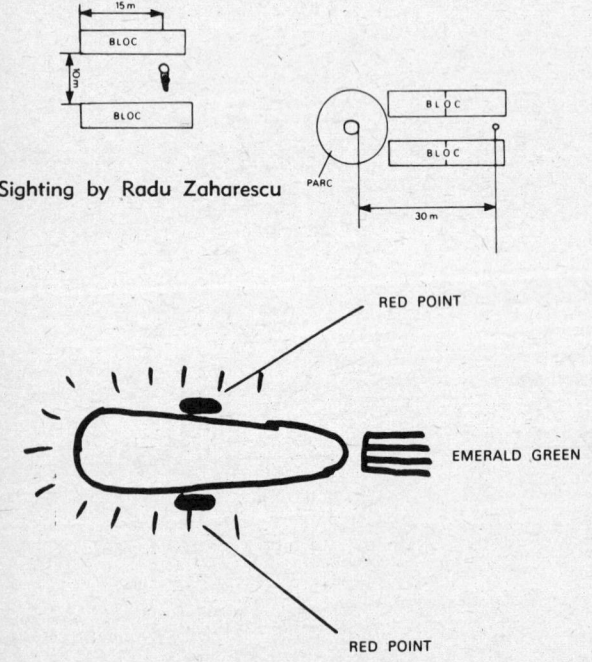

Sighting by Radu Zaharescu

Drawing by engineer Vătăman Octavian.

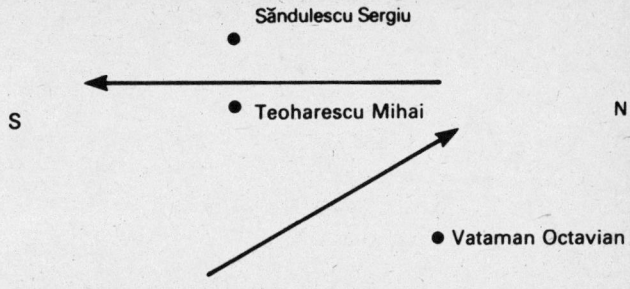

Relative positions, Bucharest sightings 1st June 1969

lessly. Average speed and trajectory horizontal, altitude much lower than that of aeroplanes (see position-sketch). Witness thinks neither height nor distance very great because object was so very clear.

1st June 1969, 02:26–02:30, Bucharest. Vătăman Octavian, civil engineer, saw together with four others in Matei Voivod Street an elongated oval object flying north at 02:26 over the houses and trees without a sound. It flew slowly and vanished behind blocks of flats in Republic Avenue. The object was bright yellow with an orange rim and it was followed by an emerald-green tail (see sketch). Its apparent size was that of an orange and both below and above there were two points glowing red. Four minutes later in the same area but more to the south a 25-year-old student called Teoharescu saw a similar object for 2–3 seconds at 02:30. Behind it there was a tail like a "halo," likewise flying noiselessly past about 20–30 degrees over the horizon, the bright red point in front this time. At the same moment the architect Săndulescu and his wife saw it at the junction of Dacia Avenue and Icoanei Street, but in the other direction. The tail was phosphorescent-green and the object must have flown low over the roofs as the places were 1 km apart. A flight reconstruction shows that either the object must have made a sharp turn (see diagram) between 02:25 and 02:30, or there must have been two objects there.

PART II
DOCUMENTATION RELATING TO FLYING SAUCERS BEHIND THE IRON CURTAIN

FLYING SAUCERS (LOTEASJKIATA TEALA) IN BULGARIA

1. 1908, SOFIA Between 13:00 and 13:30 people collected on the Maria-Louise Square because a very bright object the size of a rugby-ball (but spherical) flew slowly across at a great altitude (*Paris Match*, January 1960).

2. 1913, STRUMA VALLEY ... on the same evening a strange atmospheric object appeared over the Struma Valley. The sun had just sunk below the Albanian Mountains and the sky was lit up to the zenith when suddenly a huge astral fire-ball broke out of the sky and went down towards the frontier of Greece. At that moment all the prisoners in the Struma Valley watched as it slid slowly across the golden side of the sunset, as slowly as if its descent was controlled by a parachute (George Topîrceanu, *Opere alese* Vol. 2 page 169).

The Rumanian poet George Topîrceanu wrote this brief description while he was a prisoner. The only "strange" thing about this sighting is the slow descent: the lowest recorded speed of a meteorite is 43,000 km per hour.

3. 7th APRIL 1967, STARA ZAGORA   A triangular object stayed "suspended" above the town for 45 minutes. The staff of the M. Belinski observatory has determined path, shape, and luminous intensity. (*Nedelea*, 19th–25th November 1967.)

4. 9th APRIL 1967, SOUTH-EAST BULGARIA   Unidentified objects have penetrated the atmosphere over South-east Bulgaria. Specialists owe us an explanation of this phenomenon. (*Rindt Zwei Kurier*, Sofia, 10th April 1967)

5. 9th APRIL 1967, SOFIA   A conical unidentified object flew slowly over the capital. It was photographed by journalists and others and some days later shown on television. (From our own files).

6. 21st NOVEMBER 1967, SOFIA   At 17:30 a large unidentifiable object was spotted over Sofia shedding a bright, bluish light of the neon type. The sun was already close to the horizon when it appeared at a height of about 30 km. People began to assemble in the streets and on the squares, because the slowly-moving object seemed to be following a clearly defined route. In spite of this slow motion the observers found it very difficult to describe the shape of what they saw. It seemed at first to be bigger than the sun, but a few minutes later, when it stopped over the city, its trapeze shape was quite clear. After this it began to go north-east and editors of the daily newspaper *Trud* tried to make out its form with field-glasses which, unfortunately, did not magnify very much so it remained a mystery. A cameraman took a photo (see page 196). The sky was now becoming darker and in the middle a gigantic shape like a parachute began to appear and at its top a dark disc could be seen, around which there was a phosphorescent-green halo. This parachute or "balloon" then grew bluish-silver, changing immediately to an orange shade. The object disappeared over the horizon and we immediately contacted the Bulgarian Academy for Sciences, together with other institutes concerned with meteoro-

logical phenomena. Professor D. Simetchiev had seen the thing at the hydrological and meteorological centre so he stated the following:

At the moment it is impossible for us to say what this object could have been. Nevertheless we have been able to ascertain one thing with certainty: it was flying against the wind, which can only be explained by supposing that it possessed its own sources of energy. A second peculiarity is that the object had no perceptible influence on any of our radar installations during its flight—neither did we have television disturbance. This manifestation will of course be investigated in every detail on the basis of all the knowledge so far acquired by our research authorities.

Another scholar connected with the Bulgarian Academy, the secretary of the astronomical section, Professor Bogomil Kovatchev, said:

First and foremost I would like to stress the fact that the object which appeared over our capital was certainly not an artificial satellite of any sort known to us. It moved more quickly than a Sputnik and cast a brighter light. In any case we now know all the satellites in orbit at present—we study their movements and compile reports about them. It is a well-known fact that such satellites are difficult to see because of their great height whereas the object over Sofia was at an altitude of approximately 30 km. The colour-variations were perhaps a result of the setting sun which coincided with the disappearance of the object—the latter went out right in front of our eyes as if it had been extinguished. (*Nedelea*, 19th–25th November 1967)

Regarding the possible nature of this object we have things to say to which we shall very shortly return; but first we would refer to a strange fact which has nothing to do with the UFO itself. We have in mind information about UFO's in Eastern Europe in a more general sense. On 24th November 1967 the Russian paper *Komsomolskaia Pravda*, which is normally very reticent about Russian UFO sightings, published a lengthy article about the Sofia case. If we compare the Russian text with the *Nedelea* version, then it appears that although the descriptions are identical the former comes from a source different from the official Bulgarian one. Does the Soviet newspaper have its own correspondent in Sofia and is this an account by scientifically trained observers instead of journalists? Details in the Russian version which are different are, for instance, that the object appeared "to emit light" and that the light so emitted "made one think of the sort of light given off during welding"; that the "sphere," *after 15 minutes* turned into a balloon or a parachute and that the topmost section consisted of a "perfectly flattened disc." *Komsomolskaia Pravda* published the article without comment, as did *Nedelea*.

Professor Zigel said on being questioned about the matter:

> The thing seen over Sofia is typical of what one calls UFO's. Many sightings of inexplicable objects have occurred in our country, too, like the one in question.
>
> But there have also been sightings of discs and crescent-shaped objects etc., the nature and behaviour of which are very enigmatic. Seldom do we get satisfactory results from the use of telescopes or cameras, but in this case the Bulgarian specialist was lucky. People have detected the presence of UFO's on radar screens more than once but as yet nobody has succeeded in getting a full spectrum of a UFO which would definitely shed light on their origin. Many theories have been advanced in an attempt to unravel the mystery but we must have tests made before we can accept any of these hypotheses. It is possible that UFO's are only plasmas in the stratosphere. Many Russian scholars are interested in this problem and treat the subject seriously.

The attention given to the sighting over Sofia in local newspapers was the result of a rumour—supposed to have originated with the Bulgarian Air

Тази снимка на лотящото тяло бе направена вчера в 17.10 ч. от нашия фоторепортер Любен Донов.

Sofia (Bulgaria) 22nd November 1967. From the daily *Trud* "This photo of a Flying Saucer was taken yesterday by our cameraman Liuben Donov at 17:30."

Force—that the object was a teleguided espionage balloon from NATO sources. This rumour was taken up again in a very fierce "anti-UFO" article in the Rumanian paper *Veac Nou* on 29th September 1968. This was clearly an article, although unsigned, from

Russian sources, in view of the fact that it dealt exclusively with Russian UFO's. We feel that we cannot accept the theory that it was a balloon of any sort since the meteorological and astronomical services used instruments to determine its altitude as 30 km and at that height even the largest balloon would have looked like a tiny pin-head, if it were visible at all. The Sofia object was the size of the sun at first; that is, it had a diameter of a couple of hundred metres, in fact more like 1000 than 100 metres. . . . If we combine the two facts that it flew into the wind under its own power and that it suddenly developed a fantastic speed then Professor Zigel's theory seems nearer the truth. But what is "reality" in the world of the UFO?

7. 26th APRIL 1969, MELNIK Dumitru Trancă, general director of the Rumanian State publishing houses, and his Bulgarian colleague noticed very high in the sky at 17:26 a motionless, triangular and shining object some tens of kilometers from Melnik. (From our own files.)

FLYING SAUCERS (REPÜLÖ CSÉSZEALJ) IN HUNGARY

1. 919   An object like a flaming torch was seen in the sky, together with spheres which flew over Hungary giving out a brighter light than the stars. (cf. Ribera, *El gran enigma*, p. 356)

2. 1836, SZEGED   Spherical lights and the appearance and disappearance of what looks like a "lady in white" creates uproar in a part of the town. (?)

3. AUGUST 1940, BATA   In an article in the weekly *Tükör*, 19th December 1967, Ferenc Szakaly wrote:
    When I read the articles I have written in the course of many decades as a journalist, I find interesting similarities between what I then wrote and present-day news. Take for instance my article in the daily *Kis Ujsag* of 18th August 1940. Under the heading "Interesting sky phenomena in Bata" I read: "For several days the news has been spreading around Bata that the 'snoring friend' has returned, and is rumbling along the hilltops like a fiery cartwheel

and kicking up a tremendous row. Four years ago it appeared likewise—in the shape of a burning cartwheel. It was officially declared to be ball-lightning but the population does not wish to believe that. The unusual spectacle is apt to be seen by women doing their washing on the banks of a small tributary of the Danube. The object rolls along at enormous speed and rotation along the slopes..."
In other words flying saucers are no new phenomena in some districts. Bata is a farming village and thus the villagers describe what they see as "fiery cartwheels." These manifestations have happened again and I think we must consider them to be due to atmospheric disturbances.

This account is miraculously like that of Lucian Blaga (see Documentation, Rumania No. 9) The all-too-easy "ball-lightning" explanation can almost certainly be excluded in this case, just because it occurs again in the same place. Besides, the rare ball-lightning is accompanied by storms—and women do not usually do their washing in the open air during a storm.

4. 10th JUNE 1947, BUDAPEST   In American Air Force archives there are accounts of UFO's seen over Budapest on this date. Ted Bloecher, who reveals this in his *Report on the UFO Wave of 1947*, does not give exact details because his study deals exclusively with the American 1947 wave.

5. 15th OCTOBER 1954, GYÖR   A reporter from the weekly *Tükör* wrote on 10th September 1968:
Early on the morning of 15th October 1954 a shining object sped through the sky westwards, watched by hundreds of thousands of people, most of whom still think today that they saw a flying saucer. About 1,500 people wrote down their findings in response to an appeal from the astronomical observatory "Urania"—and here we come up against the disconcerting riddle that no two of their reports appear to be alike; according to the reports 1,500 people have obviously seen as many different objects.

Fortunately a completely objective "witness" was found—in the form of a camera. A teacher from the province of Győr-Sopron photographed the object twice. By means of this, together with reports from reliable witnesses, the people at the observatory were able to establish that the object was big, shining and reddish in colour—it could well have been a small comet—and that it went through the sky at a speed of 40 km per second along a path Amsterdam–Athens (sic). This comet only went through the uppermost layer of the earth's atmosphere before continuing its journey round the sun after a slight alteration of orbit. This case demonstrates that anybody not versed in astronomy and mechanics is not suited to discuss such a phenomenon, even though he tries to be objective. The phenomenon flew or moved at a distance of 1000 km from the observers and at a height of at least 200 km. Its speed was of a cosmic order yet not one of the eyewitnesses noticed these essential facts—everybody thought the object was much closer and moving like an aircraft.

This testimony is denied by another and equally "reliable" witness who said in the September 1968 edition of *Lobogo:*

I saw the object in horizontal flight *travelling much faster than any sort of aeroplane* (our own italics) over Vaspalya Street. It was green—like the barium mixture in Very lights—but after about ten seconds it suddenly stopped shining (Janos Horvath, technician, Budapest)

From our personal contacts with many Rumanian observers it is not possible that no two accounts are alike when strange phenomena are witnessed even when the number is less than 1,500. . . . It is not very convincing to suggest that the object was "a small comet" since its behaviour would have been different if it had been one. It is difficult to believe that an astronomical institute would put forward such an hypothesis! Especially as no other such body reported any comet along the "Amsterdam–Athens line" on 15th October 1954—not even a "small" comet was seen to alter course and enter our atmosphere, only to carry on its journey afterwards through the void. . . .

6. 27th OCTOBER 1954, UND A teacher photographed a UFO at Und. (AFP, 27th October 1954; likewise the daily newspaper *Esti-Bud*)

7. 20th NOVEMBER 1967, BUDAPEST In the 31st December 1967 edition of Hungary's most important daily, *Nepszabadsag*, there appeared the following remarkable hasty account, signed by none less than the famous Hungarian poet Laszlo Benjamin, born in 1915:

I saw a mysterious object in the sky on 20th November between 13:00 and 14:00 which I thought was a flying saucer. At first I said to myself "What an extraordinarily large aeroplane that is!" but I had to admit afterwards that it wasn't one. Since I was a boy I have always loved looking at the skies and I am no more likely to confuse Jupiter with Venus than I am a turbo-reactor with a meteorite; and I can distinguish celestial phenomena both by day and night—and this object looked like nothing so much as the UFO's people are always talking about today. It was neither cloud nor bird, neither balloon nor satellite. I saw it from Krisztina Avenue near the Danube when it was at an angle of 45 degrees over the mountain near our city. It emitted a strong, almost blinding white light and I had the impression that it was vertically or perhaps obliquely travelling. The object looked like this.

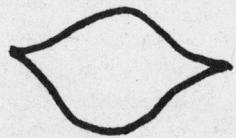

The same object was also seen by another Hungarian writer, Peter Kuczka, who gave us the same account in Budapest in October 1971.

FLYING SAUCERS (LETECI TANJIRI) IN JUGOSLAVIA

1. SEVENTEENTH CENTURY, DEČANI See page 80.

2. 25th APRIL 1898, BELGRADE Professor Michailovitch of the Belgrade Observatory follows a "Comet" which stays motionless in the sky for six minutes (Vallée, *Anatomy of a Phenomenon*, p. 35)

3. 7th MAY 1947 A disc-shaped object is seen over Jugoslavia, presumably by the American Air Force.

4. 1954, OVER THE WHOLE COUNTRY See page 90.

5. 10th NOVEMBER 1961, CROATIA On 10th November 1961 the Tanjug press agency published the following under the title "Mysterious radio-electric incident in Croatia":

Belgrade. Some days ago the broadcasts by the local radio station of the Croatian town of Vukovar were interrupted suddenly: electric lights in the studios failed or flickered for 30–40 seconds and instruments recorded an appreciable rise in the level

of static electricity. At the same time a dark grey
cloud drifted over the town but was soon blown
away by the wind.

According to *Politika* (a daily) a radio technician
recorded seeing another unusual spectacle: a number
of sodium tubes started to emit light although they
were isolated and unconnected with any electric current. No scientific explanation of this is as yet forthcoming, nor of the possible link between the cloud
seen and the disturbances in the studios.

6. 21st MAY 1966, BELGRADE An unusually brilliant and fast-moving object was seen, 80 degrees over
the horizon and apparently following the Velebitski
Canal, by the married couple Schrouet, who watched
it in a clear sky for about seven minutes. (*Gesag*)

7. 23rd NOVEMBER 1967, NICSJIC This morning
the inhabitants of Nicsjic spotted a strange-shaped
UFO. A local official, Punisja Vuiovici, was the first to
see it as it appeared over the man-made lake of
Krupat, near the town. It was conical and it emitted a
light much stronger than that of the Pole Star. Witness
made the following sketch:

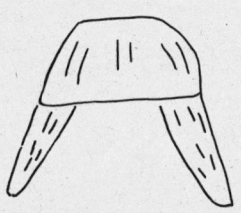

8. 26th NOVEMBER 1967, KOMOVI FOREST A
large section of the forest caught fire on this date in
spite of rainy weather in Montenegro. It was only after
24 hours that the conflagration could be brought under
control. The cause was never discovered—at least, not
officially. Various farm-workers said that a round
object flew low over the wood and the trees caught
fire as a result of the flames which the machine was
sending out. In November-December 1967 a number

of UFO's were reported from this area as far as Belgrade, but the wave does not appear to have been as extensive as the 1954 one. The object in this case resembled those of October 1971.

9. NOVEMBER–DECEMBER 1967, IVANGRAD AND ELSEWHERE   See page 91.

10. 15th DECEMBER 1967, NICSJIC (MONTENEGRO)   A large number of inhabitants south of the town saw a disc today from about 07:00 on, which stayed on the horizon for two hours. Some local officials and military personnel studied the object with the aid of a telescope and one witness, Milorad Kilibada, made a drawing of it; according to him the object was a parallelepiped with rounded corners, the innermost part being much thicker and elliptical in shape. At its broadest section there were two elongations. The object did not change shape as far as he could see. Another witness, Lucka Snedenovici, chairman of the USPM council, declared that the object made strange movements in a number of directions. A chauffeur, Danilo Popovac, noticed during the night another very bright object flying very fast across the sky.

11. 24th DECEMBER 1967, VARCONET   Over 100 inhabitants saw a saucer-shaped UFO in the southeast between 16:00 and 16:30.

12. 24th DECEMBER 1967, ZAGREB   The following was published by *Informaţia Bucureştiului* on 27th December 1967 at Bucharest:

By means of a camera the three objects seen yesterday at 22:00 over Zagreb have been immortalized. The photo was taken by the Observatory south-west of the town, the photographer being the young Zagreb astronomer Damir Gradisj, a member of the astronomical section of Croatia's Academy of Natural Sciences, the personnel of which come every evening to the Observatory to study the heavens. They could not explain what they were photographing yesterday but it actually happened and was unusual. We are now dealing with qualified observers, whereas previously we had reports about objects from lay people. While the photo was being taken another member of the Academy used a telescope for its further study (See photo, page 206).

The dailies *Borba* (Zagreb) and *Novosti* (Belgrade) supplied the following information: two of the three unknown objects, all lit up, remained motionless while the third one moved across the sky. All of them emitted an intense, bluish light and were seen by various people in Zagreb. They could not possibly have been artificial satellites because two of them did not move—that is the main reason—but also because they were together.

13. 27th JULY 1968, LJUBLIANA On Thursday evening a bluish object was seen over this city at a height of 1500–2000 metres and travelling fast in a north-north-westerly direction. It made no noise but its shape could not be determined, likewise its size. The Tanjug press agency says that members of the meteorological institute were of the opinion that the object was unlike anything they normally saw and that it could not have to do with weather-forecasting. The sky was cloudy at the time. (Ager Press report, Bucharest 27th July 1968)

14. 18th OCTOBER 1968   See page 84.

15. 21st DECEMBER 1968, BELGRADE A brightly-lit UFO was seen from 18:50 for a quarter of an hour by a group of young astronomers here. The orange-red object had a diameter less than that of the moon and was travelling south-east.

16. 18th FEBRUARY 1969, SREMCICA Around 08:30 a restaurant proprietor, Sekula Medenica, heard an explosion near his house at Sremcica (18 km from Belgrade) which made several windows break. Four

trees were burnt and there was a crater in the ground near his restaurant. The crater contained an oval object 20–21 cm in diameter, dark-grey and ribbed. It weighed 1900 gm. and seemed to be made of magnesium. Origin unknown. (*Belgrade News*, 12th January 1970)

17. 16th MAY 1970, SARAJEVO See page 89.

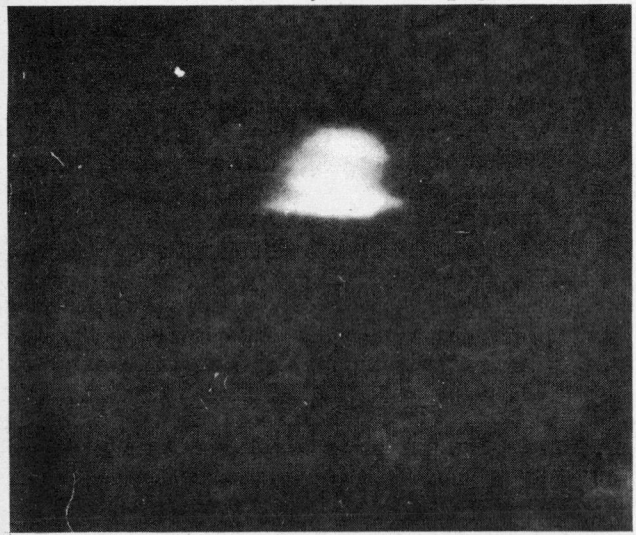

Damir Gradisj: a stationary object emitting a bright blue light.

18. 11th JULY 1970, BELGRADE Many people in the city reported an object they had seen at 20:23 over Belgrade and travelling at a speed of 400–600 km per hour. It was oval and reddish in colour—which sometimes turned orange—and kept emitting beams of differing colours. The Boscovici Observatory did not see the object, but a press cameraman took a photo of it from the 12th floor of a building in Lenin Avenue (No. 171). A journalist who saw the object for one minute at an angle of 110 degrees over the horizon from the balcony of a building in the same avenue described it as a smooth sphere or disc with flames on

the bottom. A pilot denies any possibility of its being
an aircraft after seeing the object for himself, and he
also rejects the idea that it was a balloon or satellite
as it moved horizontally. The academician Totorium
Anghelica refused to comment in view of the absence
of satisfactory data yet did say that the scientist
would naturally come up with the classical theory of
a balloon which was, perhaps, "charged with a secret
task." He also thought it possible that it was a Soviet
probe over Belgrade, which might be launched in both
south-westerly and north-easterly directions. And seeing
that the object over Belgrade appears to have
moved south-west . . . (*Nova Makedonia,* 12th July
1970).

19. 29th SEPTEMBER 1970, SARAJEVO See pages
89, 91.

20. 20th SEPTEMBER 1971, LANEJEVO On 20th
September 1971, at Lanejevo, between 08:13 and
08:21, there was a simultaneous observation at about
100 km of an apparently metallic and triangular object
made by the crews of a Genexa aircraft TU 134 and
a DC 9, 25 km south-east of Lanejevo. The captain of
the latter aeroplane, Boris Lupancic, picked up the
following message radioed from the pilot of the TU
134: "Did you see what I saw? It's flying at a great
height above us." He replied: "I can see something.
What can it be?" He described the object sighted,
bearing in mind his own position. (*Apro,* September–
October 1971)

21. 29th SEPTEMBER 1971, PULA (ISTRIA) An
amateur photographer takes a photo of a round object
with a cylinder attached underneath as big as the
object itself. The outlines are very clear to the naked
eye and the material seems to be metal (aluminium?).
It disappears as fast as it appears. The photo, when
developed and enlarged, showed a much vaguer picture
than the thing actually seen. The important daily
Novosti (Belgrade) publishes the photo on 11th
October 1971.

22. 8th OCTOBER 1971, SARAJEVO See page 89.

23. 8th OCTOBER 1971, TIMOSKA DE KRAINA
The daily *Novosti* at Belgrade on 11th October 1971 has the following:

People living in Timoska de Kraina (150 km southeast of Belgrade) saw two UFO's at 17:30, one of which was triangular and also answers to the descriptions of other objects seen in various places during the last few days. The other one was like a disc, typical of the "classical" flying saucer.

24. OCTOBER 1971, RJEKA
The Rjeka Control Tower records the presence of two unknown objects at 16:55 at an altitude of 140 degrees and 4–5 km up. The Control Tower on the airfield at Krk island also reports the presence (80 km west of Rjeka). The pilot of a YAT 440 reported seeing an unknown object on the Pula–Zagreb route (also in the same region). An object was screened on radar and its speed estimated at 750 km. (*Apro*, September–October 1971)

25. 9th OCTOBER 1971, ZADECARG SRHJO
A round and yet triangular object was seen and reported between 17:00 and 18:00 by the inhabitants of this town. (*Apro*, September–October 1971)

26. OCTOBER 1971, SOUTH OF ZAGREB
On this date an American pilot bound for London tells how he saw a luminous object about 74 km south of Zagreb; the object was round like a test-balloon and about 11,000 metres high. Shortly after his reporting it a Lufthansa Boeing 727 flying to Athens from Frankfurt sighted a silver object travelling at about 1000 km per hour. A check made with the local weather station confirmed that a balloon had been launched but that it could not have been the object in question since the latter was travelling against the wind. This UFO was followed for half an hour by Zagreb radar. The Belgrade Control Tower reported that it had received accounts about the object from

Jugoslavian and foreign pilots. (*Apro*, September–October 1971)

27. 16th OCTOBER 1971, BOSNIA On the above date newspapers reported the descent of "an instrument system" near a Bosnian village. One of the objects looked like an antenna. The Air Force removed them from the public eye, and the newspapers reported experts of the Jugoslavian Air Force as saying that they were unable to identify the objects. "It would be ticklish to tell the public anything concerning the origins of these UFO's" said the general, Stevan Roglic, in an interview with the newspaper *Vecerne Novosti*. (*Apro*, September–October 1971)

FLYING SAUCERS (LATAJACE TALERZE) IN POLAND

1. 28th SEPTEMBER 1952 Spheres, saucers and cigar-shaped objects gave rise to innumerable reports in Sweden, Poland, Denmark and North Germany on this date (Vallée, *Anatomy of a Phenomenon*, page 62)

2. 31st JULY 1953, WOLLIN A metal object 30 metres across was seen by five Poles and two Germans around 19:00 when it landed in a field near the railway. It was spherical and ringed with a flat disc with a number of openings. (Vallée, *Passport to Magonia*)

3. 1957, POZNAN Twice in the course of this year a flying saucer was seen over this town in broad daylight. (*Kurjer Polski*, 31 January 1958)

4. JANUARY 1957, MILOWKA Various witnesses saw a whitish object over the town. It was silvery, some thought, and round "like a hat." It moved with a steady flight at an estimated height of 500 metres and it had a diameter of about 20 m. The object "shone like a mirror in the sun" before departing at high speed. (From our own archives)

5. JANUARY 1957, MILOWKA A married couple were on the balcony of their flat when they witnessed three bright spheres in the sky, all of equal size and the same distance from each other. (From our own files)

6. 4th NOVEMBER 1957, CRACOVIA At 19:30, according to a number of people living in this town, a strange spherical object appeared over the town, emitting a strong orange-coloured light and flying very fast. It was one third the size of the full moon but it could not have been a sputnik. It flew to the north-east. (*Echo Krakowa*, 15th November 1957)

7. 10th NOVEMBER 1957, SKARYSZEW (RADOM) A bright, cigar-shaped object appeared over the town at 11:00 from the south. It was yellowish on the top, orange underneath. It was visible for about 30 minutes before flying off to the east and was seen by a dozen or so people. (*Zycie Warszawy*, 12th November 1957)

8. 23rd JANUARY 1958, SROARZEDZ George Barroinski saw the following early one morning before dawn: a greenish, phosphorescent cloud appeared from the north-east, the centre of which grew very bright at first but afterwards the whole thing turned colour, becoming a deep red. An oval object appeared from the depths of this deep red area and then a sort of spark, after which the whole thing vanished. Duration about five minutes. (*Kurjer Polski*, 25th January 1958)

9. 22nd DECEMBER 1958, MUSZYN   See page 67.

10. 21st FEBRUARY 1959, GDYNIA   See page 1.

11. 20th MARCH 1959, OSTRALECE Witold Sambrowski, an electronics engineer, saw with several other witnesses two noiseless cigar-shaped objects flying west in a clear and calm sky at 17:30. They were reddish-pink and in front seemed brighter. Length was about twice that of the full moon and the dis-

tance between them was three or four times their own length. They travelled horizontally at a speed greater than that of a jet. They kept just above the horizon and were 20–25 degrees over it at the highest estimate. When the two vanished a third appeared and seemed to fly along the path the others had taken. This third one was noticed by other people further away at Wojoiechowice, and all the witnesses concerned were positive that what they saw was not an aircraft or dirigible balloon. (Casimir Zaleski in *Le Courrier Interplanétaire* no. 51, September 1961)

12. 25th MARCH 1959, WARSAW   At about 11:30 J. Beck, an engineer, noticed in a perfectly blue sky an unusual, motionless object the size of the full moon. It consisted of two spheres, one of which was considerably smaller than the other, and they were connected to each other by means of a cylinder. The object reflected the sunlight and seemed to be made of aluminium. It suddenly made a quarter-turn, changed into a disc shape and quickly vanished in the direction of Mlocin. After it had almost gone it returned to where it had been before—about 400 metres above the Palace of Culture and Sciences—and re-assumed its former shape. The whole process lasted about ten minutes, each change taking roughly a minute and a half. The rest of the time it stayed motionless. There was no wind. Engineer J. Beck is the editor of the magazine *Horyzonty Techniki*.

13. MARCH 1959, KOLOBREG   Not far from here on the Baltic coast a number of soldiers saw a triangular object rising out of the sea about 4 m in width. It circled above the barracks and then vanished at great speed. (Vallée, *Passport to Magonia*)

14. OCTOBER 1960, POZNAN   A mysterious object, shining brightly, rises up over the city, sinks and changes direction several times. Seen by many townsfolk, police, railway workers and reported to the official news agencies. Mentioned by Polish newspapers

at the time. (Vallée, *Anatomy of a Phenomenon*, page 81)

15. 22nd APRIL 1963, WARSAW We live on the lower floor of a flat in a sidestreet off Smolna Street, Warsaw. I was about to go to bed at 23:00 on 22nd April 1963 and I was standing with my back to the window, the curtains of which were closed as my wife was already asleep. Suddenly I heard a woman's voice saying "Look, look!" in a pleasant way though urgently. I knew at once that I had to look through the window to the street, where there was a noise like gas escaping from bottles. Suddenly the room was lit up as if by the light of the full moon, although the curtains were drawn. Running to the window and opening the curtains I saw a strange and fearsome light. It was raining but the drops of rain seemed to be mixed up with the light which was like that of the moon. This was succeeded by a third and equally awesome spectacle— a fiery hail started to fall, with stones the size of hazelnuts which looked more like the molten steel pellets from welding than lumps of ice, both in shape and colour. The hail covered the street and caused a drumming sound on the shutters. I hoped I would be able to collect some of these "hailstones" as soon as they had "cooled." However, after they fell they kept their original form at first but then the red glare of molten steel disappeared; they turned grey and disappeared without leaving a trace. I woke up my wife so that she could witness all these strange and amazing things. While the rain was rattling and the hailstones drumming against the shutters we heard every 10 seconds an odd and gentle explosion (a popping noise) during which the rain and hail came down even more heavily. From time to time we also heard a sort of hissing and crackling like short-circuiting noises given off by the electric cables of trams and trolleybuses. All this lasted about an hour and the next morning we learnt that our neighbours had witnessed the same phenomena.

FLYING SAUCERS (LETAJICI TALIR) IN CZECHOSLOVAKIA

1. 24th APRIL 1874, PRAGUE   Professor Schafarick saw "a strange, brightly lit object which passed slowly across the moon and remained visible for some time afterwards. I do not know what to make of it . . ." (Vallée, *Anatomy of a Phenomenon* page 28)

2. 1913, MORAVIA   François Zatloukal, 20 years old at the time, was travelling from Brnoyto Zidenice in clear weather at the end of the summer. Between 21:00 and 22:00 he saw six objects very high in the sky like large fiery red stars, travelling soundlessly round a fixed point in a clockwise direction. This "star" formation was an elliptical orbit with diameter of about 1 metre (witness arrived at this figure by using his outstretched arm). He watched the phenomenon for six or eight minutes, then went on his way without waiting for the end. There were no other witnesses. (Henri Chaloupek, *Phénomènes Spatiaux* number 11, 1967; sketch p. 209)

3. **1944, KAMENSKO FOREST, BLOVICE** The War was coming to an end and the Allies were already masters of a large section of European air space including Czechoslovakia. I was 18 years old and lived with my parents at Blovice, 30 km S. E. of Pilzen. When in 1964 I read about UFO's in the daily press I suddenly realized what it was I had seen 20 years before. At the time I thought it was something to do with aerial warfare—perhaps a German Zeppelin. Round about 5 o'clock one afternoon at the end of the summer I was in Kamensko Forest and saw at least

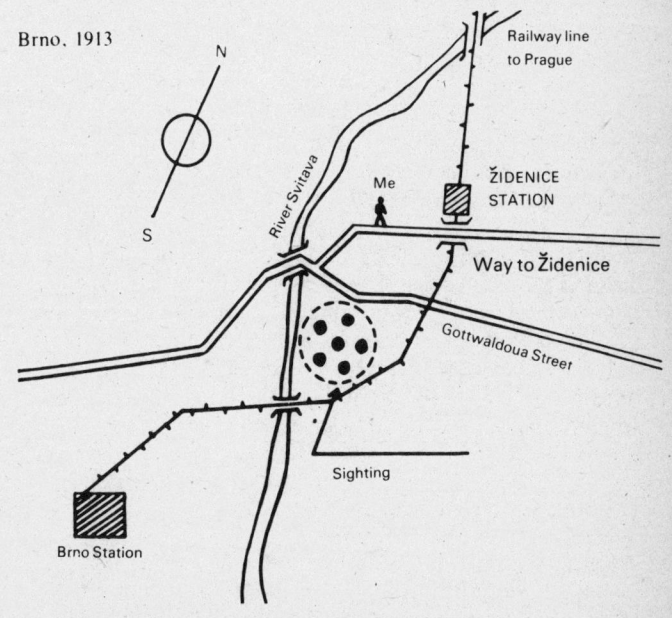

5,000 metres above me in the blue sky a cigar-shaped object glittering brightly. Although it had a stabilizer there was no propeller, rudder or wings. Its length seemed to be 100–150 metres, diameter about 50. As the sun set the object caught its light, the sunny side being silver while the one in the shadow appeared to fuse its blue with that of the sky, and yet it remained clearly delineated. The object was lit up more strongly from underneath—which was where I had supposed the Zeppelin's cabin to be—and the whole thing seemed to come slowly and soundlessly down without any detail becoming clearer. But the side facing the sun changed colour, becoming reddish and yellow. Its descent—real or otherwise—lasted about seven minutes after which the object rose up again and vanished into the blue sky. The whole sighting took about 10–15 minutes. I did of course ask myself why the Germans should have brought such vulnerable, old-fashioned and obsolescent machines as these Zeppelins into the battle. I was familiar with the use of balloons as a means of defence, since I had often seen them—but they were quite a bit smaller than the thing I now saw. Other witnesses were not present and the only people I talked to about it were my parents and my brother. (François Panes, *Phénomènes Spatiaux* Number 15, 1968; sketch p. 217)

4. APRIL 1955, HONTIANSKY-NEMCE Daniel Lazarik, a retired pilot, saw from his house an object over the Krupina Mountains. It looked like a saucer and travelled very fast at a height of about 5,000 metres. After descending an estimated 1,000 metres it vanished, flying horizontally. Witness is convinced that he saw a UFO in the most absolute sense of the term. (*Letectvi a Kosmonautika*, July 1965)

5. 1960, BRNO   See page 70.

6. 14th AUGUST 1965, LNAR At 21:10 Jaroslav Kalista suddenly sees four shining discs equidistant from each other and motionless in a straight, vertical line in the sky. The discs "go out" and five minutes later twelve spheres arise suddenly, but in a different place. They are arranged six by six in the same vertical way against the sky as the others had been. Each divides into two, after which the whole formation flies apart in various directions at great speed. (*Lidova Demokracie* 20th August 1965; map p. 218)

7. 1st SEPTEMBER 1965, KOSICE On this date hundreds of people in the Kosice district complained to the police about the glowing red and black spheres hovering over their towns and villages. Reuter published at Prague a statement about "the most recent series of non-natural phenomena of unknown origin which in the past few months have been seen over Czechoslovakia . . ." (Keel, *Operatie paard van Troje*, p. 282)

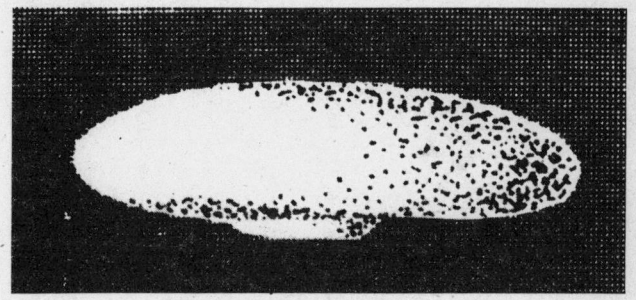

The object sighted by F. Panes.

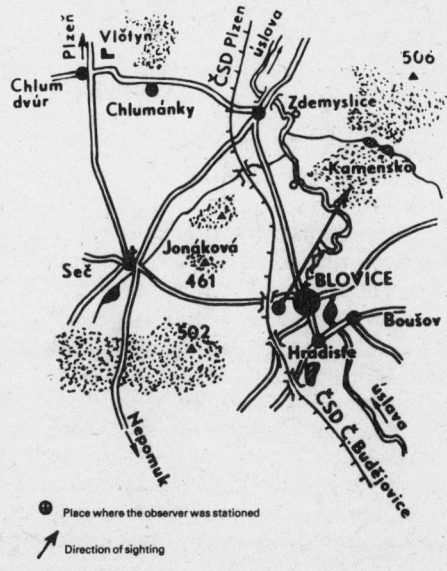

8. 2nd SEPTEMBER 1965, UKERSKE HRODISTE

In the cloudy evening sky the witness sees a round object about 20 metres in diameter, with an orange colour "as if lit up by a projector." It quickly moves away under the cloud-cover which was at a height of about 1000–1100 metres. Noiseless. (*Letectvi a Kosmonautika*, April 1966)

9. 1st JULY 1966, SNOPOUSOV

Time of sighting: 21:00. Witnesses: Mrs. Vlasta Rosenauerova, aged 56, housewife; her grandchildren Aline Jara, 9 and Jean Jara, 7. Both students. Mrs. Rosenauerova states:

As is usual with us I was with my grandchildren in our chalet at Snopousov in the country 20 km south of Pilzen. When the weather is pleasant I sit in a garden chair in front of the house and look at the sky. My late husband was an amateur astronomer and I shared his interest in the universe, with the result that I have if I may say so a more than superficial knowledge of the matter. One mild evening, with the temperature between 18 and 20°C, I went indoors after seeing nothing of special interest in the sky for the past hour. For no particular reason I

FLYING SAUCERS IN CZECHOSLOVAKIA 219

glanced out again through the window and it was then that I saw coming from the north two round points high in the sky with a reddish light like a candle-flame. They were coming down quickly towards us but they were not meteorites—I have seen the latter often enough to be quite certain of this. They kept the same distance from each other as they approached and suddenly the one on the left stopped still in the air and two or three seconds later the other one did likewise. They were about 35 cm across and distance from me about 4 km. (*Note:* According to the editors of *Phénomènes Spatiaux*, to whom we owe this extract, these figures cannot possibly be accurate—if they are then the objects must have been about 2 km across.) The phenomena were round and had a domed projection at the top. Although I was very surprised I called the children, who had not yet gone to sleep, to come and have a look at this unusual sight. They began to cry as soon as they caught a glimpse of the objects, so I had to calm them down. When they had stopped feeling frightened we all three watched the objects remaining motionless in the sky for five

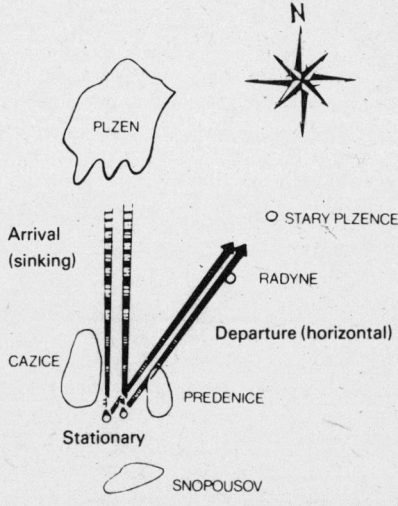

or seven minutes, after which a light plume of smoke came from the dome of the one on the left (see sketch of the spiral ascent). My granddaughter called out "Look, Granny, there's smoke coming out . . ." After the smoke had gone up the object began to move off in the direction of Radyne, immediately followed by the second one. At this point both started to emit very bright light so that the wood over which they flew turned into a fairy-like incandescence. They went away at about the same speed as they had had on arrival and vanished from view behind the trees, making no noise whatsoever. (Henri Chaloupek, *Phénomènes Spatiaux* number 15, March 1968)

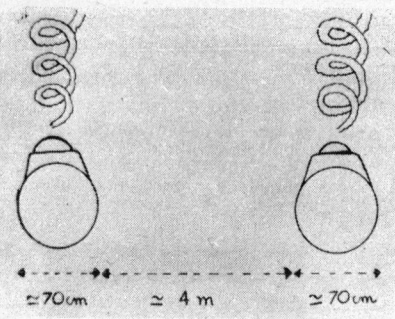

10. PRAGUE, END OF JULY 1968 A yellow, lens-shaped object apparently emitting "bluish" beams moved very quickly over the town (*Vecerni Praha*)

FLYING SAUCERS (FARFURII ZBURĂTOARE) IN RUMANIA

1. 8th NOVEMBER 1517, MOLDAVIA *Letopisețul Moldovenesc,* a chronicle about Moldavian history, states that on 8th November in the year 7025 (1517) there appeared in the western heavens "A great blue sign shining like the face of a man." It remained quite a long time in the same place, after which it "hid itself in the sky again."

2. SEVENTEENTH CENTURY MONASTERY LAINICI   See page 151.

3. 5th FEBRUARY 1709   There was a great sign in the sky on 5th February—a Wednesday. Two large columns of fire were revealed, one in the east, the other in the west, and as they moved they formed the letter A. They united after this and turned into a rainbow, emitting strong light for three hours, before their disappearance. (*Biblioteca Academiei,* "manuscris slavon" 706, f. 1.)

4. **6th DECEMBER 1737, BUCHAREST** Round about St. Nicholas time (6th December) and in the afternoon a large symbol appeared in the west, red as blood and very broad. After remaining for two hours it split up into two parts but later became united once again, after which it appeared in the west as before. (*Biblioteca Academiei*, "manuscris românesc" 2342, f. 3–4.)

5. **27th NOVEMBER 1793, BUCHAREST** On 27th November at 19:30 the world shook three times; I was dining at Florești (Bucharest) with the venerable Constandin Poenaru. On the evening of the next day at the same time the moon carried out a miracle—she made a journey along the sky for half an hour. (*Biblioteca Academiei*, "manuscris românesc" 2150, f. 111v.)

6. **1812, BUCOVINA** Towards noon a large star with many rays appeared and in the night she ascended higher and flew in the direction of the Russians; afterwards she returned and went to the west, where the beams were extinguished. Thus did the star reveal herself for four months. It was during the war between the Russians, French and Germans. Witness: Stan Irimie from Săcele-Brașov. (*Biblioteca Academiei*, "manuscris românesc" 1346 f. 2v.)

7. **29/30th AUGUST 1837, TÎRGU-NEAMȚ AND DOROHOI** In the course of this night a meteor was seen, or a *physical phenomenon* (our own italics). It was a sphere, lit up, about 12 hands long and broad (about 3 metres). It descended in the twilight and the whole field shone with a powerful light and glow. (*Albina Românească*, 2nd September 1837)

8. **5th MARCH 1843, BUCHAREST** 1. On 5th March there was a phenomenon—a sign appeared in the sky at 01:00 and lasted until 07:00 in the morning. According to some it had occurred before but this time it was bigger. There are those who say it is a comet.

2. The phenomenon appeared and disappeared in the same place. On 9th March it was accompanied by another manifestation, the latter being in the shape of a fire-ball, which vanished after a few seconds in the form of lightning.

This event was witnessed all over Europe at that time and it caused many tongues to wag. After dusk the object tended to appear in the west. It was pyramidal in shape and the side turned towards the horizon was shorter and not so strongly lit up; the other side was broader and more radiant. (*Biblioteca Academiei.* (1) "Manuscris românesc," 4043, f. 1. (2) *Albina românească*, 1843, pp. 81–82)

9. 1904, TRANSYLVANIA Long after midnight a farmer was still in his fields with a cart, and it is confirmed that he was not asleep. Suddenly he saw a fiery wheel over the Munții Apuseni coming down to the ground. The wheel approached fast, turning as it did so and the farmer stood by helplessly. When it was quite close to him it changed into the shape of a human being, who looked at the farmer for a long time without speaking.

This text is taken from *Hronicul și cîntecul vîrstelor* (Bucharest, 1965) by the important Rumanian writer Lucian Blaga (1895–1961). Blaga thinks that this phenomenon is really an account of a hallucination. In any case this farmer's experience is very much like Ezekiel's in the Old Testament.

10. SUMMER 1905, HORODNICUL DE SUS (BUCOVINA) Doctor I. P., now in retirement, and who comes from Craiova, saw one summer evening in 1905 at Horodnicul de Sus near Rădăuți an elongated, saucer-shaped object bigger than the moon. It was vividly lit up with its own source of lighting and flew steadily westwards. Witness still acknowledges that it caused him to feel considerable anxiety.

11. 2nd SEPTEMBER 1914, FĂLTICENI I saw a fine fireball (bolide) about 20 degrees long, and

white in colour, moving slowly and perfectly horizontally. Suddenly, between Aquarius and Capricorn, it vanished. (*Ziarul științelor populare si al calatorulor* 15th October 1914, page 784)

12. 1914–15 BUJOREANCA (DÎMBOVIȚA, TÎRGOVISTE DISTRICT)

A teacher who is now (1969) 68 years old was having a meal with his family in the garden in the autumn of 1914 or 1915 when everybody's attention was drawn to an object with a reddish glow which appeared when it was getting dark. The object in question was the size of a football or a man's head with a neck protruding from it like an "exhaust-pipe." It was about 20–25 metres up and travelling eastwards, causing the acacias and oaks to bend in the wind it made. It left a trail of glowing sparks about 8–10 metres long and kept on reappearing for six or seven successive days, witnessed by all the villagers. The object made a whistling noise (cf. page 151, the murals in the Lainici monastery), and appeared "out of the blue" over a particular house 800 m from where the witness lived, and disappeared with equal suddenness over another residence. On one occasion it remained stationary over one of the houses where the body of a woman was found, apparently covered with burns. (D. S. Ionescu.)

13. 1926, COLUN JUDEȚUL SIBIU

Ion Bunescu was with his horses on the way to pasture-land at Cîrța and saw at 01:00 in the night an "illuminated spear" the size of the moon. The object stayed for five or ten minutes still over the meadows and then for three or four minutes above Bunescu's head. After this the object chose to go in the direction of Arpașul de Jos (eight kilometres farther away) and after going round a small wood three kilometres from Cîrța it was suddenly extinguished. (The place where the witness saw it is a hill with very good visibility for about 60 kilometres.) The object made a whistling noise and the whole district was lit up as if it were day-light. When the object was above the witness it had the shape of a boat with a length of three m and

Iată harta capricıosului traseu al OZN-ului văzut în 1926 la Colun.

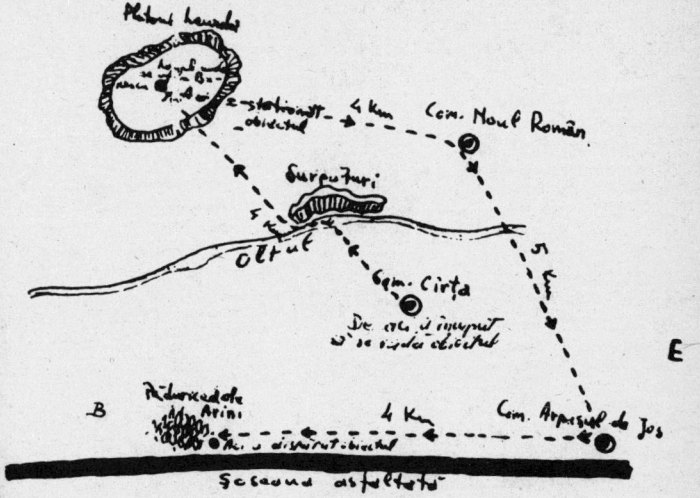

Fickle flight of the Colun UFO, which vanished at Point B suddenly or was extinguished (see no. 13).

a width of one to two m. The middle was darker than the extremities.

14. JULY 1927, NICOLAE BĂLCESCU See page 146.

15. JULY 1927–28, PIATRA-OLT One evening in July 1927 or 1928 we saw with many other people a radiant cylinder flying eastwards over the village at a fantastic speed and without the slightest noise. The object was bigger than the full moon. It was yellow and lit up the streets so brightly that one could imagine it was the middle of the day. It exploded in the air in a red shower of sparks. (Eremencu Petre)

16. 1932–33, ORADEA On a summer evening between 19:00 and 20:00 a yellow disc 200–300 metres high was seen by the witness as it moved southwest

UFO's and the Rumanian press. Farmer Ion Bunescu:
"I *did* see the thing." (See no. 13)

over the park. The disc was lit up and left a trail. Sighting lasted two to three seconds and was experienced by others. (Lucaci Victor, economist, Bucharest.)

The short duration and the trail suggest that it was a meteorite.

17. 1944, PLOIEȘTI The refinery Vega went up in

flames after a bombardment and late that afternoon after the bombardment and over the area a yellowish and pointed object was seen coming from the north, shaped thus:

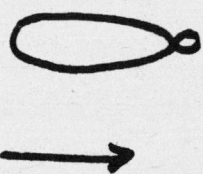

Ploieşti, 1944: cf. McDivitt's photo.

The object left a trail "like a white tail, but not shedding any light," rather like the vapour tracks of aircraft but short and vibrating. Its speed was three to four times that of the aircraft often seen over the town at that time. There was no noise and after the object had gone around the bombed area it disappeared in the direction from which it had come. Witnesses thought at the time that it was a secret weapon. (Ing. Farmache and Ing. Zmeuranu).

The hypotheses that the object could have been a cloud, aircraft, meteorite, etc., were rejected after discussion with the chief witness. The event took place in late afternoon and lasted 15 minutes. It could well have been one of the UFO's often seen in those days by German and Allied airmen in the war, each side considering the objects to be secret weapons belonging to the enemy.

18. MAY 1944, PÎNCOTA (ARAD) At the end of this month a witness saw to his bewilderment a low-flying German aircraft stand still in the air for two minutes without making a sound before continuing its journey. (Gheorghe Lucaci)

At first we thought we could eliminate this case despite the similar Russian sighting over the Ukraine 29th September 1944 at 18:00, but we decided to include the entire event because one like this is often cited in better-class UFO literature as the result of a manifestation (see Eugenio Danyans, *Platillos volantes en la actualidad,* Editorial Pomaire, 1968, pp. 54–55)

19. AUGUST 1945, VULCĂNEŞTI (CRAIOVA) I was on night-duty in the station at Plaiul Vulcăneşti near Craiova. Around midnight the special Bucharest-Craiova express passes here without stopping between Piatra-Olt and Craiova but for a certain reason it was unable to reach its destination, which is why I stopped it at Vulcăneşti. It was very warm that night, with a clear and calm sky. After I had stopped the train I went into the office to telephone Craiova and when I returned to the platform everything behind me was lit up brilliantly. I turned around and saw a large, red object in the sky, bigger than the moon and much brighter. It was over the horizon and going westwards at a ·distance of 70–80 metres. Both the guard and I were amazed. I went into the office again to fetch my colleague but he did not have time to come and have a look; when he did eventually appear the thing had vanished. I have not said anything about this for years because nobody believed me. (C. Ţîrulescu)

20. SUMMER 1945, VETIŞ This sighting was made by an elderly cowherd and recorded by Fodor Ioan, a Slatina official. For several nights in succession the cowman noticed over the fields between the parish of Vetiş and the Hungarian border a cloud about one metre across. The "cloud" was a brilliant red and moved across the fields quite close to the ground and tending to keep along the wire fences. At one of the fence stakes the cowman saw two "clouds" (illuminated traces) which moved against each other, changed colour, stood still, suddenly disappeared, etc. . . . Various other witnesses declared that they had been misled by "light" on the fields, thinking it was houses with their lights on, so that some of them lost their way when the cloud changed position. When the cloud vanished some of the wool of the cowman's sheepskin jacket was singed. (A form of static electricity?)

21. JUNE 1947, ORADEA In the 1969 November number of *Volk und Kultur*, which is a magazine for

German-speaking Rumanians, Andreas Schulhof tells of the time in June 1947 when he saw from a train-window six unusual objects flying in formation near Oradea, and so fast the witness thought they were doing "20,000 kilometres per hour."

This "20,000 km per hour" is of course "unusually high velocity" and the UFO's speed could not really be estimated. We might recall how the American Kenneth Arnold saw his famous UFO's also flying in formation on 24th June 1947, which is when he coined the term "flying saucer." It would be useful to expand the work done by Ted Bloecher on the American 1947 UFO wave so that one could get a complete and clear picture of all UFO manifestations taking place that year.

22. SUMMER 1953, SLOBOZIA   See page 158.

23. JULY–AUGUST 1953, REMETEA MARE (TIMI-ŞOARA)   A self-luminous sphere apparently twice the size of the moon came up from behind a wood (height estimated 25 m) stood still and then slowly descended towards the field. About 4 m from the ground it suddenly went out. The object cast no light and yet the orange glow could be seen over the whole surface. The sighting lasted about three minutes and was seen from a distance of about 350 m by a teacher, Florea Ion, and two of his colleagues.

24. 1955, HÎRSENI (FĂGĂRAŞ)   I have lived in Hîrseni for some time, in one of the valleys of the Făgăraş Mountains. One summer night in 1955, between midnight and one o'clock, I was on my way home with my wife. There is a small river on the righthand side of the road between Făgăraş and Hîrseni, whereas on the left side there are meadows. About 500 metres from the village we saw about 1000 m high an object odd enough to make us stand still in fright. It was an arc with a diameter of about 1.5 m and ringed with whitish sparks. It was going at high speed towards the mountains on our left. There was no sound and the sighting lasted three

Sketch of the site of the mysterious light at Livada Someș, August 1957 (see no. 25).

minutes at most. It travelled horizontally with lateral balancing movements but not rotating on its axis. Its colour was blue, with whitish-silver streaks. The night was calm and clear. I should like to stress the fact that the observation conditions were excellent so that there was no possibility of confusing what we saw with any of the atmospheric phenomena visible by day as well as at night in the mountains. (Retired teacher Dumitru Coca)

25. AUGUST 1957, LIVADA SOMEȘ Two friends camping by the Someș, river were awakened one night by a blinding light strong enough to make all the area seem bathed in daylight. It was suddenly extinguished and a receding point of light was observed. Duration and time: 01:05–01:07.

26. 1957–58 BUCEGI MOUNTAINS   See page 159.

27. 12th APRIL 1958, SICHEVIȚA Ion Secularian, then aged 25 and a draughtsman by profession, saw a cigar- (or fish)-shaped object in a clear sky. It was a clear red colour and travelled horizontally from the south to the north-east at an average speed (60 km per

hour?). Its length seemed to be about 1.50 metres and it had a "tail" of "symmetrical flames" behind. It disappeared behind a hill. Length of sighting about ten minutes.

28. JUNE 1958 OR 1959, SINAIA   See page 159.

29. 1959 OR 1960, RÎMNICU–SĂRAT   The undersigned, Doctor Jacques Kaufmann, resident at Rîmnicu-Sărat, Strada Milcov 5, states that he has seen two discs, each with a diameter roughly like that of the full moon. They were a brilliant yellow and went slowly and noiselessly from the north to the west. The discs seemed to be fixed to each other in such a way that the one behind was visible for a quarter of its surface and was much darker in colour. They were at a height of about 300–400 metres. See sketch.

Ion Secularian saw the UFO according to this sketch. The point at the front was darker than the rest of the object. Cf. UFO seen by Ion Hobana (p. 179).

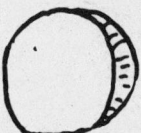

Dr. Jacques Kaufmann's two discs.

30. AUTUMN 1961, NEAMŢ   See page 167.

31. MAY 1963, FOCŞANI   About 23:00 I was out in the street at the end of May 1963 when a strong light made me turn round. A car, I thought, but realized at once, almost, that I had heard no noise. I saw behind and above me a sphere 500–600 m up which for a few split seconds came right over my head, very low, like a plane dropping medical sup-

plies. The thing seemed to be about the size of a hand-ball and it was emitting a bright white light with orange spots—it was daylight in the street, as a result of this globe which was coming from the south and moving at a constant velocity northwards. On the horizon it stood still, but kept emitting red and white light alternately, after which it vanished suddenly. There was no noise apart from a little sizzle when the red and white light was visible. During and after the sighting I was cold with fear in spite of the fact that the night temperature was pleasant. (Vasilescu Stelian, teacher, 27)

32. JULY 1963, BUCHAREST I was a third-year electronics student at the Bucharest Polytechnic and in the middle of July I went to visit a friend after sunset at about 21:00. I was near the Orthodox Church in Mihai Bravu Street, looking up at the sky as I often do, when I saw a bright, lens-shaped object 40–50 degrees above the city—over the Gheorghiu road I think—travelling S. E. at about the speed of a jet. It left no trace in the clear sky at all, which it would have done had it been a jet plane as these leave condensation trails. The fairly small and shiny object had a fiery tail like the flame of a petrol burner. It cannot have been a meteorite, travelling along horizontally for one to two minutes after which it suddenly shot up into the air at an angle of 90 degrees. Neither can it have been a jet-plane in unusual circumstances, especially since several authorities assured me that jets were not allowed to fly over Bucharest. (Ing. Strobach Iosif, Bucharest)

This witness is an amateur astronomer and the account he gives is an exact rendering excluding the possibility of any conventional explanation. See further McDivitt's photos.

33. AUGUST 1963, BUCHAREST I am used to studying the skies and since I know the times when satellites pass overhead I can even follow their or-

bits. . . . I was visiting Vasile Stoia, 61 Tabla Buții Street. He was ill at the time and I left his room to have a smoke, during which I had a look at the sky as usual. Opposite me was the roof of number 63.

63 Tabla Buții Street, Bucharest.

Towards midnight I noticed two bright objects, clearly both circular and the size of saucers. They kept the same distance from each other (about six to seven times their own diameter) I followed their course because I was fascinated by their size, which made them seem unlike stars or even satellites (because the latter appear to be much smaller and go faster). To my surprise they stopped, although keeping the same distance from each other. To gain some idea of comparison I took the two chimneys of the house opposite, number 63, and the two objects seemed to stand still between them. When I called out the niece Cornelia (Vasile's niece) came out to have a look.

Cornelia Stoia: When I came out I saw two bright objects in the sky, the righthand one moving fairly slowly towards the right—in a northerly direction. The object on the left stayed where it was. After about 10–15 seconds it suddenly went out, like an electric light. The night was very clear—be it noted. (Virgil Gheorghiu and Cornelia Stoia, Bucharest)

This report appeared in Rumanian newspapers (*Cutezătorii* 23.5.68). Two main themes—"standing still" and "going out"—(like an electric lamp—how often we find this in reports!) are so typical of UFO literature that the objects must undoubtedly have been UFO's.

34. JULY 1964, ATLANTIC OCEAN   See page 177.

35. JUNE 1966, BETWEEN ARPAŞUL DE JOS AND CÎRŢIŞOARA   About 04:30–05:00 a saucer-shaped object landed, as the sun was rising, near a dried-up well halfway between Arpaşul de Jos and Cîrţişoara. A night-watchman a hundred yards or so away ran up to it but it immediately shot away "surrounded with flames" and making "a singing noise." When the witness arrived on the spot some officials were already examining an impression in the ground which was oval and scorched. Great excitement in the surrounding villages. (Various witnesses; recorded by Julien Weverbergh).

The chief witness could not be questioned about the matter by the authors because he had left the district. Event unconfirmed.

36. AUGUST 1966, HUNEDOARA   A glittering object the size of Venus (which it wasn't!) arose at dusk and suddenly disappeared. (Ionescu Constantin)

37. OCTOBER OR NOVEMBER 1966, TIMIŞOARA   This sighting of mine took place in 1966 at the end of October or the beginning of November. I do not know when exactly but it was at the time of the launching of the Soviet rocket Soyuz. It was a clear day—about 17:00—when I saw several people looking at the sky. When I looked up myself I thought at first it was a glider but looking more carefully I noticed a white point of light on it bigger than a star. This surprised us as it was broad daylight. It was moving but at a scarcely noticeable rate. I studied the object for an hour with field-glasses and was thus able to see its triangular shape and the

multicoloured light coming from it. The object had arrived from the north-east and after circling right round the town made off in the direction of Bucharest. It disappeared whilst ascending and I could not determine the height with any exactitude. During its flight it turned in every direction and many people witnessed it. The details seen by means of fieldglasses were unfortunately invisible to the naked eye. (Dalea Ion and Stroia Mihai, students, Timişoara)

38. END OF 1966, BACĂU Witness sees about 18:00 a point of light for roughly five to six seconds coming down obliquely through the clouds, till it stops and then goes out. (Neculai Macovei)

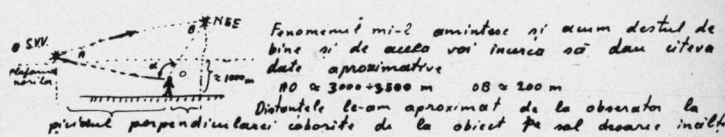

39. JULY 1967, BUCHAREST Between 20:45 and 20:55 a point of light moved for about 30 seconds horizontally south-east, fell from an estimated height of 5500 m to 3000 m, paused for about one minute, during which time it shone with a yellow glow, and then after shooting up again for 10–15 seconds went off with increased speed in a south-easterly direction. (Aurel Ghimpu, journalist).

This witness is known to the authors as a particularly trustworthy and accurate man; the object behaved like a typical UFO.

40. 25th JULY 1967, ORADEA Witness Mihai Bereş observed around 11:30 and 5 degrees over the school roof an object which was thought to be an aircraft. As it remained stationary she took a closer look and saw a cigar-shaped, aluminium object with pointed ends but without wings. When it suddenly began to move a weak light started to come from the back end and after 20 seconds it vanished behind a block of houses.

41. 4th AUGUST 1967, SÎNGEORZ-BĂI See page 156.

42. 18th SEPTEMBER 1967, DANUBE DELTA On the afternoon of this day I embarked on the ferry-boat between Tulcea and Sfîntul-Gheorghe and at about 20:30 I was on bridge on the left-hand side. There was a gentle rain falling from a uniformly grey sky and the darkness was fairly intense—no opening in the clouds for any light to come through. I was alone. At 20:45 approximately the clouds changed colour high above me and began to emit light. There was a red "margin" around them.

Suddenly but noiselessly an illuminated object appeared in the form of a pan with a tail and travelling westwards. The object then remained stationary all of a sudden 500–600 metres from my position and about 200–33 m up. It flickered like a candle flame and the disc had a diameter of 5–6 metres, likewise the tail, the base of which was half as broad as the disc, the width decreasing towards the extremity. The disc on the outside was a reddish-purple and the tail, the elongated section, was the colour of methane gas. Cloud-like sparks were coming from this tail but they went out immediately. I was very surprised if not afraid. After staying about four minutes the object turned slowly on its axis without making a sound and came back to its original position. Then it began to move again on my left and parallel with the ground, drawing its tail westwards. Again it paused for a moment after covering 200 or 300 metres and then finally vanished in the clouds without a sound or any lateral movement. The object had taken a U-shaped route. When I looked at my watch again it was 20:52. (Engineer Bîta Valeriu, Bucharest)

43. 21st NOVEMBER 1967, POENARII-BURCHII (JUDEȚUL PRAHOVA) See page 161.

44. 22nd NOVEMBER 1967, PETRILA PETROȘANI (HUNEDOARA) See page 166.

FLYING SAUCERS IN RUMANIA

45. 2nd DECEMBER 1967, BUCHAREST See page 176.

46. 2nd DECEMBER 1967, ARAD At about midnight I went into the garden. The sky was very clear and full of stars. My attention was attracted to an unusually bright object moving with amazing speed.

As it was so bright it could not have been an aeroplane—neither could it be a falling star. It was travelling from north-east to north. I called my wife, who was about four metres away in the kitchen, but before she got outside it had disappeared, a fact which suggests it had an unusually high velocity. It was cigar-shaped and its light seemed like that of the sun when reflected in a mirror. Its flight was horizontal. The next day I asked my colleagues if they had seen it but it appeared that they had not done so. (Iovana Mircea, car-factory electrician, Arad)

47. 4th DECEMBER 1967, BUCHAREST See page 177.

48. 10th DECEMBER 1967, BUCHAREST See page 180.

49. 18th MARCH 1968, CIMPULUNG Numerous witnesses saw in the evening at about 21:00 a large and intensely glowing "fire" which after some time appeared to be an orange-coloured sphere. After standing still the object made a slow horizontal movement and then a vertical one. First the sphere suddenly disappeared and then the aureole, likewise slowly (Isopescu Vianora).

A typical UFO sighting, probably with materialization and de-materialization. Compare the aureole's late disappearance with the appearance and disappearance of a UFO at Episcopia Bihorului. (See page 164).

50. 28th MARCH 1968, TISMANA In the afternoon

east of the town an unknown, bright object was seen with an apparent diameter of 8–10 cm. The base of the conical object in the sky was turned towards the earth while the axis formed an angle in relation to the ground of 150 degrees perpendicular. The object was a whitish blue but it turned red later in the evening and disappeared at 19:30. Severe radio disturbance was recorded by several witnesses amongst whom were technical students and teachers. One of the witnesses, a mathematician by profession, had a transistor (a Delta) with revolving antennae and during the sighting he carried out some experiments: the radio disturbance was noticed only when the antennae were turned in the direction of the slowly-moving object and the interference on the long wave-lengths was so strong that it blocked all other transmissions. The shorter the wave-length the more the interference diminished—and on the very shortest it was barely perceptible. The object was seen by innumerable witnesses and many groups or individuals reported their findings to Ion Hobana. The present account is based on what was supplied by a group of teachers who witnessed the spectacle.

51. 29th, 30th, 31st MARCH 1968, BANAT See Chapter 8.

52. 4th APRIL 1968, TIMIŞOARA Various students followed a bright, conical object from 19:30 to 20:00. The object went in a number of directions, sometimes at "fantastic speeds" and sometimes staying absolutely motionless. It was able to turn corners without changing its velocity and without noise. (Gheorghe Roth)

53. 7th APRIL 1968, RÎMNICU-SĂRAT A circular object, uniformly lit, moved soundlessly across the sky at great speed from east to west. (Rădulescu Lucian, economist)

54. 20th APRIL 1968, TIMIŞOARA At 08:30 witness saw about 100 metres over the ground a slowly hovering object which looked thus:

The central body-section was clearly disc-shaped with a "cabin" in the front at the end of a sort of "neck." The cabin was of a transparent material divided with slats. The tail looked something like that of an aircraft. Witness heard no noise, saw no smoke but was surprised at its sudden disappearance. (Fleşeriu Dan, student)

55. END OF APRIL 1968, BACĂU At 21:00 a light flew very fast over Bacău park and was followed by a zigzagging second one which caught up with the first. They both vanished very fast after remaining still for a short space. (Macovei Niculae)

56. MAY 1968, BISTRIŢA Many inhabitants followed the course on a clear day of a round, glittering object moving oddly across the sky.

57. 5th–6th MAY 1968, TÎRGUL-OCNA See page 162.

58. 10th MAY 1968, ORADEA For two days a UFO was seen over the town and on 10th May at 12:30 it went suddenly and at great speed north of the town in a north-north-westerly direction. It now disappeared but came back exactly one hour later to its previous position. Here it stayed hanging motionless until on 11th May in the evening it vanished. The object looked like a white spot to the naked eye and a number of scholars studied it with 10×50 binoculars between 09:00 and 11:00. Altogether it was seen for 20 hours, both by qualified observers and the general population. Those using glasses said it seemed to change shape and become roughly triangular, thus resembling an enormous pointed paper bag but also transparent. On the surface a matt colour but inside there was a very brilliant "something" which kept

moving and changing colour, from bright white to orange and red.

The meteorological service stated that no balloons had been sent up on 10th May and they supplied details about the strength of the wind at 10,000 metres, but the height of the object could not be determined. (Ing. Victor Bolcaş)

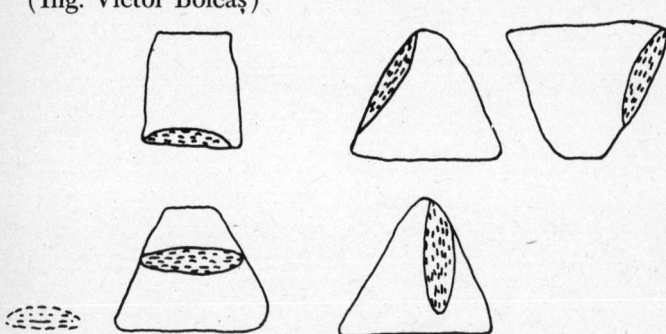

Oradea 10th May 1968. Some typical positions of the object seen. Shaded areas are zones of intense light varying from white to orange and red (see no. 58).

59. 22nd MAY 1968, BĂILEŞTI   See page 153.

60. 8th JUNE 1968, CĂPĂŢÂNENI   See page 172.

61. 24th JUNE 1968, CRAIOVA   See page 155.

62. 27th JUNE 1968, CLUJ   A round, shining UFO hangs for ¾ hour quite motionless above the town, begins to move slowly and disappears. (Virgil Hogea)

63. 28th JUNE 1968, BUCHAREST   An object, flying rapidly over the city, stays motionless for a few seconds prior to disappearing.

64. 24th JULY 1968, PIATRA-NEAMŢ   See page 157.

65. 30th JULY 1968, TUŞNAD-BĂI   A star-like body carried out the following movements at 22:10 in the apparent vicinity of the moon:

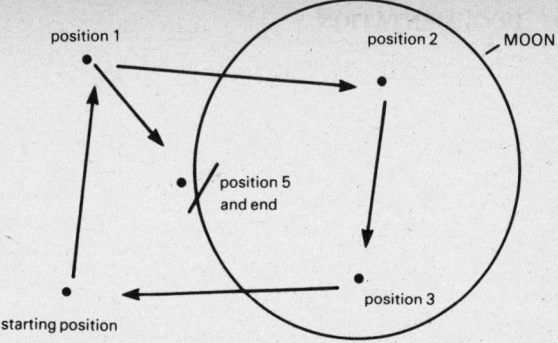

In each of these positions the object remained stationary for 2–3 seconds, after which it abruptly vanished. (Mihai Bereş)

66. AUGUST 1968, CARACAL Puiu Radu, a 24-year old decorator at Bucharest, spotted at 01:30 approximately a white object in the sky (which was clear and almost free of wind) travelling from S. E. to N. E. about one km over the horizon. Its shape was that of a rugby-ball and apparent size that of the sun. It left an illuminated tail which lit up the terrain as bright as day. Witness heard a loud hissing noise like steam from a power-station. The light went out even before the object itself had completely vanished.

67. AUGUST 1968, HUNEDOARA I am quite familiar with the stars and their constellations. One evening in August 1968 after the sun had gone down behind the mountains my friend and I noticed a very brilliant "star" moving in jerky, zigzag fashion thus:

The angles were very obtuse and the object's speed slowed each time a new "point" was reached but once beyond that the velocity increased again. (Ionescu Constantin, student, Hunedoara)

68. 16th OR 17th AUGUST 1968, IAŞI See page 182.

69. 17th AUGUST 1968, ORADEA   See page 180.

70. 18th AUGUST 1968, CLUJ   See Chapter 6.

71. 18th AUGUST 1968, BALŞ (JUDEŢUL OLT)

At 21:00 I saw a "star" in the south with a special brilliance. It seemed stationary at first but pulsated violently. These pulsations proved to be chaotic movements when I studied the object through field-glasses. I thought my hands were shaky so I sat down and supported my elbows on my knees. As a

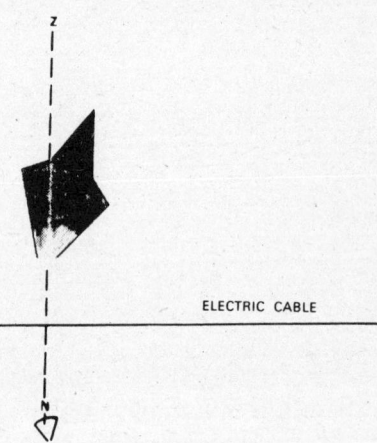

Original coloured drawing by Torcea Constantin.
Top red, body blue and lowest part yellow.

guideline I used a high-tension cable and two stars, one on either side of the object. Within this framework the hectic movement became quite clear—it resembled the flight of a bat or a butterfly and it went on "dancing" like this southwards. As it was sometimes above the cable and then below it the object projected on to the horizon was falling. The angle of 40 degrees at which I had seen the object at 21:00 was slowly lessening. The altitude I would put at seven to eight km after comparing mentally with aircraft. The colour of the "star" was interesting: red in front at the point but laterally a greenish-blue; the "back," if I may call it that, was pure

orange. I assume that over Bulgaria the object must have been sighted more clearly.
Witness then gave further details:
—duration of sighting 20 minutes
—size; larger than Venus, to the naked eye; probably about 10 cm through binoculars
—I have given you this description because I knew you were interested in the matter. However, for a long time I did not know how and to whom I should report what I saw. The observatory ought at least to have a telephone number which anybody can ring to give an immediate report of a sighting, after which qualified observers could check the phenomena with instruments. (Torcea Constantin) See sketch.

72. 18th–19th AUGUST 1968, CLUJ At 02:15 from 18th to 19th August the Megyesi family noticed three orange-coloured flying objects which stayed motionless in the sky seven minutes before suddenly vanishing with amazing speed. Confirmed by other witnesses.

73. 20th AUGUST 1968, SCHITUL BUNEA, PARISH OF VULCANA-BĂI. (JUDEȚUL DÎMBOVIȚA) Emilian Nichifor, an abbot aged 50, noticed together with one of the novices in the monastery a light and oscillating object after 23:00. It was red underneath, orange in the middle and dazzling white at the top. Now and again a projector-type of light came from the middle, the object remaining stationary 1½ hours and horizontal. Afterwards it made soundless vertical movements very fast. Shape: conical; 30 metres diameter at base. Altitude 40 m.

74. 20th AUGUST 1968, PLOIEȘTI See page 154.

75. 20th AUGUST 1968, PLOIEȘTI A brilliant yellowish-orange sphere sped through the air at 20:20 from S. W. to N. E. for about 8–10 seconds. Velocity less than that of a meteorite. Witness could not identify it. (Aurel Magdu, Ing. Specialist in technology, Ploiești)

76. 23rd AUGUST 1968, FÎRTĂȚEȘTI   About 22:30 a brilliant, round and elongated object flew through the air for five to six seconds from S. E. to west. (Popescu Victor and 4 other witnesses)

77. 25th AUGUST 1968, RÎMNICU-SĂRAT   See page 163.

78. SEPTEMBER 1968, BACĂU   A quickly moving point of light was overtaken by a similar one. They then flew on together, perceptibly slower until one of them shot off very quickly southwards and disappeared. The other remained in situ. Four witnesses. (Macovei Nicolae) See sketch

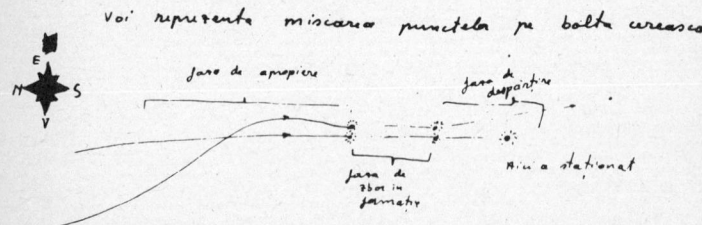

79. 2nd SEPTEMBER 1968, CLUJ   Gizela Torockzai and her eight-year-old daughter write to the newspaper *Scînteia* that at 20:30 they saw a reddish-white ball, larger than the moon, flying through space quickly and quite low. It vanished suddenly after a few minutes.

80. 13th SEPTEMBER 1968, ICUȘEȘTI (JUDEȚUL NEAMȚ)   A brilliant white oval object travelled in several directions between 10:15 and 11:05 over the town. It grew bigger and changed into a rocket shape. Various witnesses.

81. 13th SEPTEMBER 1968, PAUNEȘTI (JUDEȚUL VASLUI)   I was not the first to see the object— my attention was drawn to it by others. The object was very high in the sky and moving slowly from west to east. It was about the size of a chair (with-

out back) and none of us thought it could be a cloud. Its movement could only be determined by means of a fixed point—in this case a branch of a tree. During its flight the object rotated as if on its axis and changed its shape—see drawing. I watched it for more than half an hour, between 12:00 and 13:00, until clouds covered it. The object was seen by the whole village. (Mihai Dumitru)

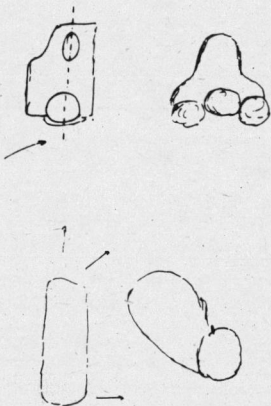

Drawing on the back of a letter by Mihai Dumitru (see no. 81)

The lenticular object seen at 00:30, by workers leaving a Rîmnicu Sărat factory (Rumania), was apparently identical with this UFO, photographed 14. 1. 1969 at Elsthorpe, New Zealand

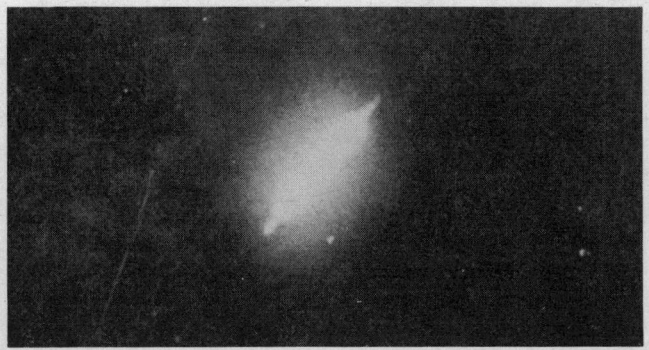

82. 14th SEPTEMBER 1968, BUCOV (PRAHOVA)
An egg-shaped, whitish-red object flew soundlessly
and at incredible speed from east to west for about
one minute. (Marin Vasilescu, hall porter)

83. 14th SEPTEMBER 1968, RÎMNICU SĂRAT
Various workers at the clothing factory witnessed
the following at 00:30 in the night as they were
about to go home: an intense white light emanating
for about 4 minutes from a lens-shaped "something"
4–5 metres long at a height of 800–1000 metres. The
thing then grew smaller and went out, but before
doing so it moved and left a kind of illuminated
track behind. There was no noise. (Buzea Stela.
Many witnesses—the whole factory. See photograph p. 245).

84. 15th SEPTEMBER 1968, BUCHAREST Around
20:30 a bright object appeared at a height of about
400 metres. The size of a basket-ball and emitting a
silvery-white light. It moved soundlessly and horizontally from N. W. to S. E., and after five to six
seconds it suddenly went out. (Mircea Acasandri)

85. 15th SEPTEMBER 1968, PLOIEȘTI See page 183.

86. 19th SEPTEMBER 1968, CLUJ, SIBIU, ETC.,
ETC. See Chapter 8.

87. 19th SEPTEMBER 1968, BUCHAREST-BRAȘOV
See Chapter 8.

88. 19th SEPTEMBER 1968, BÎRLAD See Chapter 8.

89. 19th SEPTEMBER 1968, BISTRIȚA See Chapter 8.

90. 19th SEPTEMBER 1968, JUCU See Chapter 8.

91. 21st SEPTEMBER 1968, PLOIEȘTI From the

open window of my flat I saw at 19:29 an aerial object which appeared suddenly in the shape of a disc with a light-red glow. The outlines were not very clear because of being ringed in a mass of gaseous material. The object went soundlessly from the south to the north at a higher speed than that of a jet. At first I thought it was a meteorite—of which I have seen many—but quickly concluded it was no such thing. Neither was it a satellite, in comparison with which this object had a diameter at least ten times the size. Besides, satellites coming into our atmosphere tend to leave a trail but this one had none and furthermore it moved jerkily. It vanished over our house after seven to eight seconds, my wife and son coming to the window too late to catch sight of it, although my son, having stayed by the window to keep watch, called out a little later that the object had reappeared. This time it travelled in the opposite direction and after four to five seconds it suddenly turned at an angle of 90 degrees and vanished in the direction of Strejnic Airport. (Nicolae Rădulescu, Chief Engineer, I.P.I.P. Ploieşti)

92. 26th SEPTEMBER 1968, BUCHAREST Two lyceum (secondary school) pupils saw a bright silver-yellow, oval object going through the air at high speed and leaving a tail of the same colour. When the tail vanished there appeared light, badly formed spheres in its place which disappeared rapidly. (Dan Sîrbu and Florin Jitaru)

93. 26th SEPTEMBER 1968, PLOIEŞTI At 21:23 the witness was with a friend on the Bacău-Ploieşti road. At that moment they saw an object shooting along horizontally at unknown speed from N. W. to S. E. Estimated height 2000–3000 m. It was shaped like a rugby-ball and was ten times smaller than the illuminated trail the object left behind. There was a space of about 1 metre between the parent body and the tail, the latter being extinguished only after the former had vanished. The tail looked like a red line and the whole thing was

noiseless. It could not have been a meteorite because of the horizontal flight and the "smoke trail" (Tudor Gheorghe, student)

94. 26th SEPTEMBER 1968, BUCHAREST A bright object the size of a football moved fast from west to east over the city at 21:25. It lasted five to six seconds, during which time it ejected a "sort of flame" three times. No sound. (Alexandru Andrei)

95. 27th SEPTEMBER 1968, CORABIA JUDEȚUL OLT At 03:30 the witness and his son-in-law noticed an illuminated object in the sky the size of a cardinal's hat and emitting light like the full moon. The object darted to the left twice "like a hunted animal." (Atanasie Băldescu). See sketch.

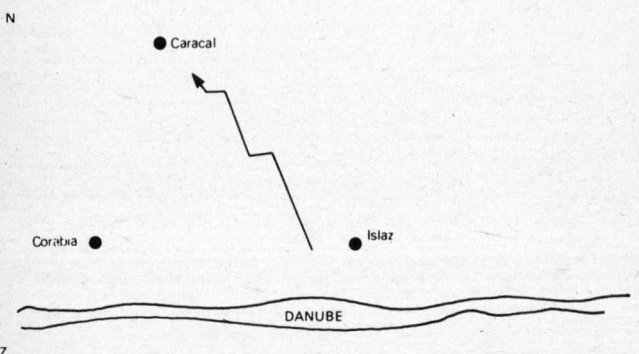

The jumps made by the cardinal's hat.

96. 30th SEPTEMBER 1968, BUCHAREST At 20:15 I could see from my garden an illuminated object in the direction of Casa Scînteia. I called my brother and we agreed that the thing could not be a star because, for one reason, the light coming from it was much too great. Nor an artificial satellite for the following three reasons concerning colour, shape and movement.

1. Colour: brilliant blue quite distinct from the

other colours pink and green which probably alternated quite regularly. The strongest beams were blue, then the pink, then green. It was all very intense and dazzling.
2. Shape: round at first, changing to rocket shape and finally into a small green sphere. Thus:

After assuming the shapes sketched it went back to the first (spherical) form.
3. Movement: Quite unlike any known satellite. At first motionless it moved on a little, only to take up its original position again. After this it went "forwards" and the candle-power decreased, but both the latter and the object's size increased when it went back to its first position. After doing all this it grew smaller and vanished. Total observation time about 30–40 minutes so it cannot have been a plane. (Ghioacă Gheorghe, chauffeur)

From 21st to 23rd December 1965 and from 17:00 to 20:30 the same object was both seen and photographed at Huesca, Spain. These drawings are based on the original photos and may be compared with those taken by Ghioacă Gheorghe. There was radio interference during the Spanish sightings.

97. 4th OCTOBER 1968, SNAGOV An elliptical object sighted above this town between 18:00 and 18:30, 50 degrees over the horizon, casting a bright light like a lamp and moving fast. It vanished below the horizon. The object could not be identified as belonging to any known phenomenon. (Mihai Valianatos, engineer)

98. 7th OCTOBER 1968, BUCHAREST The object seen at 20:15 on 30th September 1968 occurred

again on Monday, 7th October, between 19:35 and 20:20. On this second occasion the object was roughly in the same place in the north but perhaps a little to the west. Its up-and-down movement was not pronounced and the three colours—this time pink, brilliant white and green—followed each other as they had done earlier. Afterwards the object acquired a sort of tail alternately appearing and disappearing. My uncle also saw it this time. (Ghioacă Gheorghe, chauffeur)

99. 18th OCTOBER 1968, GURA VĂII Very many witnesses noticed—at 18:00—an extremely fast, shining object over the town. It appeared to follow the course of the Danube, then suddenly stood motionless about one minute before disappearing in the opposite direction. (Mih Gheorghe)

100. 23rd OCTOBER, 1968, BUCHAREST A group of workers at the Bucharest marshalling yards watched a brightly lit point from 13:10 to 13:30 which made acute angles at high speed as it travelled over the city. (Stan Nicolae and five others)

101. 24th OCTOBER 1968 We were in calm water between Madagascar and the east coast of Africa and at 15:47 just as darkness fell we were taking our bearings from the stars. The night was clear and calm when suddenly the third officer, Ștefan Anton, who was with me on the bridge to port, called out in amazement. He drew my attention to a white, shining object coming out of the south-eastern sky at an astonishing speed. When it got nearer we could see its disc shape and we reckoned the diameter to be half that of the moon. Its colour was a dazzling yellowish orange in the centre. After a few seconds the disc stopped, started off again abruptly and vanished eastwards at fantastic speed. The sighting lasted about 12 seconds and, according to the sextant we used, the thing had a diameter of approximately 17 metres and was 25 km

away from us. Most of the crew saw it. (N. Ştefănescu, Captain of the tanker *Argeş*)

102. 25th OCTOBER 1968, BUCHAREST A zigzag sphere seen flying over Bucharest for 40 minutes. (Gheorghiţă Scînteie)

103. 4th NOVEMBER 1968, BUCHAREST Chauffeur Ghioacă Gheorghe (see reports of his sightings 30th September and 7th October 1968) became so intrigued by his UFO experiences that he continued to study the skies every evening and often went to the airports to study the ascent and descent of aircraft. On 4th November he saw north-north-west of his house the same white object turning alternately green and blue and carrying out lively "dancing" movements up and down, until it disappeared, leaving a large tail.

104. 5th–6th NOVEMBER 1968, CLUJ The undersigned Danciu Horia, a French teacher living at Cluj, Andrei Mureşanu Street 24, suddenly saw a brilliant reddish object larger than the moon appear around midnight 5th–6th November. At an altitude of about 1000 m it moved very fast to the north and soundlessly for about eight seconds after which it vanished. It was oval and unlike any other object known to me.

105. 24th NOVEMBER 1968, CONSTANŢA At 20:06 we saw over the town at an estimated height of 6000 m a bright orange object with a light power stronger than that of a star of the first magnitude. The sky was slightly overcast but not enough to hinder our watching with naked eye. The object travelled very fast in an east-south-easterly direction for about 1½ minutes during which it described an arc of 30 degrees approximately (measured with a perpendicular line where we were standing). Suddenly the point of light stood quite still at B—see drawing—for about 15–20 seconds. For about the next 30 seconds it carried on along its trajectory though much slower and

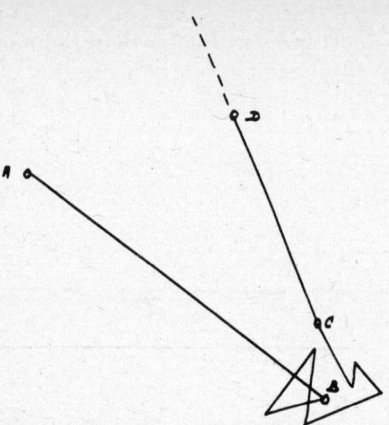

A wavering point of light over Constanţa.

irregularly. After this it increased speed again and went straight to D in a north-north-westerly direction. The object seemed to climb while in the area C-D, its size and candle-power gradually diminishing until at D it was no longer visible. Time taken to get from C to D was about one minute. This took place, as already said, above the clouds but the latter were so thin the stars could be seen. In view of the great speed of the object, its strange manner of emitting light, and also because of its trajectory and the way it moved along the path, it is quite impossible that we could have been looking at an ordinary aircraft, helicopter etc. Total length of sighting was three minutes 15 seconds. (Călin Cheorghiu, Liviu Nedelcu, engineers)

106. 6th DECEMBER 1968, SLĂNIC A bell-shaped object flew through the air at 14:00 without any noise and was seen by a man who had been a wartime pilot. He rejects any idea that what he saw was any kind of aircraft.

107. 11th DECEMBER 1968, CLUJ About 20:00 I saw from my garden a bright object over the Haia wood. It was stationary and sending out fierce rays. I noticed it for five minutes after which I fetched my wife. When I got outside again it had gone. It looked

like a parachute and was bigger than the moon. The object was absolutely quiet and emitted a bright yellow light from about 1500 m up. (L. Bucur, geographer)

108. 15th DECEMBER 1968, PLOIEŞTI A shining object moving over the town. (Andrei Manole, technician)

109. 15th DECEMBER 1968, CLUJ (20:30) A very dazzling object zigzagged soundlessly across half the sky at great speed within a time-span of two minutes (Feneşan, V.).

110. 4th JANUARY 1969, COLIBIŢA See page 168.

111. 8th JANUARY 1969, CLUJ Between 20:15 and 20:45 I saw above the town to the south a brilliant object with the following features. Apparent size—one-tenth to one-fifteenth that of the moon; thus several times greater than the diameter of Venus. Colour was whitish yellow and glittering. The light was extinguished at irregular intervals of from three to ten minutes but came back again just as strongly. The colour/light changes lasted several seconds each time. After the object had apparently stood still for ten minutes it went in a westerly direction and disappeared. No sound. I could not identify it as any form of aircraft, satellite or meteorite. (Ing. Hariuc Friedrich)

112. 11th JANUARY 1969, SIBIU See page 175.

113. FEBRUARY 1969, BUCHAREST A "star" flies over the city at frightening speed, regularly switching on and off. (Niţă Caraman)

114. 1st MAY 1969, NEGRU-VODĂ See page 161.

115. 23rd MAY 1969, BRAŞOV See page 154.

116. END OF MAY, BEGINNING OF JUNE 1969, ARAD See page 163.

117. 1st JUNE 1969, MĂRĂŞEŞTI See page 185.

118. 1st JUNE 1969, ROŞIORII DE VEDE See page 187.

119. 1st JUNE 1969, SĂNDULENI See page 187.

120. 1st JUNE 1969, BUCHAREST (01:25) See page 188.

121. 1st JUNE 1969, BUCHAREST (02:26–02:30) See page 189.

122. 2nd JUNE 1969, TUŞNAD-BĂI Several witnesses saw an object at 02:30 at night which they thought would fall on our planet as it was getting larger and larger. A tail with yellowish orange sparks was seen behind and in conical form some distance from the object itself, which was travelling at a very high rate. It vanished in the direction of Odorhei without a sound. (Radu Munteanu)

123. 3rd JULY 1969, CLUJ East of the town at 20:25 a witness saw a light yellow and red object the size of a football and with a red tail. After 20 seconds it disappeared behind a cloud. The vivid lighting was evenly spread but there were no rays. Estimated distance 10–15 km (Paul Romul, retired priest, and his schoolmistress wife.)

124. 6th JULY 1969, BUCHAREST See page 165.

125. 10th JULY 1969, EPISCOPIA BIHORULUI See page 164.

126. 11th JULY 1969, TIRGU-MUREŞ Between 21:30 and 22:00 and for 10–12 seconds the 18-year-old student Chioreanu and his friend Vaida Iancu saw an object in the Great Bear Constellation which was red and bean-shaped. The red changed to orange. It was a calm, mild summer evening and the sky was clear. The object took up the following positions:

The UFO appeared for exactly three minutes and took exactly the same time to disappear and come back into the next position and thus carry on the cycle. The witnesses got tired of looking at it after the cycle had been gone through four times so they stopped.

127. SUMMER 1969, TIMIŞOARA A conical and diamond shaped object moved all the afternoon in a clear sky giving perfect visibility from south-west to north-east. Its movement was slow and the size twice that of Venus at most. (Ida Bus, technical draughtsman. Also other witnesses)

128. SUMMER 1969, BUCHAREST A triangular object changing shape to an oval moved across the town quickly but it stopped three times for five seconds. During these five second pauses the object was approached by a "streak." Disappearance sudden. Duration of sighting: one minute. (Vlad Gheorghe)

129. 23rd JULY 1969, BUCHAREST I was sitting at my worktable at 20:37 and chanced to be looking through the open window when I saw a strange, violently pulsating light in the sky. I first thought it must be Venus, but I was amazed at its size—about 2 cm. Although I am none too familiar with the exact positions of the planets in the firmament I know that Mars or Venus are not due west as this light was. It could not have been a star because it stood out sharply against a bank of cloud higher up. The sun had set and the sky in the west was a light red so that the outlines of the clouds were fairly visible at the time. Although convinced it was not a star I stayed to watch the light until it moved; this indeed it did after two minutes of remaining motionless and it went off fairly slowly northwards. I could not possibly determine the speed but I think it was faster than that of an ordinary civil

aeroplane. I followed its route from the balcony after I had called my wife, who also witnessed it. A dark red "flame" shot out of the object in opposite direction to its flight and this flame had the candle-power of Bengal lights. The flame must not be thought of as a tail or track or flash as it was a crescent bigger than the object itself; furthermore it did not change the speed of the object in any way which remained constant. The observation point was my balcony on the fourth floor of a block of flats in the Taberei district. The initial position of the object was 2–3 degrees to the south of the place where the sun usually sets at this time. Its height I estimated by means of the ten-storey blocks of flats in the military ward one km away: about 1½ times the height of these buildings. Its distance was about 3–4 km and its diameter as I saw it was 2 cm, although I cannot possibly estimate. Its trajectory in relation to the horizon was a linear one of 35 degrees to behind the military district.

I might have been able to follow the object farther but I had the impression it was sinking or describing an arc—in any case it suddenly disappeared. My watch said 20:41 when this happened and while the light had been motionless in the sky I observed it for two minutes but I do not know how long it had been there already. Its trajectory likewise lasted two minutes and all this time there was not a sound. It is true there was a lot of noise from the traffic in the street, but on the other hand a helicopter or aircraft can always be heard above it. (Nicolae M., writer)

130. AUGUST 1969 Ganciu Moise Petre, aged 74, notices a "star" one night for 30 seconds the size of an orange and much the same colour. It stays still in the sky and is vividly lit up. After 30 seconds the "star" departs at fantastic speed, producing as it does so a sound halfway between the noise of a person panting and the whistling of the wind.

In August 1971 a group of campers in Belgium reported an identical phenomenon, including the sound.

FLYING SAUCERS IN RUMANIA

131. 25th AUGUST 1969, PLOIEŞTI Hundreds of people reported seeing a large round metal object hanging over the town between 11:30 and 15:30 and then suddenly disappearing. The witness Vladimir Stoicescu followed it with binoculars and took photos. At 13:30 the colour changed from a bright mercury to a dull metallic grey. At the same time it changed shape too; it grew smaller, appeared to split into three little spheres which finally regrouped to produce another form. See photo page 258. (Vladimir Stoicescu)

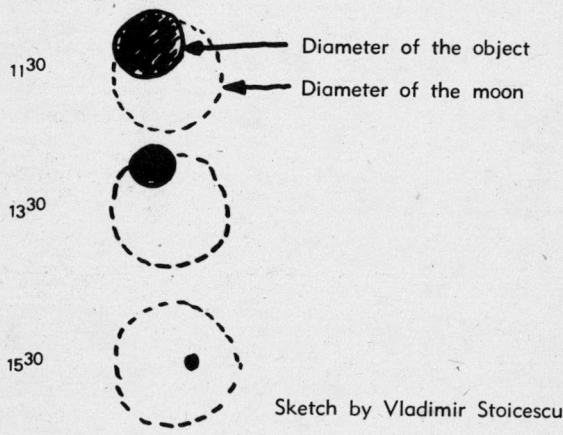

Sketch by Vladimir Stoicescu

132. 30th AUGUST 1969, BUCHAREST See page 179.

133. 9th SEPTEMBER 1969, TIMIŞOARA Between 18:17 and 18:45 I happened to look up in a north-north-easterly direction when I saw 60 degrees over the horizon a triangular, bright object with a point facing the ground. It was five to six times bigger than the largest star I know and at the time the sky was perfectly clear and calm. The sun was about to set and apart from the object there was nothing else

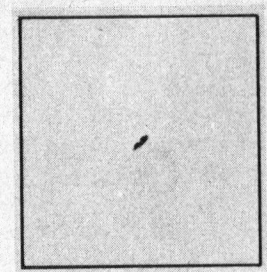

UFO after splitting; photographed over Cluj, Rumania, on 25.8.1969

in the sky. After I had found a fixed point I noticed that the object was completely motionless. As I was unable to continue watching it I do not know when it vanished. Two other witnesses will confirm what I say. The object was neither weather-balloon, star, aircraft, helicopter nor stationary satellite. I was able to follow Echo 1, 2 and Pegasus perfectly—they all moved. (Mircea Negruți)

134. 10th SEPTEMBER 1969, BUCHAREST On this date there was a sighting over Rumania very much like the ones at Banat on 29th–31st March 1968 (see page 127), at Cluj, 19th September 1968 (see page 138) and at Sarajevo, Jugoslavia, 18th October 1968 (see page 84).

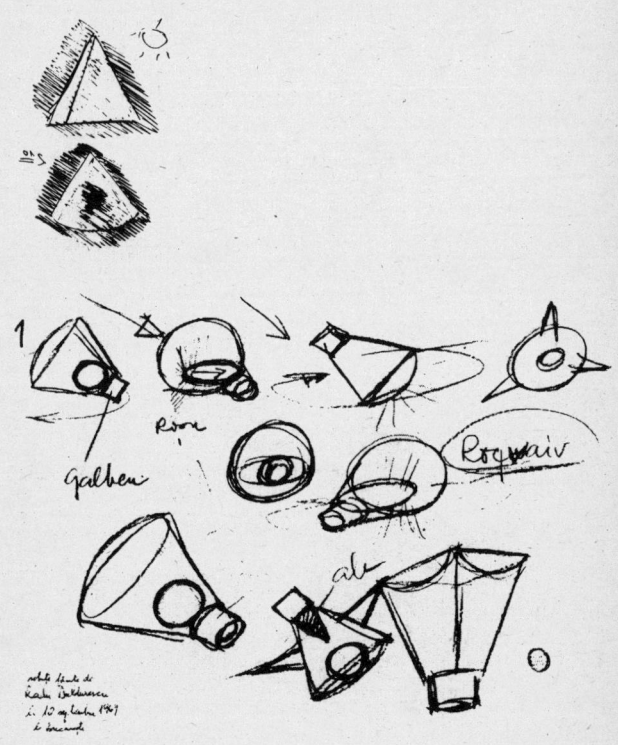

One of the countless sketches of the object which fascinated thousands in Bucharest on 10th September 1969.

In these three cases the object was seen by thousands of people and reported, sketched and photographed by scores. That it was a balloon was generally doubted. The authors are agreed about this point almost entirely. True to our principles we reproduce these cases in considerable detail, especially as it is very striking how the reports almost all agree with each other except in the very smallest matters. The use of theodolites and cameras is important because an objective standard is attained in the matter of detail and comparisons can be made with what the man-in-the-street has to say about the sightings. The conclusion to be drawn from this confrontation is important to UFOlogical research in a general sense. The man-in-the-street reports *fairly accurately what he sees,* and of course this strengthens, by analogy, the credibility of other reports—however absurd they may sometimes seem.

Concerning the object which held hundreds spellbound—Ion Hobana watched it for two hours and sketched it, as did his friend the painter Radu Duldurescu—we take three characteristic reports: one from an engineer from Sinaia, one from a working man in the district of Ploieşti and one from a Bucharest engineer who showed why, according to him, the object was a balloon.

First the account of the sighting as it appeared in 11th September 1969 edition of *Scînteia,* the most important daily newspaper in the capital and provinces.

YESTERDAY IN THE SKY OVER THE CITY

Yesterday the editor's phone rang ceaselessly as hundreds of people wanted to draw our attention to an atmospheric phenomenon. Above the city there was a UFO which was to be the main topic of everybody's conversation. We were told that the same object on 9th and 10th September had been seen over Ploieşti and now it stayed the whole day over our capital. In shape it was a tetragon and appeared to be made of some plastic material. It reflected the sunlight and could change its shape, the latter fact giving rise to discussions about pressure inside the object itself. If pressure inside had balanced the outer then it should not have altered in shape. During the course of the day it varied its position in the direction of the plane of its axis. People estimate its height to have been 20,000 m. Yesterday's sightings are being studied and we shall refer again to the matter.

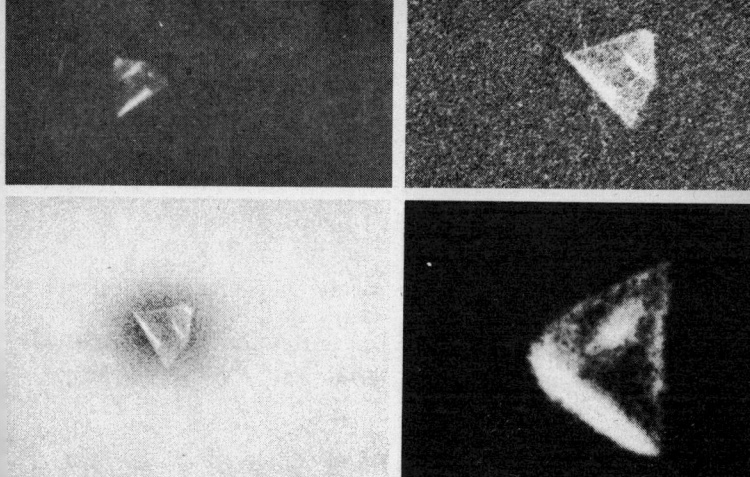

UFO photographed from the roof of the *Scînteia* newspaper; without filter; with yellow filter; with red filter. 10.9.69 at Bucharest. Compare (4th photo) Madrid, 1968.

10th September, Sinaia *The UFO Index:* 10th September 1969, Sinaia; visible: ±06:50–±08:30; colour: brilliant white; height: (from the height of the mountains) 2500–3000 metres; size: breakfast plate; movement: slowly southwards—stationary at 01:30. Other details: change of shape several times; no radio interference or disturbance on telephone or electrical systems. The meteorological observatory (height 1500 m) confirmed that the UFO could not possibly be a balloon. UFO seen by hundreds of witnesses.

The UFO was seen at the same time but from a different angle at Braşov, witnesses saying that it was over Piatra Mareberg around 07:00. One friend, a pilot, thinks it was a balloon launched from Ghimbav but he tried without success to reach it in his aeroplane. I note that on 15th September 1968 an identical UFO was seen. Engineer Emil Bellu.

10th September 1969, Mija (Ploieşti) An object was seen on this date by dozens of people on a train on

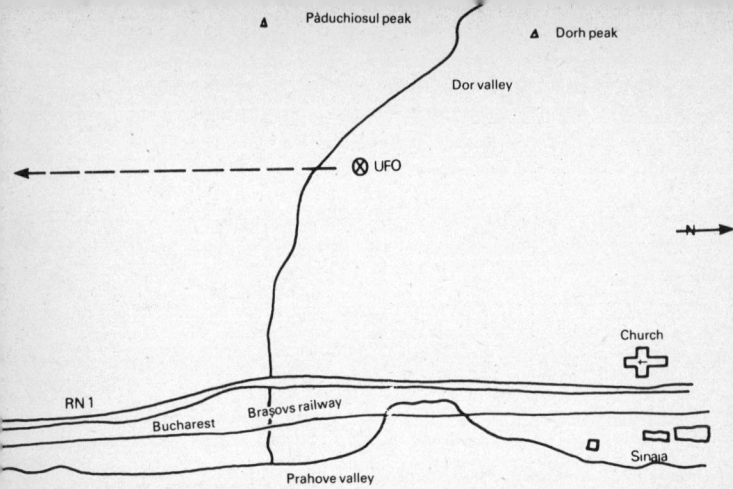

the Tîrgoviște–Rîmnicu–Sărat line at and from 07:30 on for a quarter of an hour. It was actually on the Mija–Ploiești section of the line and during the stop at Mija one of the witnesses described the object thus: 45 degrees over the horizon there was a UFO which was not emitting light but was quite visible in the clear sky. It took on various shapes: triangular, oval, square and an elongated beam form. It seemed to be gliding towards the earth without making a sound and very gently. The object when changing shape had an outline of about 25 cm., the mass remaining constant. Distance between the thing and the train I estimate at 30 km. (Trufanda Cornel)

10th September 1969, Bucharest 1. False shadows. On a clear day around 14:00 the balloon seen with naked eye revealed changing aspects; sometimes it seemed as if it was lit up on the side away from the sun. Seeing the object through binoculars I noticed that the innermost section appeared to reflect its light to the opposite side; I was able to see this reflection because the walls were transparent. People who thought the object was dull and like aluminium were wrong—they saw false shadows.
2. Changing shapes. Apart from the strongly alternating light reflection, apparently caused by the shape of the object itself, there is also the fact that

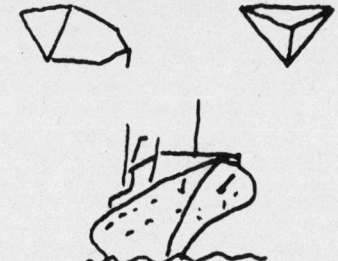

it turned very slowly. I kept on looking at the object through the binoculars, with short rests, and noticed that it moved forward but was especially amazed by its changing shapes which followed one after the other. Even now I am not sure that I can reproduce the exact forms—but see the several sketches concerned. I am familiar with the subjective "transformations" which sightings with the naked eye can "effect." Seen thus the side of the object was without any reflection—in fact it was almost invisible and the sensation of changing shape was therefore very much to the fore. The only explanation I can find for these changes is that the object, being very large, heated itself in various places and in different manners and thus brought about the transformations.

3. Typical UFO traits. The third sketch at once put me in mind of the photo taken in Madrid on 5th September 1968 at 19:00. There were the same spots—which I now interpret as the same reflections—and the identical triangular shape. The first drawing made me think of a disc with a separate light centre. The whole thing was due to inside light affecting external reflections. I now begin to understand the Sofia event of 21st November 1967 when the object had taken on different forms and radiated likewise.

Conclusions: It is understandable that many topical sightings of balloons appear to be observations of UFO's. Although some balloon shapes seemed to me at first to be inexplicable they now appear clearer and more understandable. Sighting lasted seven hours in clear sky.

During the sighting I questioned a number of people who assured me that the object sometimes stood still and sometimes moved fast. When I pointed out that it moved with a fixed speed I was not believed until I made the people follow the balloon with the aid of a fixed point. I have never understood witnesses who merely *judge* distances, heights, size, speeds, etc. In this case, however, I asked everyone for estimations of height, which was put between 500 and 2000 metres, the diameter between 0.5 and 5 metres. With the aid of the scanty equipment at my disposal I was able to *measure* the altitude of the object, which was at least 15 kilometres; and its diameter was 50 metres. It moved with a velocity of at least 25 km per hour. The candle-power diminished around 18:40. (Ing. Bogdan Paşa)

135. 18th SEPTEMBER 1969, SIBIU 4–5 km above the town a round, illuminated object the size of a tennis-ball was spotted for 40 minutes. A very typical feature is the regularly changing colour of the object—white to greenish-white and then yellowish-white to light-orange. A shower of sparks were emitted to the left of the object, after which it carried out an odd trajectory (see drawing page 265). It was a wavy movement both up and down; and all in a space of 400–500 metres. The sky was clear and calm, the temperature between 3° and 6°C and there was no wind. The sighting was in the Subarini park where it was completely dark. Three journalists witnessed it and the top of a fir-tree was taken as a fixed point. (Ghimpu Aurel)

136. 11th MARCH 1970, CLUJ My 13-year-old son Eugen woke me up on 11th March 1970 at 20:40 to watch a glittering object in the sky. It was egg-shaped, yellowish-orange and many times larger than any star. The colour and the light-intensity,

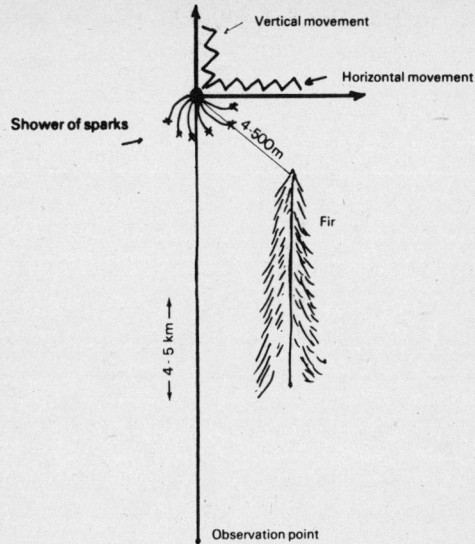

The shower of sparks emitted on the left took place when the object stood still.

too, were quite different from those of any celestial body known to me. The object fell three times very fast, only to go up again and in doing so reach a position a metre higher than its previous one. After this it stayed motionless. When the object was plunging down it shone more and the "egg" tilted into a vertical position and stayed there. The whole spectacle took about 15 minutes and from my house it seemed as if the object was over the Mănăstur district. The next day around 07:40 I noticed a sort of halo east of the town, smaller than the one on the previous evening. (Lar Maria, typist)

137. 19th APRIL 1970, TÎRGU-MUREŞ When I was watching the actions of four gliders I noticed a black object with an oval shape in the overcast sky and at a height of between 1,500 and 2,000 metres. It was visible for two minutes, at 12:30, and flew at a constant velocity quite soundlessly. (Borbath Csaba)

138. 2nd MAY 1970, CIBIN MOUNTAINS A 40-year-old engineer saw at 01:30 (in a clear, slightly frosty night sky) a "something" which he thought was a "falling star." Suddenly the "star" slowed its falling motion and went gradually down to just above the horizon. The "star" now seemed to be quite obviously a very large, luminous sphere which ascended again after a period of standing still. The object now grew so small (because of increasing distance or diminishing volume?) that he finally lost sight of it, but after two minutes it reappeared, drifted down, changed from "star" to luminous sphere, remained motionless 20–30 seconds, rose and vanished once more. Then it came back and went through the same cycle until 02:00. The sphere seemed to be biggest when it was motionless for the 20–30 seconds over the horizon regardless of whether it appeared to be nearer the observer or farther away. (Nicole Ionete)

This type of sighting often occurs in UFO literature and is also of the same order as the one at Colibița, on 4th January 1969 (page 168, photo page 171) and at Bucharest, on 7th October 1968 (page 253).

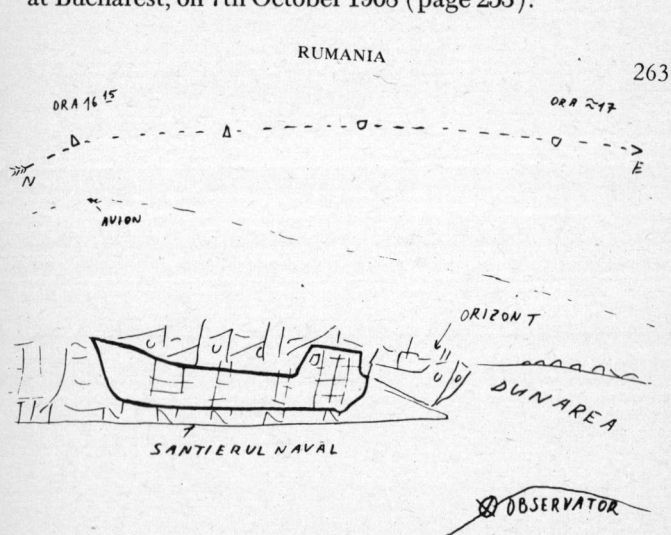

Route taken by a UFO over Galati.

139. 21st JUNE 1970, GALAȚI A merchant-navy officer reported the following:
Age: 41; Eyesight: normal.
Sighting with naked eye and with binoculars.
Weather: 80% clear sky. Light wind.
The UFO appeared ±25 km over the river Prut (see drawing).

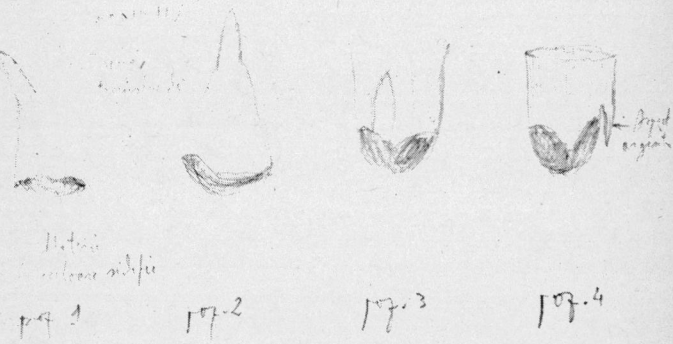

Sketch of a UFO by Nicolae Ionescu.

It was then 2 cm in size and moved with the speed of a jet which was then flying between the observer and the UFO. The shape was triangular, changeable (see drawing page 263); silverish but darker on the underside. Material looked like a plasma—if not, then a plastic. UFO appeared from 16:00 to 20:00. (Nicolae Ionescu)

140. 21st JUNE 1970, TULCEA Various people living here saw at 17:00 an irregularly shaped object of glittering silver in the clear sky which had a few scattered clouds. The thing seemed to be transparent and at first, in relation to the clouds, motionless, but after several minutes it went slowly southwards. Its apparent size was 15 cm and it must have been about 30 km in altitude. Inhabitants of the village of Telița (30 km from Tulcea) reported the same object at the same time and also moving south.

Diameter about 30 metres. The object turned a reddish orange when the evening came and it vanished about 20:30. (Moiseev Isac, teacher)

141. 28th JUNE 1970, CLUJ Witness awakened by his mother about 02:00 because there was a vividly shining UFO flying in an arc over the house, which was bathed in bright light. (Nemeș William)

142. 29th JUNE 1970, MUREȘENII BÎRGĂULUI See page 157.

143. 11th JULY 1970, BUCHAREST At a quarter past midnight I noticed an object the size of a star 45 degrees over the horizon flying perfectly horizontally from north to south with the speed of an artificial satellite. After ten seconds the light gets bigger, changes from white to orange and increases speed. After five seconds there is a short, abrupt pause till the light falls at an angle of 135 degrees in relation to the original flight. The light seems to become a sphere after another five seconds, with a tail 1 m long and a diameter of 20 cm. The sphere turned around and vanished behind houses five seconds later so that I could not follow the final phase. (see sketch) (Nicolae Ionescu)

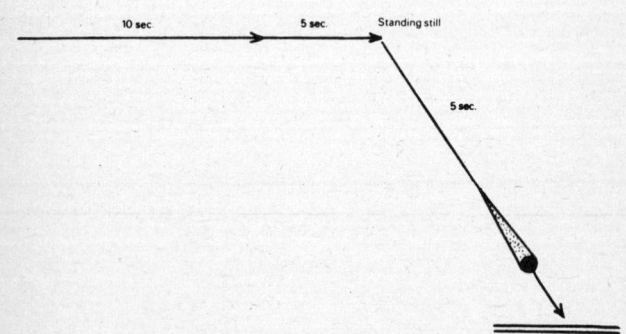

144. JULY-AUGUST 1970, BRĂILA For several nights in succession a bright, star-like object was

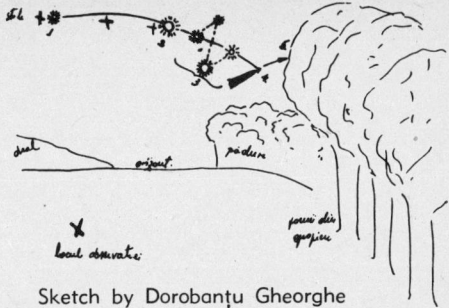

Sketch by Dorobanţu Gheorghe

seen in the sky around 21:20 in the north-east. It vanished at 21:45 in the south-east after passing right overhead. One night this routine was broken when a small shining object like a meteorite came up in the east 50 degrees above the horizon just before 21:45, flying with the "satellite's" speed in an orbit seeming to make a meeting with it unavoidable; and in fact the two objects crossed each other's paths but afterwards the smaller one never appeared again—it seemed to have been swallowed up by the other. (Niţă Caraman)

145. JULY–AUGUST 1970, BUCHAREST In July or August 1970 I saw at about 21:40 a moving object sharply outlined against the sky. I took it to be an artificial satellite with which I was familiar, having often seen them. Soon, however, I noticed the object behaving in an odd way: its speed reduced to that of an aircraft roughly and its surface turned blue. I watched it until it disappeared behind trees. After the object had slackened speed and gone blue it suddenly stood still, during which period it turned white and became bigger. After 30 seconds without moving it went on its way again with the original velocity. It carried out a few lively and odd movements and then started to change shape regularly. This I explained to myself as being due to the zig-zagging flight it made. After these manoeuvres— and the closer they were the farther away they seemed to take the object—it stood still again, I think, although it is possible that it had gone very

far away. In any case it finally vanished in the distance. I thought the sighting had finished but there was a dazzling light where the object had been, as if from a rocket. I saw it disappear behind some trees (Dorobanţu Gheorghe)

146. **17th NOVEMBER 1970, BUCHAREST** Dear Mr. Hobana, I am aware that you are interested in all sorts of atmospheric phenomena as yet unexplained. On Wednesday around 17:17 I saw a strange cloud in the sky. At first I thought it was an optical illusion but I discussed the matter with a technical colleague who was with me and thus also saw it. There was a clearly marked "cloud" in the sky about 40 cm long and 2 cm in height (taking these dimensions as from a ruler). The object was motionless and in the position shown on my sketch. However it slowly took up a horizontal position, stayed there three or four seconds and then suddenly disappeared as if somebody had taken a sponge to wipe out a large chalk mark.

If I must give some estimate of height then I would say it was somewhat lower than the altitude at which supersonic aircraft tend to fly. Its position was S. W. Whilst the object was varying its position it left no white smoke trails as high-flying aircraft do. It was just a large chalk line in the sky— that is all. I have always wanted to see a flying saucer as such, but do not know if what I saw was the realization of my wish. Ant. Belcic

147. 14th DECEMBER 1970, BUCHAREST In the night of 13th–14th December and at exactly 01:30 my wife and I were both awakened at the same time by a vividly red sky. My wife ran anxiously to the adjacent room facing the street where her mother was sleeping and meanwhile I hurriedly opened the french windows. The source of the light was on my right but invisible because of the walls of a building. I "heard" a pulsating sound (it seemed as if it was humming *inside* my ear) and noted that the red light grew white in the direction where I assumed the source of it to be. My wife and her mother suddenly called out that I must go at once and when I reached their room everything was intensely white. This light suddenly went out even before I had joined them at the window. We were on the first floor and outside on my left there was a car standing in the centre of a small square, towards which and from our direction a policeman was running. When he was within a few yards of the car it started up suddenly. My wife and her mother told me that just before I had arrived on the scene they saw a throbbing, bright whitish-blue sphere hanging right over the car but it suddenly disappeared. It was only then that they noticed the stationary car. The temperature was very mild and the sky cloudy. For the time of year it was a particularly pleasant night. Duration of the whole sighting was about eight to ten seconds. (see sketch, below) (Julien Weverbergh)

148. 5th JANUARY 1971, SUCEAVA Engineer Trofim noticed over Suceava at 20:45 a zigzagging "star" the size of Mars and crimson. It disappeared suddenly.

149. 30th JANUARY 1971, PREDEAL A light larger than a star went across the sky. After a few minutes it stood still and began to carry out some move-

ments which suggested it was springing around a central point inside. Meanwhile the light grew less and vanished after ten minutes. Did it go away? There was no noise at all. (Tiron Nicolae, precision instrument-maker; sketch below).

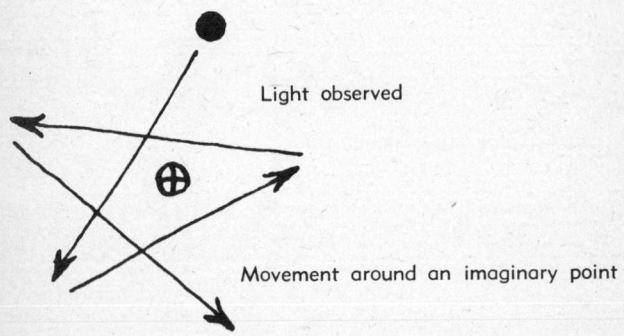

150. 15th FEBRUARY 1971, SUCEAVA At about 18:40 I was in the street on my way to a friend's house when some small children began to call out that there was something strange in the sky. There I saw a red disc the size of Venus slowly and horizontally moving from south to north across the sky, which was quite clear. The object went behind a block of flats but did not re-appear on the other side. When I reached my friend's house his wife told me all about the event I had witnessed before I said anything to her about it myself. (Engineer Trofim)

151. 18th APRIL 1971, BRAŞOV This sighting took place from the balcony of a flat, the observers being an engineer and his mother. Time of sighting: between 01:10 and 01:35. Cloudless, bright conditions. The object appeared from behind the Tîmpa hill, close to the signal-station. It consisted of a reddish-orange, pulsating body with a point in the middle, above which there was a whitish-blue, crescent-shaped light steadily gleaming and "somehow"

linked with the central body. The object at its maximum was twice the size of Venus and stayed the whole time in the same place, throbbing all the time. There were three changes of shape and the object vanished just when I had gone inside to get a glass of water; thus I did not see how it disappeared. (Dan Lucian Picu)

1. The body getting smaller
2. Growing longer, but the dark point staying the same
3. The central body is becoming larger, the point presumably smaller.

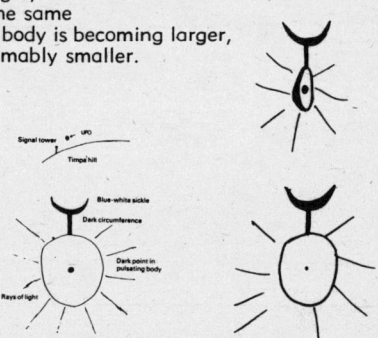

152. 12th JUNE 1971, BUŞTENI   See page 170.

153. 27th JULY 1971, CLUJ   Florea Iulia, aged 63, got up about 02:05 in the night of 26th–27th July 1971 to go to the room where her two little nephews were. She noticed that the room was brightly lit up which was not usual. On going to the window she saw a bright ball hanging in the air motionless. As this was something quite extraordinary she stayed looking at it for ten minutes, after which she went to fetch some field-glasses. Through these she could see its diameter (apparent) was 25 cm. The strangest thing about the object was that it had two rows of "little windows" which were emitting a bluish light. The object slowly went westwards after about an hour. The sky was overcast, so there were no stars. Florin Gheorghiţă, a Rumanian engineer and UFOlogist, rightly

pointed out here that the object must have been fairly low over the ground. According to him the old lady in question lives remote from reality, never reads the newspapers and had never heard anything about UFO's.

154. 1st AUGUST 1971, MANGALIA At 18:00 and in fine weather the witness saw a "star" the size of a child's head. It was still daylight and the sighting lasted several minutes. The "star" switched on and off three times, after which it disappeared from view for good. (P. Stoianovici)

155. 5th AUGUST 1971, CLUJ The Prisăcaru family from Cluj is extremely busy studying the astral constellations and related matters. On 5th August 1971 a "small star" appeared very quickly from the north and stayed motionless over the town for five seconds, after which it went off at great speed in a south-easterly direction. The same object was seen on 7th August but at 20:35.

156. END OF AUGUST, BEGINNING OF SEPTEMBER 1971, BUCHAREST Witness Agachi Faur and his girl-friend Monica Constantin sent in the following report:
Date: end of August, beginning of September.
Weather: partially overcast and rather cold.
The object appeared in the south-east, fairly high (70 degrees) over the horizon, above a block of flats and below a cloud-cover which was lying at 3000–4000 metres.
Size: a quarter to one-sixth the apparent diameter of the moon—this is twice as large as the biggest star.
Shape: spherical, illuminated and twinkling, leaving a tail of sparks as long as its diameter. Strong radiation.
Colour: almost white, the tail yellowish-red.
No noise.
Progress: the object moved horizontally for six or

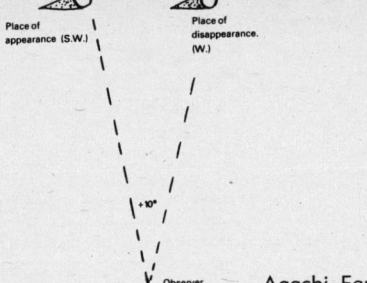

Agachi Faur's two UFO's.

seven seconds at a constant velocity and vanished suddenly. After five seconds an identical object appeared in the same place, traversed a like distance and behaved in the same way as the other had. The disappearance of both was sudden. (See sketch above).

Notes: I had the impression before seeing the first object that a flash of light had attracted my attention to the place of the sighting. The objects were lower than the clouds—clearly visible against the latter, in fact.

157. SEPTEMBER 1971, PAUŞEŞTI-MAGLAŞI A very large disc-shaped object remains quite still for two successive days from 12:30 to 14:05 over the horizon at an angle of 45 degrees. Disappears very fast. Various witnesses.

158. 4th NOVEMBER 1971, BUCHAREST A shining object remains completely motionless over the city from 15:45 to 15:48. Disappears soundlessly and at lightning speed.

159. 31st JULY 1972, TURNU SEVERIN A radiant object larger than Venus traverses a 90 degree arc of sky in six seconds at 21:45. Chief witness Professor Mucioniuilie. Unexplained phenomenon.

160. 20th SEPTEMBER 1972, BÂILE HERCULANE At 5 o'clock a radiant object seen for 38 seconds, moving very fast or remaining motionless. In the latter

stage it changed its shape and was five to six times larger than a star of the first magnitude. It was round at first, then became oval. Observer: geophysicist Adrian Nicolescu.

161. 28th SEPTEMBER 1972, VALEA PLOPULUI, POSEŞTI 69-year-old night watchman Vasile Carabuş saw an object he could not explain, just after midnight during 27th–28th September 1972, which seemed to travel straight over the fields in a clear sky until it suddenly fell down. Strange marks were found on the presumed landing area on 28th September.
Locality and site: southern slope of the 520-metre-high Odaia hill at Valea Plopului. This is a village which administratively comes under the parish of Poseşti, in the province of Prahova. This is in a relatively lightly populated part of the lower Carpathians. The geological

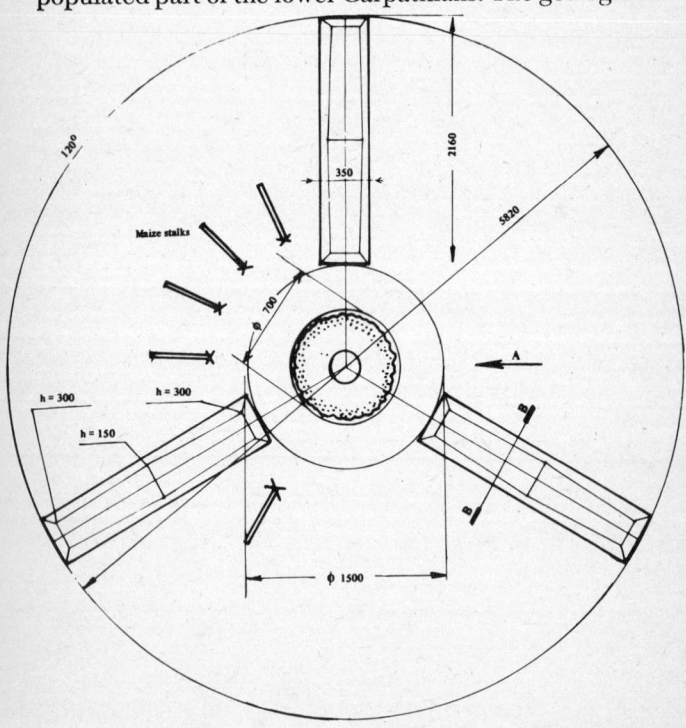

N
trajectory of the light-emitting object
2km
Vasile Carabus

ϕ 140
2160
ϕ 700
Cross-section A
350
25⁰
h
Cross-section B

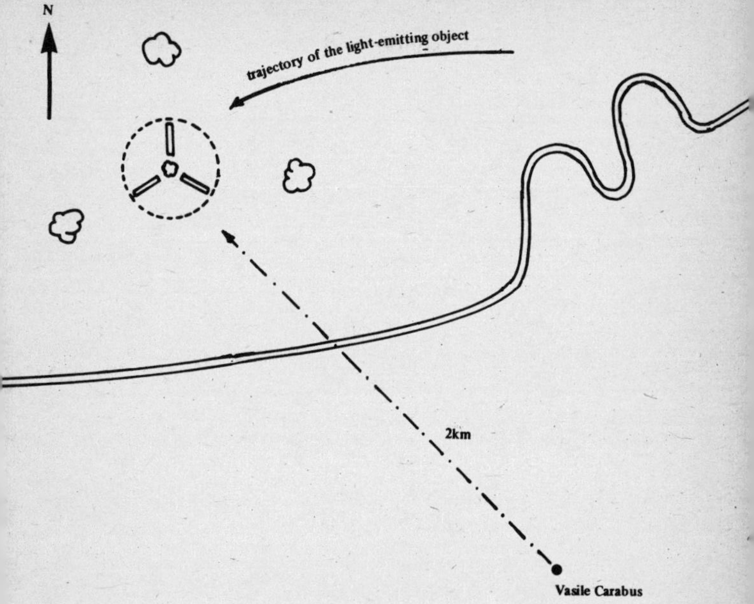

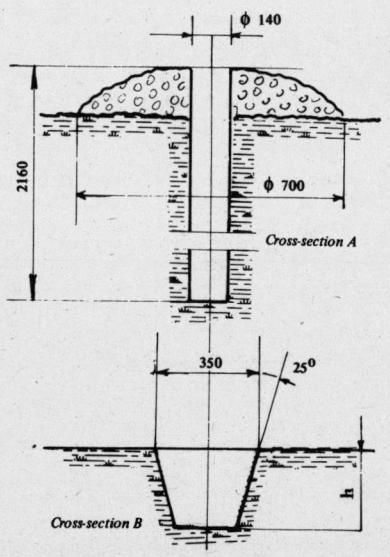

structure of the subsoil is fairly complex; very many faults and there is earthquake activity in the region. The surface of the site is simple: on the rock of the lower Carpathians there is a stratum of clay 1 to 2 metres thick and on the top a layer of workable soil 40 to 50 cm in thickness. Very rich in nitrates. Maize is cultivated in the area.

Stages of the investigation: After a number of local dignitaries—including a school-teacher—had reported the strange marks to Ion Hobana the latter submitted it to the UFO group. Professor Călin Turcu went to the site for the first time in the middle of November 1972 and an investigation was made on 3rd December by twelve members of the UFO circle.

The marks were measured and photographed, the topography studied, villagers questioned and about 20 samples of soil and vegetation taken to Bucharest for laboratory analysis.

The marks: A. The following were immediately visible (see sketch).

1. Circle of section 5.82 m indicated on the ground by irregular clay traces.

2. Exactly in the middle of the circle was a cylindrical hole of depth 2.60 m and 14 cm breadth. Walls of the hole were smooth and very firm.

3. Heaps of soil were found around the edge of the hole (a mixture of clay and friable soil) with a diameter of 70 cm. Smaller amounts of clay were to be seen here and there within the circle.

4. Three imprints together comprising a 120 degree section of the circle were found at regular intervals around the centre. See sketch for the distances, measurements and cross-sections of these. The cultivated soil around was very compactly pressed together.

5. Stems of maize (sweet corn) in the area were found partly broken or bent over about 1 metre from the ground.

6. The imprints were horizontally placed on the slope. In other words the "object which landed" had scraped a platform into the slope, so it must have been very heavy.

B. Additional facts ascertained possibly connected to the presumed landing:

1. The maize nearest the site was riper than elsewhere.
2. The grass which grew within the landing-site was "scorched."
3. The biological rhythm of nearby moles was upset; they had already begun to hibernate but now showed activity again.

C. Results of the laboratory research:

1. The samples of soil from the "landing zone" showed increased radio-activity (5 milli-roentgens).
2. The above-mentioned compactness of the soil (from the imprints) was confirmed.

D. Additional facts and conclusions:

1. Nothing special noted about the three apple-trees which were at a distance of, respectively, 5 m, 5m and 7 m. Negative results in laboratory. If there was a landing then both this and the take-off must have been vertical. Great skill in landing and avoiding the apple-trees is hypothetical however, and could conflict with the evidence given by the night-watchman.
2. The maize was not pressed flat but bent over one metre up the stem, which means that the object which landed (if there was one) had come down on a pad about the same distance above the ground.

162. 24th DECEMBER 1972, LABRADOR The whole crew of the Rumanian ship *Moldoveanu* witnessed the following phenomenon 60 degrees north and 62 degrees west: a radiant object came over the sea towards the ship very fast. When right over the vessel it slowed and changed shape repeatedly. There was a change in colour (from red to yellow, then bluish-white) each time it changed shape (from circular to longish oval). After one hour (the sighting lasted from 03:00 to 04:00 in the morning) the object shot up high and disappeared, gradually getting smaller: (logbook)

FLYING SAUCERS (LETAIUSHKIE TARELKI) IN THE SOVIET UNION

1. 15 AUGUST 1663 ROBOZERO   See pages 54–61.

2. 1842, ORENBURG   Small metal objects, perfectly hexagonal, fall out of the sky after a "strange cloud" is seen hanging over the town for a considerable time.

3. 30th JULY 1880, ST. PETERSBURG (LENINGRAD)   A large spherical light accompanied by two smaller stars or spheres, follow the course of a ravine for three minutes, after which they suddenly vanish. (Fort, *Le Livre des damnés*, page 234)

4. 4 MAY 1910, CIRNOVŢI   Dr. I. Plemely, a professor of mathematics living at the above town, saw a strange sight. On the evening of 4th May he noticed a shining celestial body approaching from the south and with increasing speed. The object climbed 40 degrees and after slackening speed went north-northwest, disappearing in a cloud at a height of 20 degrees. It was an astral type of body and shone for three minutes. Professor van Hepperger of Vienna calculated the parabolic details based on the three positions the observer drew and came to the conclusion that it might have had a diameter of 100 metres.

Victor Anestin, chief editor of the science magazine *Orion* in which this report appeared, stressed the fact that the object could not have been a bolide (meteor) because the speed, deceleration, change of direction, falling through an angle of 45 to 20 degrees, the disappearance and ascent, etc.—all these are quite different in fire-balls. Possibly Plemely saw a genuine UFO. (Our own archives)

5. AUTUMN 1938 (OR 1939) JUMINDA (ESTHONIA) An object 1 metre long and greenish-brown in colour was followed by two observers until it suddenly disappeared. (Vallée, *Passport to Magonia*, page 189)

6. SEPTEMBER 1943, PUSHKINO This sighting was made by Spanish volunteers fighting alongside the Germans in Russia—they were in the Azul division. The reporter is Oscar Rey Brea, at the moment attached to La Coruna radio-testing team. Witnesses were, among others, Jesus Arias (Asturia), Paz (Gallicia), Tomas Carbonell (Alicante). They were all in a bunker during a battle between the German and Russian Air Forces when they saw a disc-shaped object above the warring planes ("as if watching the battle" as one witness put it). Then it disappeared at a fantastic rate. (Antonio Ribera, *Platillos volantes en Iberoamerica Y Espana*, Ed. Pomaire, 1968, pages 411–12)

7. MAY 1946, NOT DETERMINED. Zigel (see page 39) places the beginning of the "modern" period of UFOlogy in Russia in May 1946: saucer-shaped objects were seen by Soviet citizens and Soviet pilots. The features reported are the same as the typical ones described today.

8. DECEMBER 1948, MOSCOW Above Moscow longish, fish-shaped metal objects were seen, reflecting the sunlight. (Vallée, *Anatomy of a Phenomenon*, page 54)

9. JULY 1949, NORTH-WEST RUSSIA A wave—see page 40.

10. SPRING 1953, MOSCOW UFO's over Moscow. Reports of angels' hair falling. (*Clypeus*, December 1967)

11. 27th NOVEMBER 1954, MOSCOW Between 16:15 and 16:30 people on Red Square saw a cylindrical object over their heads at a height of about 200–300 metres travelling in a north-westerly direction. The object climbed up with the speed of a jet, at the same time taking up a vertical position. (Vallée, *Les Phénomenès insolites de l'espace*, page 82)

12. 14th FEBRUARY 1955, MOSCOW An A.P. report:
> Not long ago a number of people saw from various parts of Moscow a cigar-shaped object at a great height which vanished after remaining still in the sky for some time. (Our own archives)

13. FEBRUARY 1955, SHLOBINE, BYELORUSSIA People working at the Gomel and Shlobine meteorological centre report seeing coloured strips in the sky. The *Sovietskaia Byelorussia* of 16th February 1955 is of the opinion that it is caused by sunlight being reflected in ice crystals. (See also: V. Mézentsev, *Phénomènes étranges dans l'atmosphère et sur la Terre*, Moscow, 1955)

14. 1956, NORTH POLE The well-known Soviet pilot Valentin Akkusatov, chief navigator for the Soviet air base at the North Pole, tells us about one of his confrontations with a UFO:
> We were reconnoitring over a strategic ice-area near Greenland when we came out of the clouds into a clear zone where we suddenly saw to our left an unknown object flying parallel to us. It seemed like a large, pear-shaped construction, or a lens with pulsating ends. Thinking we saw an unknown American aircraft we popped back into the clouds to avoid a meeting. After a further 40 minutes of

flying the clouds stopped again and to port we saw the same strange thing once more. It had no wings, antennae or windows and neither was there any trace of smoke. We decided to have a close look at the object so altered course accordingly. But while we were doing this the object also altered its course and remained the same distance from our machine. After about 15 minutes the mysterious thing shot up higher and vanished. It travelled with a speed which to us seems impossible. (*Psychic Discoveries behind the Iron Curtain*)

15. 25th JULY 1957. PACIFIC OCEAN COAST   See page 41.

16. 19th MARCH 1958, MOSCOW   Near the city a large, saucer-shaped object was seen on the ground. After a spiral ascent it flew off and disappeared. (Vallée, *Passport to Magonia*, page 270)

17. 30th MAY 1958, KAZAKSTAN   See page 40.

18. SPRING 1958, MOSCOW   A disc-shaped object falls spirally from an estimated height of 3000 metres. (*Ogoniok*, March 1958)

19. THE LATER 50's, UZBEKISTAN   See page 41.

20. 17th NOVEMBER 1958, EXACT SITE UNKNOWN   A bright object with a diameter bigger than the moon's seen descending from a great height. At first it seemed to be hanging about tree-top height before landing on the ground. (ATIC unpublished. Vallée, *Passport to Magonia*, page 273)

21. SPRING 1959, SVERDLOVSK   The headquarters of the Russian rocket base was visited for a period of 24 hours by saucer-shaped UFO's which often remained stationary over the launching-pads. They were picked up on radar and a certain amount of panic was supposed to have been caused. (*Flying Saucer Review*, May 1967)

22. AUGUST 1959, GEORGIA In the vicinity of an unnamed village in Georgia a UFO was said to have exploded, the event being witnessed by a 43-year-old farm labourer Vasily Dubischev. There were no remains apart from one ... dead monster (!) A certain Dr. Fyodor Petrov was said to have claimed it was not made of carbon but of silicon. (Robert Charroux, *Le Livre des mondes oubliés*, Paris, 1971, pages 449–450)

23. AUGUST 1959, MOSCOW The radar system at the Vnukovo–Moscow civil airport records three saucer-shaped objects near the town at about 800 m. The Air Force sends up planes after them but they are unable to make contact. Officially it is said that atmospheric disturbances are the cause of the optical illusions. (*UFO News*, August 1959)

24. 16th AUGUST 1960, KAZAKSTAN An eight-man geophysics expedition from Leningrad camped in the Kazakstan Mountains. At 23:00 on the above date a brilliant orange, lens-shaped object suddenly rose over the mountains with a diameter 50% greater than that of the moon, according to the mineralogist leader of the expedition, Dr. Nikolai Sotchevanov. The object flew south, zigzagged to the north-east, and disappeared behind the mountains after curving round. The extremities of the object were not so radiant as the centre. (*Psychic Discoveries behind the Iron Curtain*)

25. SUMMER 1960, TASHKENT A physics professor at Moscow University saw an object over the motor-way, about 28 km from Tashkent, like a large star. He sighted it between 21:00 and 22:00 flying in the north-east. It turned towards the earth emanating wavy light suggesting the "movements of a water-scorpion." The next day the witness was told that many people living in Tashkent had seen the same thing. (*Psychic Discoveries behind the Iron Curtain*)

26. SUMMER 1960, CRIMEA The same witness as in 25, this time accompanied by two art-historians and

their students, saw a UFO consisting of five separate parts. "We saw them carrying out a kind of manoeuvre in the zenith which looked like a fire-fly dancing."

27. 1961, NORTHERN RUSSIA A UFO photo taken in the north of the country attracts a great deal of attention. (*Pravda*, 8th January 1961)

28. 1961, IRKUTSK A rocket-like object on four legs was seen on the ground, together with two UFO-nauts. A doctor in a nearby laboratory was said to have taken a photo. (*Flying Saucer Review*, May 1967)

29. 1961, TOBELAK (SIBERIA) A small transport aircraft carrying four passengers and luggage vanished over central Russia. Two days later it was found intact near Tobelak (Siberia) but it seemed to have enough fuel for another two hours' flight. There was no trace of the crew and passengers but 100 metres away there was a round patch of burnt grass and disturbed soil. (*Flying Saucer Review*, May 1967)

30. 24th SEPTEMBER 1962, CENTRAL ASIA-MOSCOW Both passengers and pilots of a TU 104 which landed at Moscow from central Asia on 24th September said they had seen disc-like objects circling round their plane and then disappearing at a greater speed than their own. (*Phénomènes Spatiaux*, December 1966)

31. ±1962, HARKOV Garbaryuk noticed several odd objects in the sky. Two unequally sized balls of green and pink, flying together at high speed. A couple of years later I saw one ball of a pink shade in the Lvov district. (Our own archives)

32. 18th JUNE 1963, ASTRONAUT Astronaut Valeri Bykovsky thought he saw at some distance from his capsule an object like that seen by Valentina Terechkova but he said afterwards that it was oval. For quite a long time it followed Bykovsky's capsule and then suddenly changed direction. (*Clypeus*)

33. AUGUST 1964, HARKOV Around midnight in August 1964 one day I saw a cylindrical object flying over the village of Borovenki in the district of Lugansk at a height of ±1,000 metres. It was three times the size of an ordinary aircraft and was flying north, at first parallel with the ground but later suddenly changed direction and shot up at an angle of 60 degrees. The object was yellow and made a noise suggesting a bombardment. There was a tail of flames and the object travelled, I think, at about the speed of a jet-plane. (Mihai Oleinik in the daily *Znania ta Pratnia*)

34. 12th JULY 1964, LENINGRAD–MOSCOW A group of people on the way to Moscow from Leningrad by TU 104 saw a large bright metal disc gliding under their aircraft. A well-known UFOlogist was on board, Dr. Vyacheslav Zaitsev, who declared that the disc had a dome in its central part which looked like a cabin. (*Psychic Discoveries behind the Iron Curtain*)

35. 12th OCTOBER 1964, ASTRONAUT The crew of Voskhod 1 saw an unidentified cylindrical object like the one McDivitt reported. See also page 42.

36. 1965, CAUCASUS Dr. Ludmila Tsehanovich, geodetical astronomer, saw a glittering disc with a dome in the form of a cabin. (*Psychic Discoveries behind the Iron Curtain*)

37. 18th MARCH 1965, ASTRONAUT The crew of Voskhod 2 saw a cylindrical object. See also 42; and page 42.

38. 26th JULY 1965, LATVIA On this date at 21:35 the astronomer R. Vitolniek and two of his colleagues at the Ogre Observatory in Latvia were studying the nocturnal clouds when they saw a star-like object drifting slowly westwards. Through binoculars the light seemed to have a sharp triangular definition but through the telescope it appeared to be a combination

of four smaller objects consisting of a central sphere, two diameters of which further away were three more, similar spheres drifting slowly around the one in the middle. They went gradually through the sky, steadily getting smaller or receding from the earth. After about 20 minutes the astronomers noticed that the three external spheres went away from the central one and the whole group became invisible around 22:00 because they were so far away. They had the dull-green colour of a ruby, and were about 5 km up at an angle of 60 degrees over the north-western horizon. At first they were taken for an artificial satellite or a rocket, but in either case the speed should have been greater and furthermore the object was not one but three. Witnesses: Robert Vitolniek, scientific researcher at the astrophysics laboratory of the USSR Academy of Science; Ian Melderis and Esmeralda Vitolniek, members of the Latvia astronomical society. (*Hearing Report*)

39. 24th SEPTEMBER 1965, NOVÎI ATOS (ABHAZIA) Astronomer-geologist L. Tshehanovici saw a small disc darting over the New Athos monastery and executing unusual manoeuvres. The monastery is high in the mountains in the middle of a number of gorges. The disc's movements—often spiral—were very complicated. (*Sputnik*, December 1967)

40. APRIL 1966, ODESSA Air Force major Baidukov observed in his flight over Odessa an unidentified object which he picked up on his radar. Numerous ground-based radar installations recorded the same—an object which initially flew at a very great height. In 45 minutes the object covered a 31 to 11 miles descending flight over the earth. (*Psychic Discoveries behind the Iron Curtain*)

41. 24th APRIL 1966, TASHKENT A great deal of the UFOlogist's time is spent in trying very enthusiastically to think up new theories explaining the UFO problem instead of in busying himself with the most important work of accurately noting down evi-

dence given by witnesses and checking what they say. These UFOlogists try to prove that UFO's have something to do with earthquakes and fault-lines. On their list they include the earthquake which ravaged Tashkent in the early morning of 24th April 1966, during which there was a blinding flash of light and a sinister roar. At the same time there was even talk of an object seen by hundreds of thousands of people after most of the villages had been reduced to rubble, above which radiant spheres were seen. These were described by some as Christmas lights or balloons emitting rays.

42. 17th JUNE 1966, ELISTA (NORTHERN CAUCASUS) The geophysicist Vi Krilov and colleagues noted what had been described above, in number 38. The object executed similar manoeuvres. (*Aurora*, Information bulletin of the USSR in Rumania, March 1968)

43. 7th AUGUST 1966, MOSCOW A ball-like, brilliant object seen near Moscow during the evening by the inhabitants of Koutchina village. Evidence collected by the newspaper *Leninskaia Znamia*. The object had dimensions like an electric lamp, followed a straight course and apparently was smashed up on the horizon. This produced a shower of sparks but there was no noise at all. (A.F.P. 14.8.66)

44. 20th OCTOBER 1966, KHERSON V. L. Duginov, director of the hydrometeorological school saw, together with 50 other witnesses, a saucer-shaped object with a diameter about two to three times that of the sun and moving eastwards. (Our own archives)

45. 1967, SOUTHERN RUSSIA In the course of 1967 around 200 UFO's were seen over South Russia (*Soviet Weekly; see also Ouest-France*, 10/11, 2, 1968)

46. 8th AUGUST 1967, KISLOVODSK (CAUCASUS) Astronomer Anatoli Sazanov and colleagues in the astrophysical mountain station controlled by

the USSR Academy of Science spotted a crescent-shaped, asymmetrical object moving eastwards in the northern sector of the sky about 20 degrees over the horizon and with the hollow side of the crescent facing the direction of flight. Right in front of the object, flying at the same speed and height, there was a point of light with a candle-power equal to that of a star of the first magnitude. The object was yellowish-red and about two to three times the moon in diameter. There were vapour-trails behind, coming from the extremities. The object returned, grew smaller "and vanished for a moment." The phenomenon occurred again on 4th September, 18th October and 18th July. It was seen by numerous people in the district as well as by the staff of the Kislovodsk Observatory and of the observatory at Kazan. The crescent-shaped object was accompanied not only by the point of light already mentioned but also by other brilliant "satellites," though not on every occasion. In one case all the Kazan astronomers estimated the object's diameter to have been 480 metres, though others suggested 500–600 m. Velocity was 5 km per second, that is, 18,000 km per hour. (*Hearing Report*, p. 61)

47. 29th SEPTEMBER 1967, UKRAINE The aircraft I.L. 14 on the Zaporoje–Volgograd route was flying over the Ukraine when suddenly an unidentified object was seen overhead. The plane's engines cut out and it began to glide downwards. 800 metres from the ground the object disappeared and the aircraft's engines started up again. The rest of the journey was uneventful. (*Sovietskaia Latvia*, December 1967 and *Veac Nou*, 28th November 1968)

48. 17th SEPTEMBER 1968, ANTISIFERONA (SIBERIA) A round object sighted for five minutes over the town before quickly disappearing in a north-westerly direction. (*Flying Saucer Review*, number 1, January–February 1969)

49. 26th SEPTEMBER 1968, YAKOVLEVSKAIA An engineer saw a "balloon" at 02:00 in the morning

over the town and moving very quickly. The object had "an electric phosphorescent appearance." It vanished over the horizon. There is no possibility that it was confused with a "real" balloon. (*Flying Saucer Review*, number 1, January–February 1969)

50. SEPTEMBER 1970, KIRGHIZIA At the beginning of September 1970, many citizens observed, south of Lake Issyk-Kul, Kirghizia, a fiery, soccer-ball-shaped object. It moved above the Tersky Alatan mountains, stopped, and disappeared above the snow-covered crests in a shower of sparks.

51. JULY 1972, SIBERIA Ball-lightning is the cause of many UFO sightings according to scientific circles, since the publication of the opinion of an engineer, Klass. Ball-lightning has become the stop-gap amongst people who have never seriously concerned themselves with the UFO problem and yet have their own "explanation" of the phenomena; and this even since Dr. Menzel's theories have lost credibility as a result of analyses made by James McDonald and others. The *Novosti* information bulletin recorded a strange phenomenon on 17th July 1972 which was classified by the Russian news agencies as ball-lightning. Its behaviour had much in common with the Aveyron fireballs (France, 15th June 1966). Very peculiar traits were revealed in the latter in the course of a thorough investigation in 1970 (*Lumières dans la nuit* No. 107, 108, 109) and the final conclusion was that it was caused by a UFO. For the sake of completeness we therefore include the extract from the USSR magazine:

Ball-lightning was seen for the first time in the Arctic by people living in the settlement of Polyarny on the coast of the Tchukotka Sea in north-east Siberia.

It had been unusually hot in the settlement for a week. On Saturday the temperature reached 30°C. In the evening there was a thunderstorm.

Ball-lightning went through a room occupied by the family of building worker Yegorov at about 10 p.m. It pierced a stone wall and emerged on to the street where it was seen by passers-by. The edges of the breach in the wall were seared. No instances of ball-lightning in the eastern sector of the Arctic had been known previously.

APPENDIX A

BIBLIOGRAPHY

It is obvious that a book of this sort cannot be written without numerous borrowings from and references to other books, files and magazines. Although the reader can find in the text itself many references we have refrained from inserting too many footnotes in the body of the book in order not to burden the reader with such distractions. But the sources consulted are quite clear, especially with regard to the daily newspapers, the weeklies and the magazines reporting the UFO sightings from Eastern Europe, which have not been originally recorded by us. We did not consider an alphabetical list of this material useful as it is a matter of printed texts hardly consulted at all in the West. What we do give here is a general choice of thoughtful articles consulted by us and we would advise the critical and inquisitive reader to get to know the leading books themselves, the "Priority" volumes.

PRIORITY

1. Bourret, Jean-Claude. *La Nouvelle Vague des Soucoupes Volantes*. Editions France Empire, Paris, 1974.
Interviews with the new wave of scientists interested in the UFO problem (P. Guerin, Cl. Poher et al.) The French Minister of Defense recognizes that the French army has been following the evolution of the problem for more than 20 years.

2. Catoe, Lynn E. *UFO's and Related Subjects: An Annotated Bibliography*. Washington, U.S. Government Printing Office, 1969. 401 pages, illustrated.
This review of the most important books and magazine articles to do with UFO's has more than 1,600 titles annotated by Mrs. Lynn E. Catoe. Its compilation was the result of a request by Dr. Edward U. Condon and was produced by the Library of Congress, Science and Technology Division for the Air Force Office of Scientific Research, Office of Aerospace Research, USAF, Arlington, Virginia 22209. A copy can be obtained from the Superintendent of Documents U.S. Government Printing Office, Washington, D.C. The price is $3.50.

3. *USAF Projects Grudge and Bluebook Reports 1–12*. With an introduction by Dr. James E. McDonald, NICAP Washington, 1968. 240 pages.
These files contain twelve monthly reports (from 1951 to 1953) by the Air Force of the state of affairs regarding UFO's in the foregoing period. In these accounts, which till 1966 were secret, mention is made of military UFO sightings and observations by

pilots, astronomers, meteorologists, balloon experts, radar sightings etc. many of which could not be explained by the U.S.A.F. Copies from NICAP. Price excluding postage $5.

4. *Final report of the scientific study of unidentified flying objects conducted by the University of Colorado under contract to the United States Air Force.* With an introduction by Walter Sullivan. Dr. Edward U. Condon, Scientific Director. Bantam Books, New York, 1969. 964 pages, illustrated.

Anyone interested in the UFO problem must read the Condon Report—and not only the introductions, conclusions and recommendations which not infrequently are at variance with the conclusions drawn by various reporters. On a first reading it is possible to skip through many of the 1000 compact, concisely written pages as they give technical information about what in fact are side issues and subjects with indirect connections with the problem. The best chapters include those by astronauts on their sightings. They are written by Franklin E. Roach, the photo and film analyses carried out by William K. Hartmann, the radar analyses by Gordon D. Thayer and the historical review by Edward U. Condon. Also very good are the appendices. The Condon report is best read—or studied—after a reading of the books by Dr. Hynek and Dr. Saunders (6 and 7).

5. *Hearings before the Committee on Science and Astronautics, U.S. House of Representatives*—Ninetieth Congress, Second Session, Symposium on Unidentified Flying Objects, July 1968. Printed for the use of the Committee on Science and Astronautics, U.S. Government Printing Office, Washington, 1968. 247 pages, illustrated.

These contain the actual explanations made to the committee by Dr. J. Allen Hynek, Professor James E. McDonald, Dr. Carl Sagan, Dr. Robert L. Hall, Dr. James Harder and Dr. Robert M. L. Baker, Jr. The documents also contain the following articles or documents which were submitted to the committee:

Hynek, J. A. *Unusual Aerial Phenomena* (*Journal of the Optical Society of America*, April 1953).

Dr. Sidney Walker III. *The Applied Assessment of Central Nervous System Integrity: A Method for Establishing the Creditability of Eye Witnesses and Other Observers.*

Robert M. L. Baker, Jr. *Observational Evidence of Anomalistic Phenomena.* (*The Journal of the Astronautical Sciences*, Vol. XV, no. 1, pages 31–36, January–February 1968).

Robert M. L. Baker, Jr. *Future Experiments on Anomalistic Observational Phenomena.* (*The Journal of the Astronautical Sciences*, Vol. XV, no. 1, pages 44–45, January–February 1968).

Stanton T. Friedman. *Flying Saucers are Real.*

Stanton T. Friedman. *UFO's and Science.*

Donald H. Menzel. *UFO: Fact or Fiction?*

R. Leo Sprinkle. *Personal and Scientific Attitudes: A Survey of Persons Interested in UFO Reports.*

Roger N. Shepard. *Some Psychologically Oriented Techniques for the Scientific Investigation of Unidentified Aerial Phenomena.*

Frank B. Salisbury. *The Scientist and the UFO.* (*Bio-Science*, Vol. 17, no. 1, 1967).

The Hearing report was published by Clearinghouse for Federal Scientific & Technical Information, Springfield, Virginia 22151, U.S.A., from which copies may be obtained.

6. Hynek, J. Allen. *The UFO Experience. A Scientific Inquiry.* Chicago, Henry Regnery Company, 1972. 276 pages illus.

This book by the former consultant to the U.S.A.F. for UFO problems is not only far and away the best in its field—that is, the most critical and workman-like book—but is in itself an event in the history of the science. The position adopted by Dr. Allen J. Hynek, chairman of the department of Astronomy in Northwestern University is as follows: neither the U.S.A.F. (via Bluebook) nor the Condon team have approached the UFO problem in a serious manner although from the public's point of view it may seem indeed that they have. After more than 20 years of work linked with UFO's Dr. Hynek has come to the conclusion that the UFO is a completely new phenomenon which can only be approached empirically, though it is not as yet understood by modern science. Dr. Hynek is unconnected with any speculation about the origin of the UFO and appeals to scientific circles for more understanding.

7. Saunders, David R. and R. Rogers Harkins. *UFO's Yes. Where the Condon Committee went wrong.* Signet Books, New York, 1968. 256 pages.

Dr. Saunders was one of the most important members of the Condon team until dismissed by the latter after publication of a document, produced before the investigation got underway, prepared by the co-ordinator of the Colorado project Robert J. Low. The document contained an opinion that the final report would have to be a negative one. Dr. Saunders' book included much inside information about the activities of the Condon team and the mistakes made by same. Besides the inside story of the Colorado project the book has interesting comments about and projects for further scientific study of the UFO phenomenon.

8. Ruppelt, Edward J. *The report on unidentified flying objects.* New York, Garden City, 1956. 315 pages.

The former leader of the U.S.A.F. Bluebook offers a factual account of the investigations into a number of UFO reports and in doing so he considers all aspects of the controversy. Brought out by Ace Books in pocket edition.

9. Hall, Richard H., ed. *The UFO Evidence,* NICAP, Washingington, 1964. 184 pages.

This well-documented account contains 746 cases from NICAP files, all happening between 1957 and the end of 1963 and all investigated. The sightings are listed according to the observers. The book supports the contention that UFO's are intelligently controlled and must therefore come from outer space.

10. McDonald, James E. *Objets volants non identifiés. Le plus grand problème scientifique de notre temps?* Paris, *Phénomènes Spatiaux,* s.d., 1969. 87 pages.

A translation of the chief articles and lectures by Dr. James E. McDonald which appeared separately in English in various magazines and newspapers. Contains: "Objets volants non identifiés," and text shown on 22nd April 1967 to the American Federation of Newspaper Directors; "Science, Technologie et UFO's," a study which on 26th January 1968 was presented to the United Aircraft Research Laboratories, East Hartford, Connecticut; "Letter to U Thant, Secretary-General of the UNO"; and the theory submitted by James E. McDonald on 7th June 1967 to the UNO team for space investigations.

Price: 7.55 FF, obtainable from *Phénomènes Spatiaux* (see Magazines)

Some of the McDonald lectures in English are obtainable from UFO Research Institute, Suite 311, 508 Grant Street, Pittsburgh, Pennsylvania, 15219 USA.

11. Davidson, Leon. *Flying Saucers: an analysis of the Air Force Project Bluebook.* Special Report No. 14. Ramsey, N.J., Ramsey-Wallace Corp, 1966. 84 pages illus.

The American Air Force has published a total of 14 monthly reports about UFO's, of which the first twelve cover the years 1951–53 (see bibliographical note above). Afterwards they published an annual report, of which No. 14 was a "Special Report." It included a study of the situation from 1947 on by means of statistics, sketches, tables etc. Dr. Leon Davidson published this report in 1966 when it was released and supplied it with a commentary.

12. Bloecher, Ted. *Report on the UFO wave of 1947.* Introduction by Dr. James E. McDonald. Washington, D.C., The Author, 1967. About 200 pages, illus.

A chronological list of over 850 UFO sightings in June and July 1947 in America. Newspaper accounts supply most of the details. UFO cases which represent special aspects of the problem are discussed in detail. Numerous maps, photos, tables and graphs. Obtainable through NICAP.

13. Vallée, Jacques. *Anatomy of a Phenomenon: unidentified objects in space. A scientific appraisal.* Chicago, H. Regnery Co., 1965.

Analyses of selected UFO sightings during the course of which the French author, who is a computer expert, defends his theory that the UFO can be studied with scientific methods so that the whole problem can be approached in its entirety as a collection of unusual individual incidents.

14. Menzel, Donald H., *Flying Saucers.* Cambridge, Harvard University Press, 1953. 319 pages, illus.

The 20% unidentified objects (by the American Air Force, that is) are according to Menzel the consequence of meteorological optical effects: light reflections, refraction, reflections of ice-crystal material, etc. The author refutes the contention that UFO's are a proof of extraterrestrial intelligence. The same theme is in *The World of the flying saucers,* published in 1963 in collaboration with Lyle G. Boyd.

15. Sanderson, Ivan T. *Uninvited Visitors.* New York, Cowles Education Corp., 1967. 245 pages. (in England: Neville Spearman, London, 1969).

The author, a biologist, proposes a number of theories about UFO's and their nature, and does not reject the idea that they may have a biological structure or a "spatial" origin since many of the things achieved by the UFO's occur in the animal world.

16. Sprinkle, R. Leo. *Personal and scientific attitudes: a survey of persons interested in UFO reports.* Laramie, Wyoming, The Author, 1968. 11 pages.

An investigation into the attitudes of three groups, that is psychology students, physics students and a third group of NICAP people. It appeared that the latter demanded stricter scientific tests than the other two groups before accepting a UFO account.

17. U.S. Congress House Committee on Armed Services. *Unidentified flying objects.* Washington, U.S. Government Printing Office, 1966. 84 pages. (89th Cong., 2nd sess. House Report No. 55)

Information about U.S.A.F. activities connected with UFO's.

ADDITIONAL READING MATTER

Many UFO publications, especially American ones are entirely sensational in nature and contain details which cannot be verified—from sources equally dubious. But there are various good books on the subject for the general reader, in which the information is in general exact and often original. One does not need to agree with all the conclusions. The following books belong to this category.

18. Blum, Ralph and Judy. *Beyond Earth: Man's Contact with UFO's.* New York, Bantam Books, 1974. 248 p., ill.

19. Bowen, Charles. *The Humanoids.* A survey of world-wide reports of landings of unconventional aerial objects and their alleged occupants. London, Neville Spearman, 1969. In collaboration with Aimé Michel, Jacques Vallée, Gordon Creighton, Coral Lorenzen, Antonio Ribera and others. 256 pages. Illus.

20. Buttlar, Johannes v. *Schneller als das Licht. Von den grenzenlosen Möglichkeiten des Menschen.* Wien, Düsseldorf, Econ Verlag, 1972.

21. Carrouges, Michel. *Les apparitions des Martiens.* Paris, Fayard, 1963. 287 pp.

22. Edwards, Frank. *Flying saucers, serious business.* New York, Lyle Stuart, Inc., 1966. 319 pages.

23. Fuller, John G. *Incident at Exeter; the story of unidentified flying objects over America today.* New York, Putnam, 1966. 251 pages.

24. Fuller, John G. *The interrupted journey: two lost hours.* "Aboard a flying saucer." New York, The Dial Press. 1966. 302 pages.

25. Guieu, Jimmy. *Les soucoupes volantes viennent d'un autre monde.* Paris, Editions Fleuve Noir, 1954. 253 pages. Illustrated.

26. Guieu, Jimmy. *Black out sur les soucoupes volantes.* Préface par Jean Cocteau. Paris, Omnium Littéraire, s.d. (Collection 4e dimension) 287 p., ill.

27. Herrmann, Joachim. *Das falsche Weltbild, Astronomie und Aberglaube.* Stuttgart, Kosmos Verlag, Franckh'sche Verlagshandlung, 1962. 162 pages.

28. Jessup, Morris K. *The case for the UFO, unidentified flying objects.* Introduction by Frank Edwards. New York, Citadel Press, 1955, 239 pages.

29. Jung, C. G. *Flying saucers.* A modern myth of things seen in the skies. Translated from the German by R. F. C. Hull. New York, The New American Library, 1969. 144 pages. Illustrated.

30. Keyhoe, Donald E. *The flying saucers are real.* New York, Fawcett Publications, 1950. 175 pages.

31. Keyhoe, Donald E. *Flying saucers from outer space.* New York, Holt, 1953. 276 pages.

32. Keyhoe, Donald E. *The flying saucers conspiracy.* New York, Holt, 1955. 315 pages.

33. Keyhoe, Donald E. *Flying Saucers: top secret.* New York, Putnam, 1960. 283 pages.

34. Lagarde, Fernand (Sous la direction de). *Mystérieuses soucoupes volantes. Avec la participation d'Aimé Michel et de Jacques Vallée.* Paris, Les Editions Albatros, 1974. 318 p., ill.

35. McCampbell, James M. *UFOlogy. New Insights from Science and Common Sense.* Belmont, Jaymac Company, s.d. (1973); 153 p.

36. Michel, Aimé. *A propos des soucoupes volantes. Mystérieux objets célestes.* Paris, Editions Planète, 1967. 321 pages.

37. Michel, Aimé. *Pour les soucoupes volantes.* Nancy, Berger-Levrault, 1969. (Collection Pour ou Contre).

38. Misraki, Paul. *Des signes dans le ciel (Les Extraterrestres).* Paris, Labergerie, 1968. 318 p.

39. Olsen, Thomas M. *The reference for outstanding UFO sighting reports.* Riderwood, Md., UFO Information Retrieval Center Inc., 1967.

40. Ribera, Antonio. *El gran enigma de los platillos volantes.* Santiago de Chile, Buenos Aires, Mexico, Barcelona, Editorial Pomaire, 1966. 431 pages.

41. Ribera, Antonio, *Un caso perfecto. Platillos volantes sobre España.* Barcelona, Pomaire, 1969. 196 pages. Illustrated.

42. Stanway, Roger H., Pace, Anthony R. *Flying saucer report. UFO's unidentified undeniable.* Stoke-on-Trent, Staffs, Newchapel Observatory, 1968. 87 pages. Illustrated.

43. *The Official Guide to UFO's.* (Compiled by the Editors of *Science & Mechanics.*) New York, Ace Publishing Corporation, 1968. 189 pages.

44. Vallée, Jacques and Janine. *Challenge to science.* The UFO enigma. New York, Ace Books Inc., 1966. 256 pages. Illustrated.

45. Vallée, Jacques. *Passport to Magonia.* From folklore to

flying saucers. Chicago, Henry Regnery Company, 1969. 372 pages.

EAST EUROPE

Till now few books have been published about UFO problems in Eastern Europe, although one can find here and there in the books selected by us the occasional announcement of a UFO sighting from one or another Eastern European country. In the following numbers of our bibliography research in this field is at its most rewarding: 5, 6, 19, 40 and 42. Reference 6 contains a photo from Czechoslovakia without further descriptive details. The books in Polish, Hungarian, Czechoslovakian, Russian and Rumanian which deal with the general UFO problem are discussed in detail in this book in their appropriate chapters.

The following reference contains a chapter devoted entirely to Russian UFOlogy:

46. Ostrander, Sheila, Schroeder, Lynn. *Psychic Discoveries behind the Iron Curtain.* Introduction by Ivan T. Sanderson. Toronto–New York–London. National General Company, 1971. 457 pages. Illustrated. Bantam Books.

UFO MAGAZINES

There is no such magazine in East Europe, though a stencilled information bulletin circulates sometimes between members of the Rumanian UFO group in Bucharest who are led by Ion Hobana. In past years most of the best information about Eastern European UFO happenings appeared in the French UFO magazine *Phénomènes Spatiaux*. Special mention should be made of the Belgian magazine *Inforespace* which contained in various issues in 1972 and 1973 a very detailed study of "Tungus 1908" (see Chapter 1). This was written by Maurice de San, who has been busy with this problem for twenty years. The bibliography is impressive and comprises everything which appeared in Russia (and elsewhere) on this subject. The mathematics involved were checked for correctness by mathematicians at the universities of Brussels and Louvain.

The magazines named in this book are amongst the best in the world in this field although not coming up to the standards of scientific publications. They remain amateurish, are unevenly edited and one may find nonsensical articles side by side with others of a high scientific standard. The addresses of the main UFO magazines are:

Flying Saucer Review. 49a Kings Grove, London S.E. 15, England.

Inforespace. Boulevard Aristide Briand, 26, 1070, Brussels, Belgium.

Lumières dans la nuit. "Les Pins," 43, Le-Chambon-sur-Lignon, France.
Mufon. Brandon Avenue 8, Urmston, Manchester, L 4 ORH.
Phénomènes Spatiaux. Rue de la Tombe-Issoire, 69, Paris 14e, France.
The UFO investigator. NICAP, Suite 23, 3535 University Blvd. West, Kensington, Maryland 20795, U.S.A.

BIBLIOGRAPHY OF THE "TUNGUS MIRACLE"

1. Astapovitch, I. S., Sur la grande météorite de la Toungouska, *Nature*, 1935, no. 9, 70 pages.
2. Astapovitch, I. S., Air Waves caused by the fall of the Meteorite of 30 June 1908 in Central Siberia. *Quart. J. Roy. Soc.*, 1934, Vol. 60, no. 257, pp. 493–504.
3. Astapovitch, I. S., The Great Tunguska Meteorite, *Nature*, 1951, no. 2, pp. 23–32.
4. Astapovitch, I. S., The Great Tunguska Meteorite, *Nature*, 1951, no. 3, pp. 13–23.
5. Astapovitch, I. S., Fresh material from the flight of the great meteorite of the 30 June 1908, *Jour. Astr.*, 1933, Vol. 10, no. 4, pp. 465–486.
6. Bronchten, V. A., Courant d'air de la Météorite de la Toungouska, *Astr. Vest.*, SSSR 1969, Vol. 13, no. 4, pp. 214–222.
7. Bronchten, V. A., The Problem of the movement of the Tunguska meteorite in the atmosphere, *Meteoritika*, 1961, no. 20, pp. 72–86.
8. Conan, Clyde, Atluri, C. R., and Libby, W. F., Possible Antimatter content of the Tunguska Meteor of 1908, *Nature*, Vol. 206, 1965, May 29, pp. 861–865.
9. Farienski, Vronski, Milianov, Zotkin et Kirova, Résultats de l'expédition de 1958 sur la Catastrophe de la Toungouska, *Meteoritika*, SSSR 1960, no. 19, pp. 103–133.
10. Fessenkov, V. G., The Nature of the Tunguska Meteorite, *Meteoritika*, SSSR 1961, no. 20, pp. 27–31.
11. Fessenkov, V., A note on the Cometary Nature of the Tungus Meteorite, Smitson, *Contrib. Astroph.*, U.S.A. 1963, Vol. 7, no. 7, pp. 305–307.
12. Fessenkov, On the Cometary nature of the Tungus meteorite, *Astr. Zh.*, SSSR 1961, Vol. 38, no. 4, pp. 577–592.
13. Fessenkov, V. G., The air wave caused by the fall of the Tunguska meteorite of 1908, *Meteoritika*, 1959, no. 17, pp. 3–7.
14. Glass, D. P., Silicate Spherules from Tunguska Impact Area, *Science*, U.S.A. 1969, Vol. 164, no. 3879, pp. 547–549.
15. Ivanov, A propos des causes du changement dans l'effort

géomagnétique du bolide de la Toungouska, *Geomagn. i Aeronom.*, SSSR 1961, Vol. 1, no. 4, pp. 616–618.
16. Ivanov, Geomagnet. *1 Aeronomia*, 1962, Vol. 1, no. 4, pp. 616.
17. Ivanov, Hauteur de l'Explosion . . ., *Astr. Zh.*, SSSR 1963, Vol. 40, no. 2, pp. 329–331.
18. Ivanov, Courbe géomagnétique, Meteoritika Acad. Sci., SSSR 1961, Vol. 21, pp. 46–48.
19. Kazatsev et Kulikova, Sur le Mouvement du Météore de la Toungouska, *Astr. Vest.*, SSSR 1967, Vol. 1, no. 1, pp. 54–58.
20. Kopal, Zd., Origin of the lunar Craters and Maria, *Nature*, 1959, Vol. 183, no. 4655, pp. 169–70.

Les illuminations crépusculaires des 30 juin et 1 juillet, *Gazette Astronomique d'Anders*, 1908, Vol. 1, no. 8, pp. 61–65.

21. Koulik, L. A., Data on the Tungus Meteorite as available towards 1939, *Cpte Rend.* Acad. Sci., URSS 1939, Vol. XXII, no. 8, pp. 515–519.
22. Koulik, L. A., *The place where the Tunguska Meteorite fell in 1908*, Rep. Acad. Sci., URSS 1927, pp. 339–402.
23. Koulik, L. A., *History of the Bolide of the 30 June 1908*, Rep. Acad. Sci., USSR 1927, pp. 393–398.
24. Krinov, E. L., *Giant Meteorites*, Pergamon Press, 1966.
25. Lebedenets, V. N., and Portnjagin, I., *On the ablation of Meteoroids in the Earth's Atmosphere*, Cospar 7th Inter. Space Sci. Symp., Vienna, 1966.
26. Levin, Yu, The problem of the velocity and orbit of the Tunguska meteorite, *Meteoritika*, 1954, no. 11, pp. 132–136.
27. Macvey, John W., Missiles from Space, *Spaceflight*, no. 11, Vol. 9, November 1967, pp. 46–49.
28. Mamontoff, C., Chute de météorite en modèle réduit, *Science-Progrès*, no. 3382, Février 1967, pp. 51–54.
29. Monthly Weather Rev., *Sky glows in Europe*, 1908, pp. 219.
30. Nauenberg, M., and Ruderman, M. A., Antimatter in the Earth's atmosphere, *Phys. Let. Nother.*, 1966, Vol. 22, no. 4, pp. 512–513.
31. Obroutchev, S. V., The place of the fall of the great Khatanga Meteorite of 1908, *Mirovedeniye*, 1925, Vol. 14, no. 1, pp. 38–40.
32. Obroutchev, S. V., More about the place where the Tunguska meteorite fell, *Nature*, 1951, no. 12, pp. 36–38.
33. Plekhanov, Vasilev & al., Quelques Résultats de l'Etude . . . *Geol. i Geofiz.*, 1963, Vol. 1, no. 1, pp. 111–123.
34. Rajch, J., On the interaction layer in front of a meteor body, *Bull. Astr. Inst. Czechoslovak Ac. Sci.*, 1969, Vol. 20, no. 6, pp. 363–372.

35. The Siberian Meteor of June 30, 1908, *Nature*, no. 3210, Vol. 127, May 9, 1931, pp. 719.
36. Soberman, R. K., Noctilucent clouds, *Scientific American*, June 1963, pp. 50–59.
    Mirovedeniye, 1922, Vol. 11, no. 1 (42), pp. 142–154.
    Mirovedeniye, 1921, Vol. 10, no. 1 (40), pp. 74–81.
37. Souslov, I. M., The search for the great Meteorite of 1908, *Mirovedeniye*, 1927, no. 1, pp. 13–18.
38. Spencer, Dr. L. J., Meteorite Craters, *Nature*, no. 3265, Vol. 129, May 28, 1932, pp. 781.
39. Stanjukovitch et Bronchten, Sur la vitesse et l'énergie du bolide de la Toungouska en 1908, *Doklady Akad.*, SSSR 1961, Vol. 140, no. 3, pp. 533–586.
40. Sytinskaya, N. N., The problem of the trajectory of the Tunguska meteorite, *Meteoritika*, 1956, no. 13, pp. 86–91.
41. Voznesensky, A. V., The fall of the meteorite of June 30, 1908 in the upper reaches of river Khatanga, *Mirovedeniye*, 1925, Vol. 14, no. 1, pp. 25–38.
42. Wipple, F. J. W., On Phenomena related to the great Siberian Meteor, *Quart. J. Roy. Soc.*, 60, no. 257, pp. 505–513.
43. Young, R. A., The Airglow, *Scientific American*, March 1966, pp. 103–110.
44. Zaslavskaya, Zotkin et Kirova, Distribution des dimensions . . . , *Dokl. Akad. Nauk.*, SSSR 1964, Vol. 156, no. 1, pp. 47–49.
45. Zolotov, A. V., Role de l'onde de choc . . . , *Geomagn. i Aeronom.*, SSSR 1966, Vol. 6, no. 5, pp. 907–913.
46. Zolotov, A. V., Nouvelles données sur . . . , *Dokl. Akad. Nauk.*, SSSR 1961, Vol. 136, no. 1, pp. 84–87.
47. Zolotov, A. V., Ionisation thermique, *Geomagn. i Aeronom.*, SSSR 1965, Vol. 5, no. 3, pp. 584–5.
48. Zolotov, A. V., A propos de l'effet dynamo . . . , Toungouska, *Geol. i Geofiz.*, SSSR 1967, Vol. 175, no. 3, pp. 137–8.
49. Zolotov, A. V., *Problèmes de la catastrophe de la Toungouska en 1908*, Editions Naukai Teknika 1969, Minsk.
50. Zolotov, A. V., The possibility of "thermal" explosion, and the structure of the Tungus Meteorite, *Soviet Physics*, Doklady, August 1967, Vol. 12, no. 2, pp. 101–104.
51. Zolotov, A. V., Estimation of the parameters of the Tungus Meteorite based on new data, *Soviet Physics*, Doklady, August 1967, Vol. 12, no. 2, pp. 108–111.
52. Zotkin, I. T., Anomalous Optical Phenomena in the atmosphere connected with the Tunguska Meteorite, *Meteoritika*, 1961, no. 20, pp. 40–53.

APPENDIX B

Letter sent out to 150 amateur astronomers at the beginning of 1968 by the People's Observatory, Bucharest.

With reference to Comrade ..... Secretary of the Central Astroklub.

Knowing your interest and dedication as amateur astronomers and also as members of the Bucharest Central Astroklub we ask for your voluntary aid in support of our new foundation "BEWARE OF UFO'S." In this connection we would ask you to be ever vigilant regarding possible appearances of unidentifiable objects (UFO's) over the Socialist Republic of Rumania. When you have definitely ascertained that one has clearly appeared (and an experienced amateur astronomer will not confuse such a UFO with identifiable objects like for instance aircraft in unusual conditions, weather balloons, various cloud formations, artificial satellites etc.) then we would request you to measure it at once with all the means at your disposal, as precisely and scientifically as possible. All sightings and relevant materials (negatives, photographic plates, drawings etc.) must be sent to BEWARE OF UFO'S at once for scientific analysis for as short a time as possible. The address is: Bucharest People's Observatory, Ana Ipătescu St., 21, Sector 1, Postal Service 22, Bucharest.

We request that you establish data about the UFO's as exactly and scientifically as possible. Bearing this in mind would you kindly pay attention to the following details:

a. moment of sighting in Rumanian Time (date, hour, minute, second)

b. UFO's astronomical azimuth (fixed at 0 degrees to 360 degrees for appearance from the south—on the local meridian—and travelling clockwise, thus: south $A = 0$ degrees, west $A = 90$ degrees, north $A = 180$ degrees, east $A = 270$ degrees).

Height of the UFO over the horizon (travelling from 0 degrees to 90 degrees on a vertical line from the object to the horizon i.e. horizon $h = 0$ degrees, zenith $h = 90$ degrees)

Examples: (1) UFO Cluj (Moṭilor Street no. 44), 17.9.68, 18 hr. 14 m. 30 sec. $A = 354$ deg. $h = 61$ deg; telescope; observer E. Cuibuș.

(2) UFO Cluj (Astronomical Observatory, Dealul Aluniș), 17.9.68. 18 hr. 20 m. 16 sec. $A = 357$ deg., $h = 62$ deg.; theodolite, observer R. Irimeș.

In case the UFO is observed with the naked eye and no attempt is made to determine the angle (by theodolite or telescope) the co-ordinates can be indicated by using an astronomical chart, assuming that the observation takes place at dusk or in the night. In this case give the approximate position.

If possible would you please take photos of the UFO with a high speed film of fine grain, both in black/white and colour. You can use an ordinary camera with telelens as well as binoculars. Please describe in as much accurate detail as possible any UFO seen by means of field-glasses or telescope; the shape and colour (use colour-film), the movement, light-effects and intensity of light emitted.

So that the sighting may be useful for scientific purposes it is necessary for us to ask the observer to keep calm, report the results as quickly as possible and, above all, with maximum objectivity.

> With thanks,
> Director and President of Bucharest
> Centrale Astroklub
> Ion Corvin Sîngeorzan

APPENDIX C LIST OF ILLUSTRATIONS

p. 14, 17, 19, 22, 25, 28, Tungus, 1908, from own archives and *Science et Vie*.

p. 34, McDivitt, 4.06.1964, NASA.

p. 34, Genova, 8.09.1963, Ribera, *Platillos Volantes ante la Camera*, p. 179.

p. 34, Sherman, 2.08.1965. J. A. Hynek, *The UFO Experience*, p. 53.

p. 43, McDivitt, 4.07.1965, NASA.

p. 65, Marliens, May 1967, *Phénomènes Spatiaux*, September 1967.

p. 81, Dečani, *Borba*, 26.07.1969.

p. 82, Dečani, *Borba*, 26.07.1969.

p. 84, Mont-Athos, *Lumières dans la Nuit*, June 1969.

p. 87, 89, 90, AAAK, *Identifikacija Letećeg objekta od 18 oktobra 1968 godine*.

p. 105, 106, Flight-pattern and diameter, UFO Cluj, *Flying Saucer Review*, vol. 16, no. 5, October 1970.

p. 106, Shadow-lines, UFO Cluj, *Lumières dans la Nuit*, October 1971.

p. 121, UFO waves, 1966, *Lumières dans la Nuit*, October 1969.

p. 122, Graph, Stoke-on-Trent, Stanway, *Flying Saucer Report*, p. 43.

p. 123, Graphs and periods, Vallée, *Phénomènes*, p. 214.

p. 183, Seattle, U.S.A., *Flying Saucer Review*, Special Issue no. 2, p. 33.

p. 215, Brno, *Phénomènes Spatiaux*, no. 11, 1967.

p. 217, UFO seen by Panes, *Phénomènes Spatiaux*, March 1968.

p. 218, Lnar, 14.08.1965, *Phénomènes Spatiaux*, September 1966.

p. 219, 220, Snopousov, 1.07.1966, *Phénomènes Spatiaux*, March 1968.

p. 245, Elsthorpe, New Zealand, *Flying Saucer Review*, vol. 15, 104, July/August 1969.

The illustrations on the following pages come from our own archives:
34, 36, 37, 68, 83, 86, 91, 92, 94, 95, 101, 102, 112, 115, 124, 125, 128, 130, 133, 136, 138, 139, 144, 145, 153, 154, 160, 161, 162, 165, 167, 170, 173, 174, 175, 177, 179, 184, 186, 189, 201, 203, 206, 218, 225, 226, 227, 230, 231, 233, 235, 239, 241, 242, 244, 248, 249, 252, 255, 257, 258, 259, 261, 262, 263, 265, 266, 267, 268, 269, 270, 272, 273, 275.

Appendix D. Banat (Chapter Eight) Reconstruction of the

	date	time	place	witness	direction and angle	shape	colour	size	distance from observer
1	29	16.00–evenings	Semenic	8	East 75°–80°	cone triangle	brilliant, especially on sun side	—	
2	29	17.30–18.00	Muntele Mic	1	—	truncated cone	silver	caravelle	—
3	29	18.00–19.00	Tîrgu-Jiu	12	S.S.W. (Town) 60°–65°	triangle	brilliant, white/orange/blue	nut-apple (enlarging)	—
4	29	18.30–19.00	Tîrgu-Jiu	11	S.W.	triangle with rounded corners	white/orange/red/blue		
5	29	22.00	Ciudanoviţa	14	E.S.E. 30°	—	—	—	—
6	30	02.30	Oraviţa	5	—	—	brilliant	—	—
7	30	06.10 08.00	Oraviţa	5	N.E. 35°–40°	triangle	brilliant, white/yellow	—	—
8	30	06.30 16.00	Ciudanoviţa	14	—	truncated cone	brilliant white	half-moon diameter top 15 m bot. 25 m	
9	30	07.50 12.00	Semenic	8					
10	30	08.00	Ţarcu	3	—	weather balloon	white		
11	30	08.15 13.00	Oraviţa	5	—	truncated cone	two sides lit		
12	30	16.30	Oraviţa	5	80°–85°	—	twinkling light		
13	30	09.00 10.00	Moldova-Nouă	10	—	cone	—		
14	30	10.00 12.30	Ţarcu	3	direction of the sun	egg	dull white	—	great
15	30	10.00	Reşiţa	13	—	cone	—	280 m	40 km
16	30	10.00 11.00	Berzeasca	7	—	balloon	brilliant, like aluminium		3 km
17	30	16.00 evenings	Semenic	8	—	—	—	—	—
18	30	13.00	Berzeasca	4	—	—	—		
19	30	16.00 24.00	Ţarcu	3	—	triangle, becoming round later	see remarks		
20	30	17.00 19.30	Reşiţa	2	East	triangle	changing (lighter) blue/white		
21	30	17.30–18.00	Muntele Mic	1	45°	truncated cone	—	—	
22	30	in daytime	Oraviţa	9	S.S.W.	pear-shaped	whitish	—	—
23	30	in daytime	Caransebeş	6	S.S.E. 70°–75°	truncated cone	very brilliant	—	—
24	30/31	at night	Caransebeş	6	—	—	shining like first mag. star	—	—
25	31	01.30 11.00	Ţarcu	3	—	—	candle-power decreased as dawn came		
26	31	in daytime	Caransebeş	6	E.N.E.	—	—	—	—
27	31	06.00	Semenic	8	—	—	—	—	—

sighting.

height	direction of movement	manner of movement	type of motion of object	remarks
—	without movement	—	rocking	seen with 6 × 30 binoculars; drawings; followed also at night; see 9
10,000 m	without movement direction Țarcu	—	—	binoculars, drawings, photos. As 21
very high	coming and going	zig-zag	—	
very high	coming and going	zig-zag; slow and fast	—	lighting grew stronger as stars appeared
—	—	—	—	
—	—	—	—	
± 7,000 m	—	—	motionless	photos; as 11
10 to 15 km	without motion 5 hours; afterwards to the south	zig-zag	swaying around its axis	change of shape and colour; photos; drawings (v. diagram)
—	slowly to the south from 09.00 on	—	—	as 2 and 17
—	against the wind	unusual	rocking	as 14
—	without movement	—	very slow	theodolite; as 12
—	—	—	—	photos; followed till disappearance; drawing
—	one to two hours without movement	fairly slow	—	probably another object. Cf. 10.00 at Caransebeș
7,000 m	against the wind	alternately still and slowly moving	—	disappears from 12.30 to re-appear around 16.00. Sketch no. 1. Drawing. As 19
24,000 m	—	motionless	—	binoculars; object uninfluenced by wind; sketches
—	—	motionless	—	
—	—	slowly S.W.	—	radio contact between various weather-stations; nothing seen after 12. As 27
—	—	—	—	
30,000 m	—	constant— very fast	—	3 photos; self-lit after dusk; red-white; sketch 2; as 25
—	hardly moving	very slow	—	drawing of the object
—	motionless; afterwards towards Țarcu	slow	—	impression of self-illumination; same object as 2
—	—	aircraft speed; linear	—	
—	motionless (for one hour)	in a wide arc towards Jugoslavia	—	
—	motionless	East-North-East	—	motionless relative to the stars; visible all night
—	—	—	—	object returned same way; parallel to arrival (see sketches 1 and 2)
—	—	—	—	object returned (see 25)
—	—	—	—	as 17; disappearance as a result of thick cloud-cover

ABOUT THE AUTHORS

Ion Hobana was born in Iasi, Rumania, in 1931. He attended Bucharest University and received his degree in philology. In 1954 his first volume of verse was published. Later he wrote a number of scientific essays and a historical review of the film industry. He is scientific editor of the Bucharest daily newspaper *Scinteia*, and secretary of the Rumanian Writer's Union.

Julien Weverbergh was born in Antwerp in 1930. He formerly taught in secondary schools and has been a full-time writer since 1966. His writing includes fiction, literary criticism and essays. He and Hobana met when Weverbergh was Rumanian correspondent for the Dutch weekly, *Vrij Nederland*. He works at present in publishing in Brussels.

OTHER WORLDS. OTHER REALITIES.

In fact and fiction, these extraordinary books bring the fascinating world of the supernatural down to earth from ancient astronauts and black magic to witchcraft, voodoo and mysticism—these books look at other worlds and examine other realities.

- [ ] **IN SEARCH OF ANCIENT MYSTERIES (8376/$1.50)—Fact**
- [ ] **THE DEVIL'S TRIANGLE (8445/$1.50)—Fact**
- [ ] **POWER THROUGH WITCHCRAFT (8673/$1.25)—Fact**
- [ ] **CHARIOTS OF THE GODS (Q5753/$1.25)—Fact**
- [ ] **A COMPLETE GUIDE TO THE TAROT (Q6696/$1.25)—Fact**
- [ ] **WITCHCRAFT AND BLACK MAGIC (7996/$1.95)—Fact**
- [ ] **THE EXORCIST (X7200/$1.75)—Fiction**
- [ ] **GODS FROM OUTER SPACE (Q7276/$1.25)—Fact**
- [ ] **NOT OF THIS WORLD (7696/$1.25)—Fact**
- [ ] **GOD DRIVES A FLYING SAUCER (7733/$1.25)—Fact**
- [ ] **THE SPACESHIPS OF EZEKIEL (8378/$1.95)—Fact**
- [ ] **THE OUTER SPACE CONNECTION (2092/$1.75)—Fact**

Buy them at your local bookstore or use this handy coupon for ordering:

Bantam Books, Inc., Dept. OW, 414 East Golf Road, Des Plaines, Ill. 60016

Please send me the books I have checked above. I am enclosing $_____ (please add 35¢ to cover postage and handling). Send check or money order —no cash or C.O.D.'s please.

Mr/Mrs/Miss_____

Address_____

City_____State/Zip_____

OW—6/75

Please allow three weeks for delivery. This offer expires 6/76.

Bantam Book Catalog

It lists over a thousand money-saving bestsellers originally priced from $3.75 to $15.00 —bestsellers that are yours now for as little as 50¢ to $2.95!

The catalog gives you a great opportunity to build your own private library at huge savings!

So don't delay any longer—send us your name and address and 10¢ (to help defray postage and handling costs).

BANTAM BOOKS, INC.
Dept. FC, 414 East Golf Road, Des Plaines, Ill. 60016

Mr./Mrs./Miss_____
(please print)

Address_____

City_____ State_____ Zip_____

Do you know someone who enjoys books? Just give us their names and addresses and we'll send them a catalog too!

Mr./Mrs./Miss_____

Address_____

City_____ State_____ Zip_____

Mr./Mrs./Miss_____

Address_____

City_____ State_____ Zip_____

FC—1/75